Seed Thoughts To Consciousness

Consciousness is God.
God is Consciousness.

–Lama Sing

**A Handbook to Freedom
By Al Miner and Lama Sing**

Revised and Edited

*Seed Thoughts to Consciousness –
A Handbook to Freedom*

By Al Miner and Lama Sing

© 2014 by Al and Susan Miner

Revised and edited 2015

All rights reserved.

Cover and book design by Susan Miner

Library of Congress: 2015953555
Published in the United States of America

ISBN- 978-1-941915-05-9

1. Lamasing   2. Psychic   3. Trance Channel   4. Consciousness
I. Miner, Al   II. Lama Sing   III. Title

For books and products, further information, or to write Al Miner, visit
www.lamasing.org

Foreword:

A *Seed Thought* is contained at the top of each page, intended as a stand-alone inspiration or meditational path for the day.

The narrative from which the Seed Thought was excerpted is also included for further reflection.

This book is a summary of those readings given by Al Miner and Lama Sing from 2005 to 2015 related to Consciousness and Al's journey to reclaim Consciousness while yet finite. It is a progressive work. Each page builds on the previous. Seed Thoughts and narrative taken out of order will not be as understandable as they would be if read in sequence.

Christ/the Master – "The Christ is a Principle. It is a Spirit. It is the life. The Master has brought this Christ Consciousness into oneness with Himself. Thus, He has become the Christ. Just so many stumble over this." –Lama Sing

Father – When Al and this work employ the term Father there is no implication of gender, humanness, or religiosity whatsoever, but simply a word to refer to, call on, and address in a deeply personal way the God Source, the Creator of All, the Beloved. Al has said, "If it's good enough for Jesus, it's good enough for me."

Words – "It is important that all who might read these words understand emphatically we are using words to describe some event and actualities that have no corresponding words in Earth. So we are using the best that is at hand." –Lama Sing

The Channel – This name is used throughout the book to denote the difference between Al, the man in finite form, and the part of Al that has left his form and is in realms beyond to channel the information. It is capitalized when used in place of his name.

Lama Sing – This name refers to an individual Al has known and worked with beyond and in this and other lifetimes. It also refers to the group, others joining Lama Sing to participate in gathering and offering information from Universal Consciousness in the readings.

Form – While in "pure" Consciousness no physical-like form is present, in some circumstances, being expressed in a form that appears physical is joyful and/or useful, both to Al in his experiences as well as to communicate an understandable narrative.

In Earth – When referring to life on Earth Lama Sing uses the term "in Earth" because he is referring to Earth as a realm of expression, similar to the common use of "in heaven."

Quotation marks – In the body of this work, quotation marks were specifically dictated by the Lama Sing group within the reading. These quotation marks denote their own emphasis.

> **January 1**
>
> The power of God is the living gift within you. Use it. Give it forth. Let it pass through you.

The power of God does not lie externally, within a certain writing, a certain tablet, a certain relic, or artifact. It is the living gift of God within you. As you come unto the Earth as in this sojourn and give it, the greater is the Light that passes through you, which is of course that Light which heals and brings balance and joy.

Use it. See? Give it forth. Let it pass through you.

Find the pathway that gives you the realization that you are alive in the Earth and that you are the son/the daughter of God.

Do that then as brings you the purpose and goal according to your guidance and choice. Call it forth.

> January 2
>
> Pause with diligence to meditate often throughout the day, even if just five to fifteen minutes several times each day.

    Remember to pause to meditate often throughout each day and have a diligence in regard to same.

    This will provide more balance for the body – physically, mentally, and Spiritually – than most any supplements could, for it allows for the body, mind, and Spirit to rebalance, that those elements that are a part of the body almost constantly (when a reasonable diet is maintained) can be better assimilated. Just five to fifteen minutes several times each day would be just the ticket.

> **January 3**
>
> As one who is physically training might do, extend self: one step further into the joy and Oneness that is eternally yours.

    The body loves to be extended. It finds joy in reaching a bit further than what is known.
    If it is so with the physical, then must it not be even greater with the Spirit?
    Then reach a bit further. Extend self.
    One who is physically training might attempt to do one or two more exercises than the previous day. Then one of Spirit, one of Light, one who knows they are a Child of God and seeks that pathway to regain that Oneness would do the same.
    Take one step further, one deeper movement into the joy and oneness that is eternally yours.

> **January 4**
>
> Your Spirit is ever true. Seek, then, that which is in harmony with it, and the path will open to you.

    Be mindful not to rely on what you see or hear, for illusions can be presented to the sight and misleading sounds can be given to the hearing.
    But the Spirit is ever true. Seek that which is in harmony with it and the path will open to you in new ways.

> **January 5**
>
> Do not seek by looking for a tool that opens your eyes to be able to see. Rather, seek with a *Knowing*.

It is said, *In the beginning was the Word and the Word was with God.* These are written words that have meanings of some diversity, which we would perceive in this way: In the beginning, everything was one with God, and then creation went forth.

In the beginning, we did not know what was "beyond" because we did not consider anything could be beyond God. We did not revere God or look to God in the manner as religion would at present because we did not know God in a sense of separateness or distance. We then, as now, consider God and ourselves in oneness.

In our particular journey we sought to understand how anything could be separate from God. We began that process because we saw that others had begun to move, and we considered to what they were moving and to where. (It is difficult to convey to you at present, but we know that your Spirit will understand.)

The issuance of the Word of God is not a force moving apart from God, nor is it a force extracted from the body of God and penetrating the nothingness in order to create. For all that is, always was; all that shall be, is. We know that, if you dwell upon this, it perhaps could stretch the credibility of your sanity – or *consciousness* (with a note of loving humor) – and yet, it is so. We offer this here to help build an understanding.

Do not seek in the sense of moving backwards in time. Do not perceive by looking for a tool that opens your eyes to be able to see. Rather, seek with a *Knowing*.

> January 6
>
> Step over the current belief and habits, past the veils that separate you from Consciousness and oneness with God.

The awakening to Consciousness is the unburdening of self of that which has been collected in the current sojourn, or journey in Earth.

Some would argue, what is the point of the journey in Earth? Our answer to you would be, quite simply, the point of your journey in Earth in the current time is whatever you choose it to be.

One seeks and finds and uses tools, wonderful treatments, exemplary methodologies of sight, sound, meditation, prayer. These are all stepping-stones.

In this specific work it is Consciousness that you are "seeking" and the stepping-stones or the methods, the treatments, all can help you step over the habit, over the current belief, to pass beyond the veils that separate you from Consciousness, which is, was, and ever shall be one with God.

> **January 7**
>
> Shatter the illusion. Release it by affirming your oneness with that Consciousness that does not know limitation.

    Those who deny the Completeness of their being one with all that is are denying their own existence and, therefore, they must perish.
    In other words, their belief in their limited nature leaves them only one way out. And the only way they can move forward, then, is to perish. Because of their belief in such limitation, the incompleteness of their Be-ing, they cannot continue on in a sojourn in the Earth or any other realm without it having defined beginnings and defined endings.
    It is through the experiencing of these beginnings and endings that understanding is built. Thus, the Wheel of Life, or Karma and reincarnation and such as this, are methodologies that have been put into place in order to facilitate these beginnings and endings.
    Yet miraculously, some will shatter the illusion of such limitation. How? By a simple pause to affirm that which is always theirs – their oneness with God – and by releasing, and moving into the Consciousness that does not know limitation.

> January 8
>
> Consciousness is being explored at micro as well as at macro levels. Yet one who knows Consciousness knows all.

    The Consciousness of God could be explored at the sub-atomic level, and in finer, and finer particles.
    There are those who seek it within these.
    And in the macro or larger scale, there are those who seek to know God in that which is beyond or above, rather than within.
    Yet how does one explore or examine Consciousness?
    That one who knows Consciousness knows all.

January 9

Can you walk upon the Earth and yet sustain your oneness with God? Do you believe you can?

If you question, "How did the Master, our Lord called Christ, sustain His oneness with God and yet walk upon the Earth?" the answer is just as you are doing.
But He believed.
Do you believe?

(That is given in a spirit of love and compassion.)

> January 10
>
> Passing through Consciousness, which has no references, the assurance that the path ahead is right must come from within.

In the search for that which has meaning there often will come about the need to make reference to that which is known or has been experienced by others.

So is it that, as one might pass through that level of Consciousness that has no historical references or experiences that can be sought out from one's peers, there is that which must come from within Self to be that power and that which gives assurance that the path ahead is aright and the course is appropriate.

> **January 11**
>
> Now is the time to explore the Colors of Creation. They go far beyond pigment. There are the colors of love, sadness, joy…

    Colors can be recognized of a broad array in the Earthly sense. You consider certain primary colors and others to be derivations or combinations of these.
    Yet you know not some of the expressions of "Color," for color is not limited to pigment or light.
    There is the color of love. There is the color of sadness. There is the color of joy, and on and on, and these colors are about you now. Yes, in many instances you will perceive or experience these "Colors" with the traditional color. Your guides help to bring these to you in order that you might seek one or two steps beyond that to know Self, to know the path.
    Now this is the time to explore the Colors of Creation… swirling, cascading masses of energies steeped in the intents or lack of intents that abound in the mass-mind thought of Earth and those thoughtforms that surround it in nearby or adjacent realms.

> **January 12**
>
> Experiences color our lives including those from the past, but what colors would you ride to the Consciousness you seek?

    Each entity is comprised of colors from the collage of experiences that constitute their memories.

    In many instances, if not all, the experiences from past events and circumstances such as past lives are also to be considered here, for they, indeed, color the individual as they enter the Earth. Thus, it cannot be said that one enters as an empty canvas, though the colors present are not necessarily specifically formed at that time but, rather, present moreso as influential reservoirs of potential. (We note that much thought might be given to that as just given, but be mindful not to become too intense or scholarly here. The intent is to *free self*.)

    So what can be meant by our commentary about colors and how they influence the individual and the nature of one's walk through Earth as a lifetime?

    It is not that you should look to the colors alone or to the emotions or energies that, for the most part, perpetuate them. It is moreso what "colors" would you ride to the Consciousness you seek? Which of these would you choose as a pathway for your journey?

    Know that not one is greater than the other.

January 13

Which is the greater, the Light or the Darkness? Which is the path? Does it lie through both, between, or a moderation?

In terms of pigment, you consider the basal colors to be the darker – the blacks, browns, grays, and such as this. When you look about the Earth the color scheme does include as its foundation the stone, the rock, the earth and, as you progress from that, the greens, more browns, etc. This might logically suggest that one would see this as a basal structure upon which the other colors might rest.

As you begin a journey in meditation, there is often the perception of naught and of darkness. Yet by the influence of conditions in the consciousness of Earth or by accepted standards, the darkness is considered not the best of all.

Which is the greater then, the Light or the Darkness? Which is the path? Does it lie through both, in between these, as a moderation of both?

When you seek in meditation the next time, *look* for the darkness. Let that be your quest, your ideal. And, if light is present or any color, see these to be step-stones and move to the darkness. (It is just, we believe, a pleasant little exercise.)

> January 14
>
> From whence do you draw your need or your reliance? As you fine-tune your intent, the familiar can actually be barriers.

Dependence upon, or need for, or reliance on, or expectance of the familiar... Such mechanisms, in Consciousness, (however subtle) can become significant barriers, as the tuning of Self becomes finer and finer and as you move beyond the scale of adjustment of attunement, so that new scales must be developed.

Then it is important to understand from whence have you have drawn these references, and do you control them at this point? The familiar essences that are not so easily defined... Are these within your control, or have you become so familiar with them that they are given carte blanche, free access to be a part of you wherever, whenever?

Which brings us back around to why understanding the Colors is valuable.

> **January 15**
>
> When you seek Consciousness, as you pass through color and sound, consider their origin, their intent, what they seek.

  Sound is a stimulating force created by those who intend to portray a thoughtform. Sounds created through the forces of nature are different from this to an extent, and yet the mass-mind thoughtform that is embraced and given life within the force of nature does bear qualities of this. Then sound might well be looked upon as another aspect of thoughtforms attempting to gain support for their existence. As one is sensitive to sounds, they can be freeing or severely limiting, moderately limiting and accepted or non-existing in the consciousness of one who does not affirm them.
  When you seek Consciousness, it is good to know, as you pass through color and sound, where these come from and where they are going. In other words, what is their intention? What is their thoughtform? What do they seek to gain or create? Consciousness, in the unlimited sense, would see these without differentiation. Whether the color is light or dark, the music harsh or melodious, the sound an outcry from an animal on Earth or words from an individual who walks upon same, these would be seen merely as that which is in that spectrum.
  The importance derived from the color pink is dependent upon the emotions one has gathered relevant to the color pink. In the level of Consciousness you are seeking, you can look back and see all these rather like undulating filament-like curtains, as though a gentle breeze is giving them sustenance. If you were to take them outside of those filamental curtains (using these terms very loosely), they would not exist.
  Pure Consciousness knows all because it is all. But it is not living within the color pink. The color pink is living because Consciousness, shall we say, *acknowledges* it.

> **January 16**
>
> As you *Know* through Universal Knowledge, Consciousness, what shall you do with that Knowledge?

    In the general sense (moving to a somewhat different level here), you are seeing the manifestation of the color of emotion in the Earth again and again at polarities.

    There can be the joy of a child just born in a hospital maternity ward, or the cries of a child who stands in the midst of the rubble of an earthquake that has just transpired. What colors would you portray these as? If it is a girl-child, perhaps the color pink we mentioned earlier would come to mind. But the child standing in the midst of an earthquake's aftermath is also a girl-child of a few more years. Would you color her pink, as well?

    How would you color yourself when you are joyful versus when you are sad? What are the colors of those with whom you share your life... your mate, your friends, your children, your relatives? Would you give them a color? Do you think that color would have meaning to others who know them as you do? It is a wonderful little exercise.

    As you *Know* through Universal Knowledge, what shall you do with that "Knowledge," the ultimate Consciousness or Universal Awareness?

> January 17
>
> In healing: The connection is not between healer and dis-ease; the connection is between the healer and the Law of Grace.

    Sacred Truth is the master sight, that one who is dis-eased might be seen in the completeness of their current state of being: If they weep from the dis-ease, are these tears coming from the immediate, or from the past; are they coming because the dis-ease gives them a means to be recognized and heard; or is it that the soul has done all it knows to do, and now is met at these crossroads, that a dis-ease has challenged the soul beyond its measure to respond, not through fault, not through error, and perhaps not at all by choice in any form
    Then can cometh one of righteousness and see this, and say, in the Law of Grace, "All that is, is restored to you." And the sight of that – which is an illusion unto one of righteousness, such as in this example – heals them.
    The connection is not between the one of righteousness and the dis-ease, for the dis-ease is meaningless. It is very important to understand this.
    To one awakening Consciousness, see it as the colors, the sound, behind the living curtains of Consciousness, knowing that you are not a part of it, unless you wish to be, knowing that it lives because its existence has been permitted.
    To those who would seek to know the colors... Be gentle with yourselves, and look about, and look within. Look at that which is, perhaps, still a part of the familiar.

> January 18
>
> What color is fear? Habit? Pain? At some point you become Free from limitation, and *you* are the creative force.

    At a certain point in your passage, you come unto that Freedom from limitation from whence *you* are the creative force.

    You could look back over creation into the Darkness and know it to be good and, seeing within the depths of it, creation yet unfolding like gigantic waves of light rolling forward. Yet at the periphery, are the veils of finite creation, level upon level of limited consciousness: *this* veil is a consciousness surrounded by a curtain of fear, *this* curtain surrounds those within it by habit, *this* is the curtain of pain, *here* is a curtain of celebration of the attainment of goals and ideals. What color are these veils? *Here* another curtain filled with conflict, and the colors swirl in a collage with no single definition.

    Or you could find yourself in the midst of the purest of Pure, the darkest of Dark, from whence one small thought is as a burst of light that is alive and soars and turns this way and that, creating sound and radiating rays of itself off into the Darkness, stimulating laughter here and there, as others who have claimed Consciousness observe it and see it to be good.

    In the movement of the Earth know this: The dawning that shall follow is one of goodness and beauty, and is that Light in which you shall see the Promise return.

> January 19
>
> In the finite, color was created as a tool to enable definition, expression, and communication by the user.

Color has consciousness.

What, you might ask. *How can pigment have consciousness?* Because they are not pigments. They are the very foundational aspects of life. They are those things that give definition and dimension to existence.

The colors of pigment are not in place by chance, by some curious freak of the universe in its creative formulation. They are by intent, by choice, by design. The colors are for the expression of what is relevant to Consciousness.

In other words, Consciousness, as it moved into finiteness, created those as tools to enable definition, expression, and communication in the finite, for there was the rapid recognition that Consciousness unto Itself could not communicate in finiteness or form without instrument.

Color, then, has life according to the intent of the giver, the user. Color is a living thoughtform arrayed with the collective mass-mind thoughts that have been associated with them. You probably are involved with their creation, but in your current finite consciousness or expression these are not recalled or not recognized.

Color and sound basically comprise the mechanisms of creation. Many of them have not yet manifested. In other words, they are as unused tools.

> **January 20**
>
> Consciousness is not confined. You don't find it by following a rote or dogma but by freeing yourself from rote and dogma.

    The pure Light of God has no color. Then what is it? And Darkness, does it have color? Not so as to be known.

    So we have light and dark... words, phrases, definitions. Do not stumble over them.

    Consciousness is not confined nor limited. You don't find it by following a rote or dogma. You find it by freeing yourself from rote and dogma.

    The threads that bind are those things that are deep within you, things that you have come to accept as requirements, mandates, expectations, or the comparative measure in Earth. These, in a manner of speaking, have force. They are like a whirlwind that has suction that pulls you down into itself, into its embrace, and the more you relent and move into this, you are giving it life. If you do not give it life, it will not perish, but it will not be a line that tethers you, a thread that binds.

> **January 21**
>
> The expansion of one's joy is most recognizable when it is reflected, when it is amplified by the presence of another.

    This is a sacred Truth: The expansion of one's joy is most recognizable when it is reflected, when it is amplified by the presence of another.

    When that one who is with thee has less consciousness, the gift is diminished. When that one is of greater consciousness the gift is accelerated. Yours is the opportunity to limit them or to join them.

> January 22
>
> One can speak of light, can argue over it, but until one experiences the light and returns, no one can know it in its truth.

Consciousness is God and God is consciousness.

Oneness cannot be equated by the standards of Earth.

It would be difficult to feel a sense of complete Oneness, true Oneness (without some reservation), with one who is a child molester. But were you to move beyond the Earth to the Sacred Silence and see this child molester, there would be no hesitation or reservation.

The differentiation, then, lies within the consciousness of self and the Consciousness of the Oneness that is being contemplated.

If consciousness is from a position at the bottom of a well, how much of the world (the world being Consciousness) can you truly perceive from the bottom of a well? You would need to move out of the well and stand beside it, that your consciousness can be more expansive. You can know the well but have no need to be in it, unless of course you find shelter, comfort, some sense of protection or ease within the well.

In the example of cave dwellers, they can speak of light, they can talk about it, they can argue over it, but until one experiences the light and returns, no one can know it in its truth.

So the question is, does one then claim Oneness from the bottom of a well, from the depth of darkness in a cave? Or do they consider that the position must be comprehensive in order to embrace and encompass... *encompass*, see... creation.

> **January 23**
>
> Experiences felt as monumental in finiteness, in Consciousness are known as momentary, like grains in a sand mosaic.

    Through a one-way glass, seeing a child molester answer questions in an interrogation you would be steeped with emotion if you knew the details of the crime.

    But to look at the child molester from the Sacred Silence, you would see this in the perspective as a gigantic mosaic, as some of the Buddhists make in the beautiful sand paintings and then erase them because this symbolizes the nature of Consciousness and existence.

    It is momentary. It is a few grains of sand in the mosaic of finiteness, which is embraced within Consciousness. It becomes a minute portion of something, which is a minute portion of something, which is a minute portion of something, et cetera, until we move from the minuscule to the maximum, which is Consciousness.

> January 24
>
> Generally, one chooses challenges such as fear, sadness, war, dis-ease, etc. because they "need" it in order to become Free.

If you look from a position of being "seated beside God" (so to say) off into the wonder of Consciousness of all that is, you can see only the beauty of all that is.

Or if you wish, you can look off in this direction or that in an immeasurable "distance" (as you would know it) and see the veils of illusion or separateness, and you could know that the primary intent of these veils are the choices of those who dwell within same. For them, it is the shelter of the depth of a dark cave. They do not have to deal with anything other than what they have accepted and constructed.

You could ask, *why would anyone wish to deal with fear, or anger, or sadness, or war, or dis-ease?* In the general sense, because they "need" it in order to become Free.

> **January 25**
>
> To shatter the immutable, call forth the love and laughter of the Child within. This is the strongest force of all.

    The realms of darkness that surrounded the Earth, called the Shadowland, were swirling masses. Then the creative power of God within the darkness became filled with the laughter of the passing children, the children of the tsunami.

    In their short tenure in the Earth, these children yet had their gifts of God... their youthful vibrancy, their love, their compassion. As they left the Earth, filled with their gifts, and passed through the adjacent realms, they were still in conformance to the "Universal Laws" of finiteness, and so their gifts could not be denied. So the Veils were rent, cracked, if you will. Their laughter and joy seeped into the Shadowland and reached out.

    Those who had been dwelling in the Shadowland (some for eons and eons) who were willing were carried off to wheresoever they would be capable of moving, all the while surrounded by the love of God in the form of the laughter of the child.

    To doeth the work, let the laughter of the Child within be the strongest force of all, for it can shatter the immutable. That which is insoluble can be melted away with the love and laughter of the Child within.

January 26

Punch a hole in Earth's precepts of limitation and look for the path that brings you to Freedom. Re-member Consciousness.

The Master gave it: These flowers afield are filled with the radiant beauty of a loving Father, and yet they labored not for it. They simply are. No greater can be manufactured in Earth than what is given as the freely given gifts of God.

Yet in the journey called life there is a thoughtform that hangs over all those who enter and, though some can find the measure of their child within in spite of this, most struggle. They manage to make their way a few steps, and then return again and again.

Now, in these times, the predominant thoughtform will be shaken and some will make the way passable. Some will find the way to use their own inner laughter and joy to transit and become Free. This is, as we see it, what you are seeking in this work of "re-membering" Consciousness.

In the Earth, you are given to the precepts, the massive all-pervading thought that overrides all else. Punch a hole in it. Look for the path that brings you to this Freedom. When you are hesitant, the Freedom is not present because the Law is perfect. In other words, if you deny It, that is your right; when you choose It, that also is your right.

January 27

All that you seek and greater awaits you. You have that power and right to seek any of it, all of it, or to create even greater.

Recognizing that all that you seek and greater awaits you, it becomes a question of recognizing that you have that power and right to seek any of it, all of it, or to create even greater.

The Seeker shall open because the Seeker chooses.

The Reader shall tell it because the Reader chooses and, in the telling, they manifest it.

The Listener receives according to their willingness, and their reception of what you read is that which can guide them to the vestibule of Freedom that lies beyond the doorway.

Those who experience what is said become the finite expression of the thoughtform.

But if the Reader says, "Let there be Light," the interpretation of that statement becomes the product of the listener, not the product of the speaker.

In the knowledge of Sacred Truth, there is no thing that can be in any sense limiting because the Sacred Truth is that one is Free. When one claims that aspect of the Sacred Truth – Freedom – then, to answer a call, as with and in the Master, it is a (perhaps you might call it) *no-action event*: The call is answered as the caller gives it. The Master's presence is the reflection of the Truth that makes the way passable.

> **January 28**
>
> To journey to Consciousness there must be the willful-ness, not simply the willing-ness, to so do. Go, then. Journey.

For a journey to Consciousness, there must be the will*ful*-ness, not just willing-ness, to so do. In other words, the choosing along the way in order that the way is made open and passable.

It is good for each one who seeks to understand the intent, the ideal, for any work: *What is my intention for this work?* So is it, then, important to know, as you seek Consciousness, what is your intent?

If you seek to move into Consciousness and observe and look for the limits, the walls, as one would look for the walls of a large room in darkness, then your journey will not be as joyful as it might otherwise be. If you go to Consciousness primarily, if not singularly, for the experience itself, then all things will become known to you.

Do not – and we underscore this – <u>stumble over intellectualizing this</u>.

Go, then. Journey. Close down the last vestiges of finite consciousness and move forward.

In the Consciousness of the non-finite, there is the presence, first and foremost, of a sense of awe, a sense or feeling that one is in a holy place. We do not mean holy in the sense of tradition, mores, religion, cults, dogma, creeds, and such as are in the Earth, but holy in the sense that the Self within is awake or is awakened, that it is from this position of the Self (capital S) that one is Conscious.

In a meditation to Consciousness, a part of the journey is knowing what *is* Consciousness, for there are no sensory mechanisms known at the Earthly level. There are only those things that are eternal. The "only" has to do with the Consciousness that can move without limitation, instantly, fluidly, with only the subtle intent to so do.

> **January 29**
>
> A part of the journey is to consider: What *is* Consciousness?

[Note: From here on, we are including some of Al's experiences as recounted in the "Consciousness" readings. These numbered journeys refer only to Al's journeys in his intent to recover Consciousness while yet finite. Prior to these readings are thousands of others, and hundreds more since.]

[Journey 1 begins:]
 The perception at first, as our Channel journeys, is one of a vastness, indescribable as might be presumed.
 Yet there is some sort of linear expression that seems to demarcate varying points, not so much as literal things but as shifts in Consciousness. These shifts in Consciousness are very, very diverse, as you would measure them from finiteness, and the distance between them is as though to make them alone or utterly separate, yet in Consciousness they are not. They are, in essence, the byproduct of others who are in Consciousness at this point in time, as you measure it.
 To this, our Channel, these are seen as angled, almost vertical shimmering sheets, subtlety different than the void of Consciousness as it was initially perceived. Then there is the capability of perceiving this more and more as he allows his consciousness to enjoin with it, taste of it, feel it, experience it. (One needs to be mindful that so doing in pure Consciousness can draw one into another's creation or others' works... this given for reference.)

> **January 30**
>
> Any work that engages the right of Free Will of others triggers finiteness. The desire to do good works is hauntingly sticky.

[Journey 1 continues:]

Over to the other side (using this for reference only), there is another sheet, more luminous and of a lighter color. It is like a beam of light in a foggy nighttime, a concentrated beam but in a sheet form, very subtle. This is angled a bit greater than a 45-degree angle from a right angle. The reason for this angular definition is that it is how it is perceived, and that has to do with the effect and influence upon the Earth.

These are Prime Energies drawn from Consciousness and being directed into finiteness as a benevolent intent. These will manifest in the Earth in the form of the energies defined as color or emotion or thought or energies of perception. The intent of these is to bring about an awakening, that entities who are in deep routine, not knowing of their right of Free Will or who have relegated same, would come into consciousness of these potentials.

The Channel moves away from these, sensing that he does not want any limitation. Though his curiosity is peaked, he has moved away from them and moreso into, as you would define it, *pure* Consciousness. He has recognized that to move from pure Consciousness into intention is to become limited. Albeit subtle, it is s a limitation. It is not relevant what the ideal of that intent is, for any such work that engages the right of Free Will of others precipitates finiteness. It is hauntingly sticky, the desire to do good works.

In the journey that he has moved to at present, he is exploring Free Consciousness, and as such is... well, simply is.

> January 31
>
> Replacing all thought with a state of simply *be*-ing invokes the Spirit within and brings a sense of joy and Oneness with God.

[Journey 1 concludes:]
  We are perceiving the peace and joy that is radiating from him. It is deeply engaging. There is a powerful field resonance that is profoundly fetching, causing the perceiver, the viewers, to be drawn unto it. It is not so much that there is a command, a statement, an intent. Rather, the absence of it.
  You might find that the elimination of all thought and the replacement of thought with a state of simply *be*-ing invokes the Spirit within, the Light that is eternal, which brings forth a sense of joy and the Oneness with God.
  Here, in order that we can perceive him, Consciousness is giving us an image of him. It is a beautiful sphere, luminous from within, delicate rays of light first appearing as small colors upon the luminosity, and then softly reaching out from the central core of his glowing brilliance. There are so many that the sphere is seen as having rays of energy coming out from all around and about it, but not so many so as to obscure the perception of the sphere. It is lazily turning, simply being.

[Note: After the reading Al explained to his wife, Susan, as he recalled his experience in the reading that, at this point, he was attempting to reach out with his beingness to <u>Know</u> Consciousness. The colors (he suspected) represented his various reactions.]

  We move a bit further away in order to sustain communication with you, for connections between souls are powerfully in place at this level of Consciousness, and those that are invoked or created by Free Will Choice remain. They *remain!* In Consciousness, they are paths, paths of sharing and such. So from here, a movement in Consciousness away, we can tell you that he is at peace.

> February 1
>
> There is intent from beyond Earth that is engaging the shifting energies, aiding understanding of the gifts of change.

    The energies in the Earth that are shifting and moving, with more forthcoming, are intended to be gifts.

    The angled Wave of Intent we recently spoke of passes through the Christ Consciousness, or the Sacred Truth, into the Earth, accumulating energies that allow the "colors" of Consciousness to manifest.

    In other words, the angled Wave provides for the gifts of change to be understood amidst the thought and emotion and desire and these sorts of things that are the rod, the measure, of Earth in order that that which is hidden can be seen and understood.

> February 2
>
> To know Self is one of the greatest journeys of all. To "move into" Consciousness enables that process.

There is considerable wisdom in asking to be in Consciousness, for to know Self is one of the greatest journeys of all and to "move into" Consciousness in the individual sense enables that process.

When one interacts with others, that interaction produces a by-product. In other words, two entities interacting create something that is not the thought of one but the thought or product of the two, which becomes, in essence, a third.

When you add another and another and another, this becomes more and more expansive and this is very empowering. Hence, the Master's statement, *"Where two or more are gathered in my name, there am I."*

But to know Self is, indeed, a very beautiful thing.

The Master knows Self.

> **February 3**
>
> No thing is impossible. Limitations cannot be associated with the journey in Spirit. Consciousness is oneness with God.

Those things that can be burdens or limitations that befall one in the Earth cannot be associated with the journey in Spirit or Consciousness. They are not so interactive as one might assume. It is more that, as one knows a thing and becomes it, then that is like a shield, a greater force than the predominant force that is environmentally encompassing that one in their expression.

For the Channel to have an experience here that is considered powerful, spiritual, pure, and then to return to the Earth and have a tooth fall out, is not relevant. These are independent. Are they a matter of concern? Of course. But when was the journey of the issue of the tooth begun? See?

This is not to evade the power of God and the promise of thy Brother. It is to put things aright. How deeply does the habit, the concern, the doubt, the fear, the question reside? How great is the consideration of the byproduct or after-effect and how it will manifest?

Consciousness is oneness with God, and thereof no thing is impossible. Yet no thing in the limited sense is present; all things are present in potential or possibility.

(You will understand this more and more as you progress but sufficient for now, we believe, is what we have given.)

February 4

Does your environ have an effect upon what you believe or what you experience? Who chooses the environ?

[Note: We will begin including communication to the Channel that was repeated on the recorder for Al's benefit upon his return. Some may find interesting the directions, suggestions, and shared experiences that sometimes occur during a reading between the Channel and the Lama Sing group. Generally, the Channel's side of the conversation is not recorded. Ellipses have been included to represent the space, the pause, in which the Channel is pondering or communicating.]

[Journey 2 begins – To the Channel:]
The Light shining down comes from Consciousness. It is the invocation of that which brings to you the next phase of realizing that Consciousness is the All, or, all of Consciousness is of God. ...

... You have seen this and experienced it in the sense of "no thing," the "Nothingness" (as you have titled it), and now there is the light. The contrast is to illustrate the contrast of polarity, which is imbedded in all potential, all that can be and could be created. So there is now this potential for reference, seeing these different experiences as polarities. ...

... As you turn about now in the light and find it to be (as you have called it in past) delicious, how is it deliciously different than what you experienced previously? The point here is not to create a distraction for you in your current wonder, but for when you return to the Earth to consider: Does the environ have an effect upon what you believe or what you experience? Who chooses the environ? ...

... In midst of the journey from Earth to here in future meetings [readings], you might explore this, perhaps choosing a color or colors, or choosing to not feel the need to be devoid of any thing in order to "qualify" to enter here (humor intended).

February 5

> Those who would dominate pound thoughts of limitation into the Earth century after century. The Truth is Freedom.

[Journey 2 continues – To the Channel:]
 The Ideal leads the way and makes it passable.
 You stated, "I seek Consciousness." That ideal as your choice blends with the ideal of the soul, which is service. So the service is shifted to service to self. The knowledge of service to self and the fulfillment of same are empowering to the service that follows: service to others. ...
 ... The continual denial of self in service is a greatly limiting factor. Even though the Law of Just Return applies here, to what end, if it is returned to a cup that has no opening in which to receive? ...
 ... These are subtleties imbedded deep within the foundational structure of the thoughtforms prevalent in Earth, pounded into it by generation upon generation, century after century, of intended thought directed by those who would seek to dominate rather than to free. The true intent is to free.

> **February 6**
>
> To manifest something in finiteness do it first from beyond, from whence it then enters back into finiteness.

[Note: This entry and others ahead have to do with a group of four – Al, Susan, and another couple – that began exploring the abilities of humankind that are more or less latent, including the ability to heal wholly and completely or, better, to awaken our true and perfect nature while yet finite. Entries dealing with manifesting Consciousness stemmed from this group exploration.]

When one seeks to manifest in finiteness, there needs to be the realization that it does not occur from within finiteness. It occurs from beyond and then enters back into finiteness.

It begins with the Consciousness as a principle, as an ideal, as a playing field, if you will, into which the players can move (that given very colloquially). Only then can the manifestation that is a part of the physical truly take root and manifest according to that which is being sought.

But even here, we find that there are those qualifiers that are deep within each that need to be met. These are numerous and each would find them unique unto their own nature.

> February 7
>
> Even things that are of joy, satisfaction, and pleasure to you can be a limitation when seeking Consciousness.

[Journey 2 continues – To the Channel:]
 ... Now, take a form and experience Consciousness in form. ...
 ... As you turn your head up to allow the light to irradiate you and you feel the beauty of it, to what are you turning your head? ...
 ... You see? Even here there is the subtlety of influence that tells you the flow of God's loving Light is above you. Is it? Could it be behind you? Could it, perish the thought, be below you? ...
 ... Now, give up your form again. Without a reference of finiteness, form, you do not look up. You simply reach out, sort of omnipotently, in all directions simultaneously and you feel the flow of that light or energy to you from all directions, from all reference points. ...
 ... Shift, now, back to a form. ... Yes, a physical body. ...
 ... Look at your hands. See them made of light? They are not of flesh, yet, every detail, every finite aspect of it, is present. Bring your hands up closer. Look into them. Turn them over. Do you see the life, the vibrant energy? ...
 ... Put your hands together with palms facing you and see your own reflection in them. Do you see glasses? ... No. Do you see youth? ... Of course you do. Why do you not see this when in Earth? ...
 ... Now, give up this body again. ... Aha! Is there a hesitance to do so? Do you find that something that is manifest and is of joy, satisfaction, and pleasure to you is more difficult to give up once it is yours? ...
 ... So being formless and being Consciousness lost its allure for a moment there. Isn't that curious? And now that you are back in Consciousness, do you feel a sense of something missing? Do you feel a sense of loss? ...

> February 8
>
> Definition gives understanding. Definition offers the seeker tools by which they can comprehend.

[Journey 2 continues – To the Channel:]
 ... Now, if you would, move. Just begin moving in whatever direction you would consider.
 ... Yes, your normal intent would be forward or backward. Move forward, then. ...
 ... Do you *feel* movement? ...
 ... But you are moving because you intend to move. Do you see anything passing you by to indicate movement? Would it help you to see anything passing by in order to know you are moving? ...
 ... Then pause for a moment. Perceive yourself moving through a beautiful grand, very broad corridor that has no ending that you can perceive in the distance. To the right and left, ornate columns reach up to a wonderful array of facades and architectural designs with patterns and colors. Beautiful, isn't it? ...
 ... Now, move again forward. Do you see all this passing by? Do you know, now, that you are moving? Of course. So then, it could be said (as a premise, at least) that definition gives understanding about one's action. Definition offers to the seeker tools by which they can comprehend. ...
 ... Let us now release that thoughtform. It is gone, and yet you are moving. Do you feel the same? ...
 ... Well, then, take form. That very nice form that you just had, bring it back. ...
 ... You create it by your recall of it. *Be* it.
 ... Very nice, isn't it? Energized, powerful, filled with light, and yet so soft and gentle strength of immeasurable description, yet it is gentle enough to birth a flower from its seed in the palm of your hand. ...

> February 9
>
> For there to be sound, color, fragrance, feelings of warmth or coolness, must there be a conventional source?

[Journey 2 continues – To the Channel:]
 ... Now, let us move again. This time let our movement be through substance. Let the Consciousness about you have substance. ...
 ... Simply know it to be until you can feel it moving past your form, perhaps a bit of subtle movement of your hair. You can feel it as a wind from the Earth gently bringing you sweet fragrances of what lies beyond. You can feel the warmth of something that you are moving towards. You begin to become aware of aromas, of feelings, of tastes, of sounds, of colors. Why do you feel these things? Why do you know them? Is it because Consciousness has substance and you have form? ...
 ... Now, let us move instantly back to what is generally called a formless state, and let us allow Consciousness to be "pure."
 ... You are still moving, aren't you? ...
 ... Do you hear the sound of peace? ...
 ... Do you hear the sound of sweetness and joy? ...
 ... Do you see these? ...Can you taste them? Feel them? ...
 ... Not without creating it first, true? For you are pure Consciousness and, in the *purity* of Consciousness, any such creating might be thought of as a limitation and a movement from pure Consciousness. Is this true?
 Or is it possible that you can, in pure Consciousness, choose to experience these things in any form or manner as is your choice? Would it then follow that any of the perceptions known in the Earth could also be used here if you choose to use them?
 The point in all this is, must there be the reference point in order to know movement? Must there be a source for there to be sound? Color? Fragrance? Feelings of warmth or coolness?

> **February 10**
>
> If Consciousness is the beginning and ending of all Creation, then all must be within you and a mere choice or two away.

    If Consciousness is the beginning and ending of all creation, then all of this must be within you, a mere choice or two away.

    Is it, then, that your thought of having such choice creates a concern within you? Would you, perhaps, consider this to be approaching the level of God? That, in Pure Consciousness, should you make such choices and create such actions or intentions, you become the Creator? And, of the potential that lies within such a consideration, would you be fearful? Would you question whether or not your motive, your intent, your ideal, your purpose, your goal, any or all of this are equal to that of God?

    For, isn't it written or taught that God has none of this, but is the sweetness, is the joy, is the love, is all of this with an open heart, an open hand, that grants absolute free will choice?

    Then is there concern if you are in Consciousness, which is God, and you make choices, that these choices would then be perpetuated, would precipitate out into finiteness and impact others, and thus you could be doomed to centuries of karmic return?

> February 11
>
> You stand as a wondrous being of light in the midst of Pure Consciousness. Make your choices, do your works, from *here*.

[Journey 2 concludes – To the Channel:]
   ... Take form, again. Now, hold out your hand. ...
   ... We place into your hand a tiny grain of seed. Close your hand around it. Feel it in the palm of your hand. ...
   Its potential is defined only because it is believed that it is defined. The plant from which it was born or propagated placed its own thought within its seed, and then, with faith in the All, released its seed, which is as to say, released itself.
   You stand now as a wondrous being of light in the midst of Pure Consciousness, and in your hand is this simple seed. Is the potential for its life within its definition, or in your willfulness to open your hand and say, "Be as thou would. Be that which thou can." ...
   ... Do it. ...
[Pause]

   ... Do you see the flower and the plant in your hand? Do you see it to be good? Give it, then, to finiteness. ...
   ... How? Look off to the side in the distance and you'll see the veils of separation embracing finiteness. Send it there, just as if you would toss a gift to someone off to the side. Only, this is different, for it sort of creates its own movement. It moves into the energies that are, as you look upon this, connected from Consciousness to those definitions. ...
[Pause]

   An "adept" might learn to do the same, according to the choices of finiteness, and make those choices and manifestations *from here*.

> February 12
>
> An adept begins the exploration by studying those things that are wrong. A master never does this, for there is no wrong.

It doesn't matter whether you are in the Earth in physical body, deep within the realms of limitations about the Earth, or in the midst of the most pure Light of all. It still has to do with what you are willing to accept, what you believe in, what you have come to constitute as your reality.

Discovering what those parameters and defining boundaries are is no small undertaking. Many in the Shadowland became trapped because they continually energized that very thing that was limiting them.

What differentiates, for example, a good, beautiful, joyful journey in sleep versus one that is lumpy with the gravy of life (with a note of humor)? The precept is the same: that one begins with a consciousness and ends with a result. If it was less than of sweetness, one of several limited choices follow, either the entrée into the sleep period was not with a precursive thought of sweetness, or the will of the Spirit opened the way to make it possible to search out memories, fragments of limitation, any areas of concern or doubt so that the nights' dreams were actually in answer to the soul's request, little guidances.

You ask for guidance, you ask for awareness, you ask to be enlightened, and so it is given, given, given.

The adept soul knows they are adept, first and foremost. The master soul *is* a master soul. Knowing, believing, practicing and all that sort are not considerations.

If you are a fish in water, why would you ask to be a fish in water?

You are already what might be asked for. An adept begins the exploration by studying those things that are wrong. A master never does this, for there is no wrong. You might want to reflect on that.

> ## February 13
>
> If you believe that you must work at it, then your belief makes it so.

    If you believe that you must work at it, then your belief makes it so.
    But if you *know* that you *are* it, then you will *be* it. And the fruits will fall from the tree according to the tree, not according to what passes by the tree.

> **February 14**
>
> In the beginning all was God. In the ending all is God. What is in between?

In the beginning all was God. In the ending all is God. What is in between?

> **February 15**
>
> Look upon all that is with an open hand, open mind, open heart. Release the need of any thing and be Free.

[Journey 3 begins:]
In this journey with the Channel, we intend to afford him some of the gifts of Consciousness that he has not accepted to the present time in his incarnation in Earth.
[pause]

We pass through the bands of beautiful color that represent influences of finiteness. They are becoming thinner and thinner and we recognize that the sense of freedom grows with the thinning.

As one releases the need of any thing, they are much more free. It is not to say that one must abandon or cast aside but, rather, to look upon all that is with an open hand, open mind, open heart manner.

Any of you who may read these works and who consider that you have done these things, then, it follows that you are free! Do you *know* that you are? Therein lies a pivotal point. In the knowing that one is free, one might ask, *Where do I go from here?*

It may be possible that our brother will recall that, woven into the color in this journey, was sound, intentionally so in order that there could come the grasp of the influences of sound and color as they interplay. Once they are seen (so to say) at arms length and are used as a *means of movement*, their position in Consciousness becomes different.

We are pausing here, and the Channel is moving off into the beauty and wonder of Consciousness, where we shall allow him to be.

> **February 16**
>
> How do you recreate within your memory sounds, odors, tastes, feelings tactile and emotional. How real is it for you?

Look about you in Earth and see what is there. Then close your eyes and see what is there.

Listen to music, the sound of nature, children laughing, people talking, a symphony. Then cover your ears thoroughly and listen to what is there.

Smell the odors of the Earth... fresh bread, a sumptuous herb, fresh mown grass. Many different things come to the forefront. Smell the fragrances of various flowers, perhaps a spring rain. Now, cover your nose. What is there?

Feel a bit of silk, a bit of velvet, feel a handful of sand, run your hand over a stone, lift it, feel its weight, its density. Grasp a handful of leaves and close your fingers on them. Now, open your hands and let them be free. What do you feel?

Taste a bit of sugar, then a bit of vinegar, a bit of salt, and so on. Then irrigate your mouth so there is no taste remaining. What do you taste?

The point of this little exercise is to indicate to you how temporary these perceptions can be. The wind can carry a fragrance to you and just as quickly stop, and the fragrance is no more. Music begins and ends (in the consciousness of Earth) for the most part, as does laughter, and on and on. But when you think about these things in your mind, they become real once again. You can explore how you recreate this and discover that, within your memory, you have colors, sounds, odors, tastes, feelings both tactile and emotional, and see how real it is for you.

The point is, when you move upon the Colors as was suggested to the Channel, you are not only moving in the dimension of creation in which you dwell but upon something you have accepted, chosen. It is a part of you.

> **February 17**
>
> As you move, willfully releasing all memories and references, you become more empowered to command everything.

[Journey 3 continues:]

As you move, it is important for you to be capable of releasing all memories and references. As you release everything, you become more empowered to have or to command everything. It is the <u>willing</u>-ness to <u>willful</u>-ly release: Is there any thread that causes you to hesitate? Is there some inner twang that you feel when you are about to release something that is deeply loved?

There are many aspects in the consciousness of an individual that have become so much a part of memories, thoughts, feelings, emotions, that they are almost inseparable. You, our brother, have learned how to separate your consciousness from those things, those aspects, for the purposes of doing what you call readings. Now, as you seek to know Consciousness, you are coming to realize that, within Consciousness, all of these are, that the level of existence or expression is dependent solely upon the choice, *your* choice in Consciousness.

Now, universally, those threads that could limit or tie you to a state can be released through Grace. The power of Grace creates an action that brings about harmony. Grace transmutes (so to say) karma or balances that which is imbalanced. Viewing Grace as orange (for example), you would perceive action. In the blues you would find something that is foundational, the essence upon which other expression can be manifested. Blue is very much a color of service. It provides the means for other colors to manifest and express and to be perceived.

> February 18
>
> In Consciousness movement is not definable by passing something in a linear sense. Movement is will-full. You *will* it.

[Journey 3 continues – To the Channel:]
 ... Notice how, as we are closer to you now, that your perception of Consciousness, or your oneness with Consciousness, is altered just a bit. ...
 ... The awareness of others in your presence, whether you are in finiteness or in utter Consciousness, has applicable relevance according to your choosing of it. ...

[To the reader:]
 If you are in a group of people in the Earth who are speaking, you can choose to speak or not. If someone directs a question to you, how does that change your sense of Freedom? Conversely, when the conversation follows a course of discussion you disagree with, how does that feel? Does an energy rise up in you? When you are feeling the call to offer an alternative, even to disagree, what does that feel like? That is a Color. What Color is it?

[To the Channel again:]
 ... As you continue to explore Consciousness, we are moving you. You feel something growing within you, so to say, "defining" movement. In Consciousness, movement is not definable by passing something in a linear sense. Movement in Consciousness is a will-full thing. You *will* movement. ...
 ... You are willing movement now because we are connected, and we are the influential force because you permit it. Our choice to move you is as though *you* have chosen to move. You are experiencing, in this moment, a building of perceptive consciousness. It is consciousness that is known because we are choosing your state of consciousness. The point at which you were joyful, peaceful, awed, you were submissive. ...

February 19

> By moving through Consciousness you are gathering an increased perception of it. Employ your abilities to perceive.

[Journey 3 concludes – To the Channel:]
　... Now, there is the influence of our empowering you. In other words, in a manner of speaking, were you to have a rheostat control on a light bulb in a lamp and you slowly turn it to increase the lumens of light being emanated, this is somewhat parallel to what we are doing. ...
　... No. It isn't that you have moved (the lamp hasn't moved), but where there was a dimness of perception, the "increase of the dial" increased the "lumen output," and so the field of perception becomes greater. ...
　... By moving you through Consciousness, you are gathering an increased perception of it even though, in the traditional sense, there is only the peace and joy and laughter and love that seem to be perfect no matter where you are. So are we stating to you that you are gathering more and more perfection? Or is perfection like finiteness, like, *here's a bit of perfection, here's another*, like grains of sand, that soon we have a bucket full? ...
　... To Know Consciousness, employ your abilities to perceive. Then let these be step-stones to build those perceptions that you aren't quite so familiar with or that you don't recall quite so well. ...
　... This is not complex. It is not distant. It is not something one must study intently. It is simply that, in the being and doing *with perception*, one comes to gather within self Consciousness.
　If you come to a difficult place on a path you are traveling, you walk around the obstacle to understand it better, to see what can be done, what is the easiest path.
　In this instance, there is no obstacle. There is only the continuity of perfection. What are you gathering, then? What are you experiencing? ...

> February 20
>
> The Children of God reflecting to God that which is, *is* God... yet different. What is this difference? What is its nature?

[Journey 4 begins:]
    Consciousness knows Itself.
    Consciousness knows all that is.

[To the Channel:]
    ... Wherever you move in Consciousness, there is that which is the potential: that which is thought of, and that which is then expressed. Yet *pure* Consciousness does not dwell on these, does not hold on to these. Therefore, they are not in form (as an expression in finiteness might hold a creation). ...
    ... We will pause with you that you can look about. ...
[pause]

    ... Now, feel the potential, as we call forth the creative potential. Let us, first, feel joy. What does it feel like? ...
    To assist us here, Zachary has come forward.

[Zachary is well known to the Channel, as he is one of his guides. They have often been together in past lives and now in these works, called readings.]

[Zachary To the Channel:]
    "Now you know what joy feels like, because it is reflected to you.
    "The Children of God reflecting to God that which is, is God. I, in the singular sense, am speaking to God. You, in the singular sense, are God listening to me speak to you. So it could be said that God speaks to God. Yet we know that it is different. What is this difference? What is its nature?"

> **February 21**
>
> You can move from the subjective to the empowered, from the yielding to the claiming... one is no greater, simply a choice.

[Journey 4 continues:]

If you are an architect and you reflect, and then create drawings, plans, blueprints, a color scheme, have you actually created it? If you design a multi-storied building, when you have completed the plans, is it a structure? Have you created it? Or could we say that you have made the way passable for it.

The presence of Zachary with our brother makes the way passable for Consciousness to know itself, to expand itself: As the Channel moved through Consciousness, he accumulated Consciousness because he was moved from the subjective expression to the empowered expression, from the yielding to the claiming.

Which is the greater?

There is no "greater." It is the choice that determines which shall be.

Several of our group have joined with Zachary and the Channel, and we have moved into a "place" in Consciousness where we intend to build a consciousness, literally create it.

Gathered together in a small geometric formation intending to manifest, each of us contributes something to the center of our group.

Zachary reaches behind himself, pulls a handful of beautiful butterflies forth, and laughter is all about. The Channel, then, getting the idea, waves his hand across and creates a stunning rainbow... in the midst of Consciousness, mind you! Now all gathered are doing the same, some offering sounds, others offering other things, and as we look upon them a light is building around them.

This Consciousness is a collective intent, increased because more than one participant is present. The number increases the potential because of that position in Creation.

> **February 22**
>
> Be one with Consciousness and let the memory of Consciousness, which knows all, be that which contributes through you.

[Journey 4 concludes:]
The brothers and sisters gathered here in this "place" in Consciousness are in discussion as to whether they have called some memory forth as they created.

The light grows as this discussion continues about where it was that they each got their contribution, and the now boldly shimmering light in the midst of Consciousness is drifting, we might say, off to the side. This "place" is no longer *pure* Consciousness. It is *expressed* Consciousness, a collective intent. Each member of the group is free, so they are creating from a position of Freedom.

The beautiful light has no color. It is, in essence, a veil, a *realm* of Consciousness. It has no color because there is no color for it to be, because it did not come from finiteness. It came from Consciousness.

Consciousness knows all. Consciousness remembers all. Consciousness is all. So, knowing this and remembering the rainbow that was created, do you believe it was created from the Earthly memory? Or did Consciousness offer it when the Channel was asked to contribute something? And what is its composition? Color? Light? Each contributed something unto the collective intent that gave it even sound and substance.

It is much like this in the Earth. The purer one is in their conscious ascension, or reclaiming, the more pure is that which they create.

One can draw on a memory and use that memory to do a work, to create a thing, and it could be something of contribution. Or you can be one with Consciousness, and as you see a need or feel called to contribute, you can let Consciousness contribute through you, not your soul memory and not your singular memory but the memory of Consciousness, which knows all.

> February 23
>
> Dwell not too long on that which limits. Spend great quantities of time on that which sets you Free.

    Consciousness has the potential for all expression. (We are referring to Consciousness and creation.)

    It is often said in realms of finite dimension that wherever one encounters another who is in a state of dis-ease that the creation has gone awry, has been influenced by something less than Consciousness. But from Consciousness comes the answer to all that anyone would ever meet, for the creation of what *is* flows from Consciousness. Thereafter, it is formed and fashioned in whatever ways have been the choices of those involved.

    The point here is the beautiful Law of Free Will. Then what is sure to follow is the question: What shall we do with Free Will?

    The Master does a work because He has stated, *"I Am. I and the Father are One."* In other words, *I Am Consciousness.*

    Dwell not too long on that which limits; spend great quantities of time on that which sets you Free.

    None of this is offered that you would labor nor that you would struggle but, rather, that you would *not* struggle.

> **February 24**
>
> The initial prerequisite to enter Earth (to set aside the higher Consciousness) can give way as one gains tenure and chooses.

We realize it is very difficult to comprehend how it might be that you need only do several things and all that you seek and greater are yours. Yet it is so. How? You "build" a thing by recognizing it requires your participation. It requires momentary (or longer) pauses throughout a given day in order to strengthen it, to give life to it, no different than one who tends a crop and would, on a regular schedule, tend those to see that their needs are met.

The dedication to a work cannot be measured in the sense of one's anticipation of a "reward," but rather that, as one seeks to become that for which they are striving, they become the instrument of that, augmented by its attainment.

In seeking mastery, the journey is equal in importance, if not even greater, than the attainment of that as a goal.

You are in the Earth by choice. You have chosen to accept those predominant forces integral in the consciousness of finiteness. In order to enter into finiteness there is the prerequisite that you set aside your higher Consciousness. (Understand, now, we are going to use such terms for reference, not to be stumbled over.)

You enter into the Earth having been through all that is involved in preparation and you assume the consciousness of the Earth, nurtured by that which is surrounding you. That consciousness is, at the onset, preserved by Universal Law. But as you gain in tenure in the Earth, that initial preservation begins to give way to the forces that were known in the review of the life prior to entry, that were known and chosen for that lifetime. Then, as you progress through that life, various things can awaken you, challenge you. You choose, through free will, how to respond.

February 25

Finite consciousness is limited. But God lives. The greater Consciousness is the true power, the true and eternal life.

The Master's entry into the Earth in the lifetime as Jesus was immediately into the blessing of the Expectant Ones. He was known to be the Promise. He was continually supported and nurtured in every respect in order to fulfill the Promise, the Prophecies.

His journey through that work as the Christ, brief as it was, was to demonstrate to those in the Earth:

- that God lives
- that there is that which is worthy of recognition while one is in the Earth
- that the spiral of finite consciousness, which was and is nourishing itself, has only limited form
- that the greater Consciousness, which is eternal, is the true power, the true life.

February 26

Do not judge whether or not this or that is a miracle. You are the miracle. Recognize and celebrate the master that you are.

Now is that point that the Light comes.
Be at peace with this and celebrate it.
Let your faith be that Light that you give to make the way passable.
And do not judge whether or not this or that happens miraculously. You are the miracle, that your path has brought you to this point.
We humbly encourage you to see and to recognize and to celebrate the master that thou art.
[pause]

Healing is a matter that comes up oft in the Earth. There are many issues that can be brought to the forefront in discussing healing as a topic.
As prayers come to you, answer them, and do it in a manner that you *know* you are answering the prayers. Do this. Do it with love, with laughter, but *with a certainty* and a faith that, as you ask it, He will give it.

> February 27
>
> Consciousness includes the finite realms of expression. It is only they who dwell therein who choose to ignore it.

Consciousness is so beautiful.

Remember, Consciousness *includes* the finite realms of expression. It is only they who dwell therein who choose to ignore it. Yet there is no life without God, without Consciousness, no existence without His presence.

> February 28
>
> Look at any stumbling block and see it from Consciousness: a tool to use to rise above who you've come to believe you are.

    Use what you know to use. Use what is before you. Use that which you believe in.

    When you find yourself stumbling over something that you have stumbled over in past, now is the opportunity for you to stop and truly claim dominion over it, to identify the role it has played in your life, and then to place it as a stepping-stone for you to move beyond.

    In other words, as one might stumble over something again and again or find something limiting to self again and again, deal with it in the manner as described, using the wondrous presence of the Sacred Truth to see it for what it is, not as the "limitations" that the emotion or habit have evolved so that you would perceive them as such, but see them through the Consciousness of the Sacred Truth. Pick these things up and see them as keys, tools, to help you rise above who and what you have come to believe you are.

> February 29
>
> How can Consciousness be absolutely pure if Consciousness contains the All?

    The Channel is not alone in his journeys in Consciousness, of course. But he is correct that he is, in *his* consciousness, alone there because he does not choose to move beyond the level of Consciousness to any form of finite memory.

    The Channel is currently defining pure Consciousness as simply being... simply being one with the All, the creative potential of God. See? There are memories in Consciousness, his and others, but he is choosing not to "know them." Very poignant if not powerful, because, as has been stated, *"As it is here, it is also within."* And if the Channel is here in Pure Consciousness and he goes within in that same intent and he chooses not to know them, what is it that he doesn't know. See?

    We have in past talked about knowing self and knowing that which is thy intent, thy goal, and the importance of same. Here, the Channel chooses. It is his intent to be in the utter purity of Consciousness.

    How can Consciousness be absolutely pure (in that sense) if Consciousness contains the All? It is that his *choice* of Consciousness is the relinquishing of all awareness in the sense of Knowing and, rather, choosing Be-ing.

    There is a choice involved, and it is very powerful.

    So then, if the Channel chooses to be in pure Consciousness, it is because he *Knows* pure Consciousness. Knowing pure Consciousness means that he remembers *Be-ing in* pure Consciousness.

> March 1
>
> A bond of Light with others in your world or beyond awaits only that you would know of it, claim it, and choose it.

[Journey 5 begins:]

Only those who have a very powerful bond of Light connecting to him – fashioned out of a living love that forms only through the experiencing, and passing through the veils, of finiteness, the "colors" of finiteness – can reach the Channel in his choice of Pure Consciousness.

So he found, to his utter amazement and delight, a dear brother present in the midst of Consciousness, who is known by the name of Jude, or Judas. The sweetness of this bond was built out of pure love: the willingness to sacrifice all for others.

Think about this a moment… How many could fulfill the prophecy by being willing to take the role of Jude in his lifetime with Jesus that had the conclusion in finiteness as is so widely believed? So in a similar way both of these, as brothers in that lifetime, were willing to give all they had to give, and did so. This offered them a bond of love that is virtually unbreakable, so they are eternal brothers. That bond of Light is strong enough that Jude saw, and knew, and chose to express in a form of reactivating that love, and the Channel now sees him.

Then came Zachary with an equal bond of Light, differing circumstances in that lifetime with Jesus in some regards, yet equal. So he, too, was able, according to the Law, to reach the Channel in pure Consciousness.

Now, there are many other bonds of Light, lines of Light. They are not lesser or greater in any sense than these three brethren. It remains only for all or one to know it, to claim it, and to choose. See?

> March 2
>
> Color is produced by emotion. In times of heightened emotion, colors can be swirling masses with no direction.

With Color you find a means of expressing. Colors are produced, in effect, by emotional reaction, by emotional habit, and by the defined and agreed upon definitions for emotion.

You have the colloquial terms: *I am feeling blue*; or, *I am seeing red*; *this has been a golden day in my life*. These colloquial uses of Color do have relevance to finiteness.

Regarding levels of Consciousness, these Colors are likened unto actual realms. Not as in a brown realm, a green realm, etc., but more as reference points. As one journeys from finiteness in the Earth, some (not all, see) are aware of passing through the Colors. Usually those souls who are aware are capable of perceiving these Colors as reference points as one moves through the energies, the emotions.

Here's an example of some Colors of emotions: Visualize a small group of children playing at the seashore in the sand, building little structures. As though they are miniature gods they create, in a matter of a few minutes, an entire realm of finiteness in the sand, and through agreement amongst them (though perhaps unspoken), they all see it as a castle or some such and so it *is* for them. Then an older child chasing a ball comes racing across their creation, and perhaps with a bit of ill intent and mischievous laughter, not only chases the ball, but also stomps their creation to bits.

There is a moment where the younger children are numbed. For a brief time, that was their consciousness. It was a reality that they had agreed upon between themselves and had created. Suddenly, in a brief moment, it is gone.

In a moment such as that, Consciousness is very fluid. The Colors are not separate but swirling masses of emotion with no direction.

> **March 3**
>
> The color of a habit, the color of remorse, the color of a need, the color of domination, the color of... See? Nothing but color.

    The creation of sand of the small village or castle that the children had carefully sculpted is now gone, and they are stupefied. Most of you can recall seeing small children in that state. They might sit there for a moment and, then they begin to wail their woe at the destruction of their beautiful creation.

    One is demonstrating anger, throwing a small pail and yelling threats at the larger child, who is ignoring this completely. Another is sobbing at the loss... such differing arrays of reaction here and there in this small group.

    But look over here at this one little girl. Her face is blank. She looks from one to the other without reaction and then down at her portion of the creation, now shattered. Without a word, she quite happily bends over to begin fixing it. She scoops the sand up carefully and pats it back into place. The tiny flag that was atop her creation is uncovered beneath the sand and carefully, lovingly, thoughtfully placed atop the creation again. Oh yes, the creation is not quite the same, but it doesn't matter to her, for the creation is not where her joy is. Her joy is in the being, the doing, the reaching out and feeling this wondrous day, the warm sun and the water lapping up to the edge of the seashore. No time to be angry or despondent, for she knows that what she created previously she can recreate and perhaps even add a new dimension to it.

    After a time, she stands, brushes the sand off her hands, and runs off to find her parents. She doesn't even think to tell them of a bully. One of the other children has run sobbing to their parents, another has gone over to a larger child and is kicking sand at him but not so with this little girl.

    You see? Nothing but Colors.

> **March 4**
>
> We paint with emotion. We paint with words. We paint with thought. We paint our life, our experience, with Color.

What is finiteness? Why have you chosen it? What is the level of Consciousness that is a part of finiteness? What are the levels that the Channel could tell you about that he passed through for this reading? What is it about? Why does a body ever have to experience dis-ease?

All of it has to do with knowing the potentials that lie within the Colors, what their source of origin is, and how they manifest.

Colors... Colors are the tools with which one in certain levels of Consciousness can paint their reality, just as an artist with oils and canvas could paint a scene and you, viewing it, would feel what the artist is trying to share with you. A grand sunset, a path leading through the crowning embrace of wondrous majestic trees lining a pathway through a forest, the splashing of water over rocks along a creekside dotted with flowers and small children...

You see? We only have to tell you these words and you immediately create. Isn't that true? And of what do you create? You can't say, in truth, that you are totally recalling a memory, can you? So we have given you a gift of color. Don't you feel a bit different now than before when we said this to you?

We paint with color. We paint with emotion. We paint with words. We paint with thought.

March 5

The wonder of potential is the urge that spawns finiteness. It is Perfection knowing Itself.

In the dance of the Colors there are many things to be discovered. It is your choice whether you find joy in the moment, whether you see the moment as bringing you blessings, wondrous life-giving rain, sunshine that feels so wonderful upon your face and hands.

Colors... in the pure Consciousness all these things are. *Knowing* them, see, brings you into finiteness. It is the wonder of potential that is the urge that spawns finiteness.

The journey into finiteness should never be looked upon as a burden, as a penance, as something less than Perfection knowing Itself. It is the reluctance to see in this way that is limiting. Everything in the experience offers a gift that can lift you up.

So if something happens and your sand castle is smashed, know that you are the creator, and that what you create might be even better than what was.

March 6

> Change is the movement that bears the fruit of discovery. See the balance and harmony offered in all change and claim it.

The only way that Truth is truly known, in order that a soul grows in its beauty and in its brilliance of light and knowledge, is by its movement.

Change is the movement that bears the fruit of discovery. Then see the balance and harmony being offered in all change and claim that. No matter what comes, keep your eye and your heart joyful in the center of that balance.

> March 7
>
> You are becoming awakened. You are asking yourself: *What is Consciousness and how do I Know myself within It?*

[Journey 6 begins:]
There is a "bridge of consciousness" within each entity. It is a bridge that spans the breadth and depth of the unknown in order that one can move from that which they know in the current to that which lies beyond.

The nature of the bridge is dependent:
- first and foremost, upon whether or not the seeker is truly or *consciously* seeking or if this is more passive
- secondly, if this is an active seeking, though the focal point may lie beyond the current knowledge, that it is nonetheless the cornerstone of that one's faith.

[The Elders to the Channel:]
As you discussed with your mate earlier this day, you look upon Consciousness as a state of being that is near perfect.

But as you also discussed, you are cognizant of something that lies beyond where you are in your current state of awareness. You are becoming awakened and, from this, asking, *What is the nature of Consciousness, and how do I Know myself to be within It?*

Some ways might be relevant to sensory perceptions as are known in Earth such as sight, smell, taste, and feeling... perhaps as the feeling of warmth or cold or neutral, and feeling as might relate to emotion.

What you are wisely avoiding is exploring and knowing Consciousness through memory, through remembering.

> **March 8**
>
> Deep friendship, companionship, can be a profound "force" even in Consciousness.

[Journey 6 continues – The Elders to the Channel:]
  Movement is apparent to you in this journey, and as you know it, you are recognizing that you are knowing it without the usual conscious reference points that would be indicative of motion.
  And this time, as you had asked for the companionship of your brother called Lama Sing (but who has other names as well, of course, as do you), his companionship with you is manifesting a difference compared to your previous journeys when your intent was to experience it alone. Your movement into Consciousness is impacted now by the presence of this one who is so loved and who has in past been so meaningful to you and you to him.
  As you continue to move, there is a subtle but evidential force that seems to be attracting you both. That force could be described as having some magnetic force to your very being, to your Spirit. You two are, in effect (by definition in Earth), embracing one another and the movement is continuing towards a distant destination.
  We can hear your communication (although it would not be *heard* in the normal sense). You ask Lama Sing, "Have you a perception of what is pulling us? I find it very curious that I know I am moving, as though I have moved beyond my previous position in Consciousness. How is that possible?"
  We perceive Lama Sing's response. "I believe the force giving us momentum is the point of our primary junction."
  "So the point at which you and I became friends?"
  Lama Sing merely smiles.

> **March 9**
>
> Any limitations are those *you choose*. The subtle imposition of those limitations becomes yours, then, wherever you journey.

[Journey 6 continues:]
"I feel a slowing, Lama Sing. I feel we are now stationary in Consciousness." The Channel is struggling, it might be said (with a note of loving humor), not to think too much.

"Why not let go of any struggle to balance? We are in the embrace of God."

"I need to be in this new position in Consciousness. I need to be... to *be* it. Do you understand, Lama Sing?"

Lama Sing (in essence) moves to the side of the Channel in a way so as to be utterly neutral. If you were able to perceive, you would not perceive Lama Sing in this moment, for this state of neutrality is at the level of God, and he is extremely adept at so doing.

The Channel is perceiving, qualifying, but perish the thought he would call it *thinking* (with another note of loving humor). In a moment, he realizes that any limitations here are those that he chooses and that, after the choosing, the subtle imposition of that limitation becomes his.

In the realization of this, he begins to softly laugh and he begins to perceive lumens of color dancing here and there all about. He communicates softly, *"Lama Sing... !"*

[pause]

"Yes... Beautiful... Very beautiful."

> March 10
>
> From Al: Spirit, when it chooses and creates, endures long past the physical ability to perceive it, perhaps forever.

[Journey 6 continues:]
   "Lama Sing? Would you laugh for me?"
   A soft bit of laughter rolls out into Consciousness from Lama Sing. Golden and silver flashes occur here and there.
   Off, very far off, the Channel can hear something. As though he were reaching out with his own being, suddenly *he is* what he hears... He is the gentle sweet laughter of his beloved Lama Sing, coming from far away.
   He *is* it.
   He feels himself moving in free form, expanding and contracting, turning upwards, then downwards.
   He feels the different colors.
   He knows the different tones, but they are no longer the sounds that would be made of a physical body laughing. They are something far beyond this. They are as the wind in some sort of crystalline tubes or something that he has no explanation for... something very, very beautiful.
   "From early times," a voice speaks softly.
   In that moment, the Channel realizes that Lama Sing has been with him the entirety of this experience, yet he continues to soar, to sail off as the colors and sounds and energies of the laughter remain. They haven't diminished as a laugh in the Earth would.
   On and on it continues.
[pause]

   Then there are some flashes of light, some curious sounds, as Lama Sing "touches" the Channel.

> March 11
>
> From Al: The absolute Freedom found in Consciousness is immediately conditioned, limited, by rational thinking.

[Journey 6 continues:]
    The Channel begins to consider what he has been experiencing. A bit of an inner struggle ensues as he so does, and the brilliance of Consciousness seems, to him, to be changing...
    And changing...
    And changing...
[pause]

    All about him now is the brilliance, the beauty of this gathering place, and he sees instantly that it is as though he has fallen, not as one would fall from a high place to a low place but *fallen* in Consciousness to that which is moreso defined. (*Moved*, might be the better word for the Channel to use, *chosen* might be even better.)

> **March 12**
>
> The thinker is the creator. The substance of the thought is the substance of what is created.

[Journey 6 continues:]

The Channel is being greeted with great embraces and loving comments by some who have chosen form. Some place their hand beside his head and lean forward to touch their forehead to his. Others make gestures from their heart to him and other greetings of love that they have shared over eons.

Jude comes and takes the Channel's hand and the Channel flushes with the energy that occurs as their hands meet. "Jude, what is that?"

"That is our recognition of one another and the gifts we intend to each other. They are meeting at the juncture of our hands. In Earth, you use your hands as implements. In truth, your hands are an extension of your Spirit. If you employ them with that as the ideal, your hands empower you to go beyond your native energy, your life-force. But come."

The Channel is back in the expanse of Consciousness.

> March 13
>
> In Earth, knowing comes as a response to stimuli to what is engaged; in Consciousness, Knowing is through receptivity.

[Journey 6 continues:]

The Channel finds he has returned to the expanse of Consciousness with such speed that he turns to see where he has come from.

Jude notes this. "Involuntary reaction, right brother? In Earth, you look back to see what you've gained. It helps to tell where you are on the pathway, if you have chosen one. If you haven't chosen one, looking back helps you to know where you are on someone else's pathway."

Little sparks of light slip from the Channel, whishing, crackling, soft but audible, which the Channel hears and notes with a bit of chuckle.

"As has been given so many times, thoughts are things. The substance of your thought is the substance of what is created. Those sparks were your curiosity. You were delighted by the experience and the sparklets of energy were created by that, and the reason there were many small ones is because there wasn't one primary intent."

"I understand, Jude. I know what you are saying, not just by hearing it as in the Earth. I am *knowing* it here."

"Knowing," continues Jude softly, "is not necessarily the same at every level of one's expression. Knowing is somewhat aligned to the willingness of that Spirit (or that soul) who has the willfulness to be receptive and not just responsive.

"In other words, in the Earth, knowing often comes about by a responsive reaction to what is encountered, what is being engaged, the colors on the pallet of your life that you can draw to that moment. The colors are interactively involved, closely associated to all the other sensory mechanisms, and to all the emotions, and to memory, to history, and on and on.

> March 14
>
> From Al: Memory can be limited in its completeness. *Knowing* in Consciousness never is; it is always complete.

[Journey 6 continues:]

Jude communicates to the Channel. "Be in my thought with me."

The Channel does and he can feel the sweet tranquility of Jude. Suddenly, the Channel is everywhere, and as far as could be perceived and beyond that and beyond that, he is capable of Knowing.

He feels Jude do something curious, as though he is embracing all of these places, simultaneously. Though the Channel cannot quite conceive of how this is done in the technical sense, he realizes that Jude is placing himself everywhere simultaneously and then *calling* to himself (in a manner of speaking). As a parent might call to their scattered children lovingly, *Come to dinner,* an action of love intending to nourish the children, Jude is nourishing creation, all of Consciousness, *with* Consciousness! In a manner of speaking, Jude is loving himself, everywhere simultaneously, with joy.

In that moment, the Channel realizes that Jude is claiming Oneness with God and, instantly, he can see Jude's laughter. It is so similar to the earlier laughter of Lama Sing, yet carrying different essences and energies, moving in somewhat different ways, as best he can recall.

Jude reaches out to the Channel. "Don't try to remember it. Lama Sing's laughter is still here. Simply Know it."

Instantly, the Channel can *see* the laughter of Jude and Lama Sing as though they are dancing together.

> March 15
>
> From Al: Allowing, believing, and Knowing are tools that can set you Free to the Consciousness that awaits.

[Journey 6 concludes:]

Up, down, sideways, as some remarkable bird of the Earth might fly in such changing patterns, yet in perfect harmony, the movement for the Channel is a lazy one. In great spiraling arcs he swirls.

And he Knows that he is laughing, and he can hear the laughter of others. Lazily he moves and soars.

He is moving, moving, down towards the familiar, and he Knows that he is moving. He Knows it because he allows himself to Know it. He Knows it because he believes he can Know it. And in this moment he is Free.

The gift he has claimed is Knowing (with a capital K), and the Knowing has set him Free. In this state of Freedom, his Consciousness can move as it wishes, yet, even though it passes now, soaring in great lazy arcs through the Sacred Truth, he is not of it.

With a simple intent, he sharply swerves upward to spiral, still laughing. Then he turns down again to claim his oneness with his mate.

They embrace and clasp hands in the nature as he knew Jude to do with him and their energy becomes as one. Off they go, soaring gently as one might soar lazily across a great plain covered with flowers and fragrant shrubs, and then over the mountaintops and down, gazing at one another, rolling about as they soar, laughing.

> March 16
>
> There is naught that is without Consciousness. Believe that you *are* Consciousness. Believe that you *are* Free.

    If one believes something to be possible, it is possible. If one believes something is not possible, then for them it is not possible.

    If you believe that Consciousness is a place that is demarcated, separate, and has only this quality or that nature, any of which might be violated causing the one in Consciousness to leave it, if that is the belief, then so is it for the believer.

    But the power of Consciousness is omnipotent. There is naught that is without Consciousness.

    To be wheresoever you would choose to be begins with the belief that you *are* Consciousness, and that that Consciousness can set you Free.

    In this time, in this day, in these works, you are Free.

    Remember it often.

    And when some matter in the Earth is challenging or limiting, remember that you are Free. None can take this Freedom from you, for you *are* it, *if* you can remember and claim it and be one with it.

> March 17
>
> Join the celebration that this way is being opened.

[Journey 7 begins:]
    For reference, the entry of the Channel into these realms has been met with dazzling joy, celebrating the presence of him, his mate Susahn who travels with him, along with those from the Earth who are beginning to awaken more and more as these words are known and lived, including those who will come to this work later.
    Some present are the guides of colleagues from the Earth. Others are guides for those the Channel does not know at present in his Earth consciousness, though, here he knows them well. The celebration is that this way is being opened.
    One of the larger groups in this meeting is comprised of the Holy Maidens (from a "past time" of some distance), and they are gleefully greeting the Channel and attempting to lure Susahn into their group again for an outing of their own, so to say, not unlike some outings they shared in past.
    Several others have come to the Channel and are moving him to more of our group waiting to greet him. Of particular interest to the Channel here is the presence of Michael. The Channel moves up to him. They embrace, and now they are communicating. A moment, please...
[pause]

    The complete communication cannot be given in the constraints of this meeting, but the sum of it is, the Channel asked what brought Michael to this gathering.
    Michael smiles, communicating that the Channel only presumes Michael not been present all the while, and Michael begins to move the Channel more and more rapidly.

> March 18
>
> From Al: Previously, we were made aware that memories can be limiting. Now we are shown how some can be Freeing

[Journey 7 continues:]

The Channel feels the movement accelerate and looks about to determine how it is that he knows of this movement.

Michael merely glances at the Channel, yet the Channel hears, "The parameters of Consciousness are not defined by substance, as you know emotion and color and sound to have substance, nor is it (as those in Earth have defined) relevant to particles and waves. For all of this has to do with the nature of those who have defined it and perceived it and such. As you look forward (since we are, you might say, angled in that direction), what comes to your perception?"

While Michael has kept his gaze upon some point to which they are moving, the Channel had been observing the remarkable features and countenance that Lord Michael has displayed for him here, the way his hair sweeps backwards and seems to be ever-so-slightly being blown by an unfelt wind. Now, following Michael's gaze, the Channel looks ahead. He perceives only vastness. He, then, looks all about. The (he would call it) Nothingness is astoundingly clear with awe-inspiring depth and peace, and an embrace of a nature the Channel has not ever recalled; yet, something somewhere in him seems to *Know* it.

Michael draws the Channel's focus back upon the distance (as though towards a horizon, though there isn't such). "You have avoided the aspect of remembering in order to feel. Have you considered that there are memories within you that would not be limiting? Rather, would be freeing.

March 19

When one knows Self, all else that is can be known.

[Journey 7 continues:]
After Lord Michael has conveyed that some memories can be freeing, a rush of energy passes through the Channel.

"*Now* look, Channel."

The Channel focuses, and in the remarkable clarity here, he thinks he can perceive a shimmering, as though somewhere the sun or a star or some planet were refracting light upon the very body of space itself, *this* space of Consciousness! A swift review of all he can perceive and he Knows there is none such here... no sun, no moon, no stars, just this grand spaciousness. Yet he can feel it, a subtle essence.

In the next moment he knows they have come to a stop. He realizes Michael is looking at him, smiling softly in a way only Michael seems capable of doing. "From here, you must go on alone, for that is your choice. It is the nature of what you have set as your ideal: knowing that you are never truly alone. In the sense of your ideal, then this is completely valid. For when one knows Self, all else that is can be known; yet the Uniqueness of Self not only remains but is empowered.

"The value of creating an ideal has its breadth and depth of merit in the realizing of it. As one does so, the ideal that is attained becomes the step-stone to that which lies beyond it. But you cannot know the next step in the fullness until you attain, become, the ideal that you have set forth.

"Know that I am ever with you."

Before the Channel can speak, the energy that is Michael begins, in essence, to dissolve and is gone.

> March 20
>
> Cleave unto your ideal, for it can sustain you through all.

[Journey 7 continues:]
    There is a period in which the Channel engages in some rebalancing activities, which he knows well from decades of honing such skills for the purposes of the works (the readings, meditations, and guided meditations) he has done.
    He feels himself balancing with the dimensional absence of one expression that is dearly loved, and he engages in the cognizance of his oneness with Michael, even though that dimension of recognition is no longer functional. Thus, he shifts himself for a moment and "recreates" Michael, and Michael is present. Michael does not speak or communicate, but the Channel communicates to him, and then releases the thought of Michael, receiving, as the presence is released, a smile and a nod as though to say to the Channel, *Well done.*
    The Channel, realizing what he has just done, begins to glow a bit. There are subtle collages of self-consciousness but very subtle. Most perhaps could not even perceive it, but since we are one with him in this way, we can recount it to you.
    After a time, he readjusts and draws to the forefront his ideal. The ideal, you see, gives strength to one who finds a disruption on their path, the rod of God that can be used to set the way aright and to give one dominion over any thought, thing, emotion, or whatnot that would try to gain life from you by being recognized and held. Thus ever is it encouraged to those who might hear these words—know the ideal and cleave unto it, for it can sustain thee through all.

> March 21
>
> He realizes something wondrous: that he has only just begun one of many journeys into Consciousness to *Know* God.

[Journey 7 continues:]

The Channel realizes the wonderful gifts Michael has brought him. As he bathes in this, other potentials come flittering about as though to lure him to give them life, to create them, yet he only smiles at them.

One thought seeking to be born is, *I am not worthy.* Another seeking life from him is, *This is all impossible. You are a fool!* But the gaiety and joy filling the Channel make a purity here, and the thoughts swiftly fall away, for they have naught to sustain them with life-giving thought or energy.

A memory then comes to the Channel that resonates with his ideal: Consciousness! And his movement is resuming... this time, alone. A lightening bolt of tempting thought regarding aloneness passes through him but he gives it no footing, and he falls into peace, *the* Peace of God, the Peace of Consciousness and, all the while, he knows he is journeying.

He reflects upon what he experienced with Michael, filled with the essences of Earth – color, sound, light, scent. Though sensational perceptions have no footing here, nonetheless, there is the yellowish glow... subtle, subtle, subtle, that seems to be pulsing, gently, no particular form, just freely, way out there in Consciousness.

Suddenly, he is in it! He realizes that he is spinning and soaring, moving, and all about him are glorious rays of this silvery yellow, wondrous energy.

He knows there is more, so he reaches for his ideal...
Consciousness. ...
Consciousness. ...

In this, he realizes something wondrous: that he has only just begun his journey into Consciousness, that this is only one of many perspectives, and that the sum of these is God.

> March 22
>
> All that is known and all that can be known, let these be a quest within you.

[Journey 7 concludes:]
    The thought of all that he has been experiencing is but one of many perspectives that sum to God, and the quest for definition and the quest for understanding, causes him to shift. As though one would take their child and move them from here to there with loving tenderness, and then set them free to be, the Channel begins soaring and spiraling, aglow with the joy of his journey.
    Some of the silvery yellow color remains with him and he touches it. It is as though he breathes it in, taking of its scent. He holds it, listening to its song. And he is filled with laughter.
    The embrace of the Maidens is as though they raced to catch him and give him support as he begins to slow in his movement, his journey, his experience, back into his service with Our Lord, with his brethren. Each of the Maidens jostles him a bit and offers a small quip or bit of humor, and he does nothing but laugh.
    They continue until Susahn comes forward from the midst of the Maidens and embraces him. They turn, arm-in-arm, to bid farewell for now and soar off together in a magnificent spiral, acknowledging the colors, the levels, the realms as they pass through them, turning to laugh with one another as they feel each of these and memories come, old challenges that were overcome and now are step-stones, the peacefulness of accomplishment, the joy of knowing that all is aright, and the harmony of their love bringing them into a state of ease.
    They pause, for on the periphery, to his delightful surprise, the Channel can see ever so clearly our Lord Michael accompanying them now, bringing them back to Earth.
    And so we conclude this journey. All that is known and all that can be known, let these be a quest within you. For surely, as you so seek, all these and greater shall be given unto thee.

> March 23
>
> Mind is that quality of Spirit that has an intent to be manifest and to understand its manifestation.

It has been asked: Do I have mind in Consciousness or is it something different, like knowing?

Recognizing that the question is asked from finiteness (or from consciousness in Earth), from that perspective there is the need to understand in order that you can comprehend the answer. Mind in the Earth is like an activator, in harmony with the Spirit, with the heart, with the emotion, and with the choices or will of the individual. Mind, then, is conditioned in terms of your definition of that word in the Earth. Therefore, our answer is no, mind does not exist here in Consciousness in the sense that you define mind in the Earth.

Mind is a tool of Consciousness when Consciousness chooses to manifest itself into the finite. Mind is that tool that is used by Consciousness to create.

Mind is that which seeks to know itself in finiteness and, as such, becomes cognizant of itself in Consciousness.

Mind is that quality of Spirit that has an intent to be manifest and to understand its manifestation, and thus to comprehend the nature of the dimensions of finiteness.

Mind is that which can see and do according to the will. The will is associated to Spirit, so Spirit is intended to have dominion over the mind. Mind in the Earth often does not accept this and is subjugated by the "mass-mind" thought, the collective nature of those forces or energies which either are used or unused. The power associates with the strongest, most dominant.

March 24

Consciousness *Knows*. *Knowing* does not require thinking, evaluating, adjudicating. Consciousness *Knows*.

Addressing a statement we have heard, that all things have already been created and that all that is occurring is that we are choosing different plays to play in...

Considering Consciousness with a capital C – in other words, Consciousness beyond the finite, beyond definition – Consciousness *Knows*. *Knowing* does not require thinking, evaluating, adjudicating. Consciousness Knows.

When you *are* Consciousness in the Earth, you are the Christ in a manner of speaking.

If you perceive from finiteness it is understandable that you could consider that all that is or ever shall be is already in existence, for finiteness has, by the matter of its own definition, definition. See?

But Consciousness is unlimited, ever expanding, ever unfolding, and always alive.

To consider that all exists that ever shall exist, and that movement through existence is merely a sort of random or serial selection of what should be explored next, is a part of the cognizance of finiteness. It could be called an illusion.

Existence is alive, as God is alive, as Consciousness is ever a part of that which is open, creating, unfolding... manifesting, yes, but willing manifestation, no.

Consciousness is that force that goes before all of existence and makes it possible in a manner of speaking.

> **March 25**
>
> You have a *song*. The song is You.

[Journey 8 begins:]
The Channel is being greeted by a Child of God... delightful, beautiful, no form, only pure Consciousness.

This is a Child of God who has not experienced finiteness, though not an angelic being as that title would infer to you by definition in the Earth. The Channel is being greeted as this Child of God would greet any other such Child of God, and the initial impact upon the Channel was that he was awestruck by the beauty.

The greeting was to call out his song, for this Child of God and all others know him and he knows them.

Because a portion of his being is focused in finiteness in order to sustain the expression as a life-form in Earth, he is (in a manner of speaking) incomplete here, thus the momentary imbalance at the encounter.

This Child of God is the fulfillment of sweetness, an immeasurable quality of innocence and purity creating an environment for the Channel that is quite alluring. This is very precious, wondrous, spontaneous.

It is an occurrence of Consciousness not planned, not expected.

It is a very beautiful, beautiful, primary event.

March 26

Being Consciousness means reclaiming that you *Know*.

[Journey 8 continues:]
　　The Channel has pursued more questions than had been asked verbally prior to this reading. He has been questioning here but in the sense of Knowing, reclaiming that he Knows more than he has asked. In that, he opened himself beyond what he *had* been open to.
[pause]

　　Excuse us. We must digress a bit to share this event, for it is profoundly beautiful.
　　The Child of God has become one with the Channel.
　　The Child of God is reaching into all of the consciousness of the Channel.
[pause]

　　You may feel the Child of God touching you at this moment, Susahn, as this Child now Knows you.
[pause]

　　The Child of God is passing through all the consciousness of her brother, the Channel, and in (as you would call it) the twinkling of an eye has reached out, through him, to touch every member of your group, pausing to bless each one.

> March 27
>
> You are a Child of God. You are God in a form of Uniqueness of God by intent of God.

[Journey 8 continues:]
    The Child of God now invites the Channel to Know her.
    (We will attempt to remain in communication with the Channel. If this is not possible, we shall conclude relating this work auditorily so as not to disrupt them.)
[pause]

    All that is experienced is indefinable in your references, huge arrays of dazzling light and colors and beautiful sounds.
    Something is occurring with the Channel that might possibly be understood as showering the body from the inside with the essence of Peace. You in the Earth would perhaps think of it as love if it were manifest in finiteness. But here, it is something far more profound.
    The Child of God is now moving off just a bit to leave him in his individuality as an honor to him and all of those whom this Child of God now knows and, as well, this work, which the Child of God knows and offers blessings to.
    You could think of this Child of God *as* God in a manner of speaking but by intent of God, in a form of Uniqueness. This is who you are, each of you. You contemplate Consciousness and existence serially so. To honor that perspective: This is you as you were when born of God in the pure form.
    This Child of God is stunning. The beauty is beyond measure or description. The Channel is infilled with it.

> March 28
>
> The essences of the Principles of "Masculine" and "Feminine" are but one of many Colors of a Child of God.

[Journey 8 continues – To the Channel. Again, the ellipses before and after comments indicate pauses, during which communication is occurring between the Channel and the Lama Sing group. Of course, the group responds to the Channel non-verbally. They are only providing words for our reference and for Al's upon his return to physical form since he does not always recall the entirety of his experience:]

   ... No. You cannot bring this back into finiteness. Not in this form. ...
   ... Because the Laws of Manifestation, Universal Laws, cannot permit this, lest all the free will of mass-mind thought is violated. ...
   ... No, it would *not* be benevolent. ...
   ... Yes. If you can manifest it such that it is within you, that, then, complying with the Law, *then* you can do this. ...
   ... Be in the peace of it then.
[Very, very long pause as the Channel experiences the Peace]

   ... Yes, of course there are others. ...
   ... The Child of God found you because she chose to find you. ...
   ... We call her *she* because she's defined as an aspect in the Feminine Principle. ...
   ... No. It is only a definition when expressed in finiteness; as a Child of God, it is a quality, an essence. ...
   ... If we were to define it for you, it is as a collage of many, many particles of color. The Feminine Principle would be as *a* particle of color within that Child of God, and thus we do not choose to call her she. For interpretation, we use this reference that we know would be understandable to you, but we only use it as a form of translation and communication. ...

> March 29
>
> Letting go of the familiar is part of the process of reclaiming Consciousness while yet in finiteness.

[Journey 8 concludes – To the Channel regarding the issue of Masculine and Feminine:]

... No, it is *not* limiting, it is not overstepping. It is merely to perceive and to attempt to define perception. ...

... We would define you as *he*, yes. ...

... No, not in the sense of exclusion but in the sense of the Principle. That particle is moreso the active, defined, from your consciousness, as the *he* Principle. ...

... No. Both of you are balanced equally in (what you call) Masculine and Feminine. But there is the uniqueness, you see. ...

... We do not know how God chooses that uniqueness, but that is a good question. Might you ask that of she? ...

... You would ask of she in the same manner as you are asking of us. You would only turn to her, and ask it. If you will hold the question, she will answer you. ...

... If you do not perceive her in the moment it is because you have moved away from perception of that nature. To return to it, simply choose it. ...

... No, you do not need to remember it. It always is. In the Earth, you remember; here, you simply Know. ...

... No (that is humorous). Not thinking it, knowing it. ...
[pause]

Very well, the Channel has chosen to rest for a time, so to say. He is simply dwelling in Consciousness, trying to dissipate fragments of finiteness, with a note of loving humor.

Isn't it curious... When you move into the infinite the tools of finiteness are often the first ones that you seek to employ.

> ## March 30
>
> Lines of Light are those pathways that exist between entities eternally.

The question has been presented, *Why is it that the Channel has not encountered many others?*

Understand this... Consciousness does not manifest form except as Consciousness chooses to create or to perceive in that manner for the purposes of specificity unto the choices of that Child of God. Therefore, the Channel, in the midst of Consciousness, is in the midst of numerous other entities (we shall call them). But since they have not expressed form, there is naught to see.

Can he Know them? Of course. He has not chosen to.

His brethren, Jude and Zachary and certain others, including his mate, can join him because of the "lines of Light," so to say, the eternal pathway that exists between them.

Do others have such a pathway with him? Yes. To date no others have, to our knowledge, chosen specifically to be with him in Consciousness. In order for them to do so, the same release of finiteness must take place as is known.

> March 31
>
> In Consciousness, it is not about thinking but about letting the limitlessness of Consciousness flow from and to you.

[Journey 9 begins:]
 The movement of the Channel is swift and he is in the midst of Consciousness, knowing the peace, knowing the joy of it, gathering it to himself that it flows all through him. He is joyful, laughing, and his laughter opens many pathways.

[To the Channel:]
 ... It is good for you to explore the question that you brought with you about seeking out that first Child of God. ...
 ... You would do it by calling to her (if you don't mind us referring to her as her). ...
 ... You are over that as an issue? Very good. ...
 ... Place yourself in a position that you can replicate what you experienced in past. In other words, in Consciousness, *Know* it. ...
 The Channel communicates that he is not aware of her.
 ... Are you thinking about it? Don't think about it. Be it. Let it flow from you and to you. Consciousness has no limitation. If you bring a limitation to Consciousness, then you are not in the *purity* of Consciousness. ...

 The Child of God is not responding to the Channel, though he now can feel her presence.
 Then – quite remarkable – the Channel is gone!
 He is (in your terms) soaring through Consciousness. He is not seeking the Child of God. He is seeking nothing. He has released all his thoughts and questions and is merely being one with Consciousness.
 You might ask, *how will he know this when he returns?* It will be dependent upon the clarity of both of he and his mate, Susahn, when they return, the degree to which they are capable of knowing the answers.

April 1

The Gift of Free Will Choice is as prime in Consciousness as it is in finiteness.

[Journey 9 continues:]
  Lama Sing: A few points to mention here:
• Jude is with the Channel, though the Channel is not choosing to focus upon him or acknowledge his presence. You can be in Consciousness surrounded (in a manner of speaking) with others, yet not perceive them. It is a matter of choosing to perceive. You might consider this "levels" of Consciousness, though they are not literal levels. They are merely choices of where to place your Knowing.
• The Channel had brief encounters with doubt and worthiness, and we are pleased that he recognized these as stepstones rather than limitations. Questions about Consciousness come when examined from finiteness; in Consciousness there is nothing to question. The Knowing is complete.
• The Child of God the Channel engaged in his last journey (just as a reminder, using terminology here only for your understanding) is aware of the Channel's presence. Because she knows the Channel so well and also the Channel's mate she chooses to be cognizant of them, to know of their immediate presence and activity.
• A question that might be floating about there in the Earth... It is one thing for the Child of God to be expressed and another for the Channel or his mate, or any of you, to be expressed here. You have chosen and continue to sustain a connection to finiteness, an expressed form therein.
• There are other entities here who have connections to different levels of finiteness. As with many of you they, too, have chosen service, but they serve those who serve, as one might be a guide or teacher to a guide. That is quite an intimate relationship and often cannot sustain a connection with pure Consciousness.

> April 2
>
> In Consciousness there is no time, space, location, or other such quantifiable measurement because it is all present.

    Movement through time and space is a measurement of finiteness; from Consciousness there is no such measurement because it is all present. It *is*. The unfolding of Consciousness is immeasurable by time, space, location, and other quantifiable measurement. To what would Consciousness be creating? In other words, would it be in this direction or that? Would it be at the edge of finiteness or beyond? These things are not relevant in Consciousness. Consciousness can unfold creation within itself, which is (we might say a bit with tongue in cheek, if you understand this) one of the favorite methods of choice.

    How does one unfold creation within one's self, you might ask? How does Creation create within Itself? Easily, because it is not limited by boundaries of time, space, and dimension. If you look to, for example, what might be thought of as an oasis in the midst of the sea of finiteness such as the World-Between-Worlds (as it's called by the Channel's mate), you can find Consciousness co-mingling, so to say, with (small c) consciousness because of the level of choosing on the part of those in finiteness who are present through acceptance.

    (Small c) consciousness entities cannot obtain presence in the World-Between-Worlds without certain choices having been made and certain qualities of Consciousness, the absence of limitations that permits them to accomplish this position of awareness and this presence with those who are outside of finite form.

[Note: In meditation on limitlessness, Susan discovered a "point" that was neither finite not totally unlimited, neither here nor there, and gave it the title World-Between-Worlds.]

> April 3
>
> Laughter from one who is not in physical form is like a stimulation, a gift of love, that is offered to all of Consciousness.

[Journey 9 continues:]

The Channel is pausing. He is... (Very difficult to place in words, please bear with us.) He is slowly rotating, you might call it, reaching out to other expressions of Consciousness all about him and he perceives, knows of, a number of other Children of God. The Channel calls out to one and they are Knowing each other. As there is absolute access, instantly, both Know the other to considerable depth. The Child of God is not choosing to Know the Channel to the depth you might expect, and this permits what you would call questioning and answering.

The Channel first seeks to know whether or not this Child of God has engaged in finiteness... in other words, has taken form, and determined that this one has not.

This Child of God then *probes* the Channel (so to say) to ask what is the difference like... Knowing it and being it?

The Channel responds that perhaps this one might wish to Know his group in the Earth and their recent experiences as they explored Consciousness from finiteness.

The Child of God does just that and laughs, to the delight of the Channel. This laughter is not as hearing *Ha ha ha.* You who are reading this might experience laughter of one not in limited expression, incarnation or form, as rivulets of (by your definition) light and color and sound. Actually, the Child of God offers forth a stimulation to all of Consciousness, a gift of love. The Channel *experiences* this as laughter. He then reciprocates generously, which delights in kind this one, as well as several others who have chosen to be a part of this sharing.

> **April 4**
>
> How long do you intend to experience the not-knowing, which is the essence of finiteness?

[Journey 9 continues:]

Another Child of God present in the sharing poses the inquiry to the Channel, "How long do you intend to experience the not-knowing, which is the essence of finiteness? And what is it giving you?"

"I would not ascertain that from here, for if I did, that would create the effect of that in finiteness because I have a connection to it, as you can see..." and the Channel shows the Children of God his connection to his physical body.

They look and marvel over it.

"If I answered that from here, I would create that there. I do not wish to create that from here. I wish to do so from within my current journey of finiteness, for that embraces the Law and all who are dwelling within it there."

"What Law," one Child asks?

"This Law. " The Channel shows the Child of God in a manner that the Child can choose to Know it or not. The Child of God chooses, and now knows of what the Channel speaks, the Law of Manifestation in finiteness called Free Will.

It is incredible to relate this to you in the Earth, for we realize the potential impact of all of this upon many of you.

Some of you will not be impacted per se but perhaps will smile knowingly.

Others of you will seek it and that is a worthy intent.

> April 5
>
> You do not have to be without (capital C) Consciousness. To give up Knowing is a choice.

[Journey 9 continues – The Channel has returned to Zachary and Jude. They have all chosen to be in form:]

"What did you learn?" asks Zachary.

"I learned what I Know and brought it to an understanding I hope will serve me in the Earth and, perhaps, others."

"Well, would you like to share that?" quips Zachary.

"Of course, but I know that you already know it."

"But sharing it with me, the others will hear and know it."

The Channel begins blurring a bit at the mention of the others and finiteness.

"Why are you blurring, Channel?" asks Zachary. "Just a few moments ago (by finite measurement) you made references to your own physical body and were with it instantly. Why, now, are you blurring?"

"I guess, because I am... thinking... I am finite-ing."

"I see that."

Jude moves very close to the Channel. "You do not have to lose (capital C) Consciousness when you do that."

"Tell me what you mean."

"It is a choice."

"How can I choose, when I know that I have a physical form right over there?" pointing towards finiteness.

"Ah, but you are choosing to remember and to think and, in essence, giving up Knowing."

The Channel chooses and is instantly "gone," so to say, back in pure Consciousness. But this time he hasn't moved away from Zachary or Jude or his mate.

> April 6
>
> Thinking uses polarities to understand. That understanding comes by categorizing, boxing in answers to digest them.

Relinquishing thinking is releasing the polarities that are cleaved to in finiteness. Thinking uses polarities and memories to understand. That understanding comes about by categorizing, boxing the answers in so they can be digested. Thinking is sort of a digestive system of finiteness.

There were and are Children of God who choose to move into greater detail of expression that could be, in a manner of speaking, independent of Complete Consciousness in order to better know the expression of uniqueness.

Consciousness flows into finiteness according to the pathways presented for it to move. Those who go through formal study in the Earth are creating pathways for specific consciousness to flow more easily to them. Contrary to the belief mechanisms, it isn't so much that one is learning what will be given to them. It's, rather, that they are making the way passable for it by creating understanding and, through understanding, acceptance. Much of this comes about through thinking, which is the building of reference points. Therefore, Consciousness is limited in its flow into finiteness because of the need for definition to be a form of communication.

[Journey 9 continues – There has been a very long pause and Lama Sing dialogues with the Channel:]
... What does a Child of God do for fun? Well, they don't do anything for fun, for there is no absence of fun. You don't go off and do something fun because everything is fun. ...
... No, these particular Children of God are not interested in moving into finiteness. ...
The Channel then offers the information that they already know it. Because they have never stopped being one with their brethren who *have* moved into it, they know it.

> April 7
>
> From Al: In expanded Consciousness, reaching back to where you came from for answers may lessen the experience.

[Journey 9 continues – The Channel resumes his dialogue with the group of "Children of God" again:]

"Do you not wish to, as we say, smell the flowers?"

"No."

The Channel tries to question them as to why not, and they do not answer. Their statement of choice stands alone and requires no justification, no follow-up commentary.

The Children of God then address the Channel, pointing out that, in the Earth, the energies of uncertainty seem to enhance the experience of finiteness. They ask the Channel why he is dabbling in that.

The Channel chooses not to answer (with a note of loving humor) which, of course, they immediately accept.

[pause]

What is occurring here is that, as a part of this current journey, the Channel is "experimenting" with approaching finiteness and thinking, or finite discovery, to give his finite self some points to contemplate.

From here, he does not see this as indecision but, rather, the consideration of multiple choices. When expressing this to the Children of God gathered here and they inquired of him, he chose not to answer because he wisely knew that, to so do, he would have to delve into finiteness to such a depth that he considered it would be challenging, if at all possible, to sustain two such powerful choices of focus – the finite simultaneous to the infinite.

> **April 8**
>
> Whatever you cling to, limits you. Your consciousness is attached and portions of your potential remain with that.

[Journey 9 continues:]

The Channel is moving closer to us now and closer, doing so in a linear measure so that he can assess it, that he can Know it.

Any one of you who are choosing to Know can Know. The degree to which your knowing is clear to you is dependent upon those same factors we have discussed repeatedly:

Whatever you cling to limits you. Your consciousness is "attached" and portions of your potential remain with that. Therefore, your potential moves forward incompletely.

> April 9
>
> Consciousness gives birth to expression, wherein the energies of Color are continually being created, forming, interacting.

[Journey 9 continues – Lama Sing dialogues with Susan:]

Lama Sing: Do you hear us communicating with you, Su-sahn?

Susan: Yes, I do.

Lama Sing: Have you any comments on your experience or what has been shared, if you recall it?

Susan: I'm aware that I was hearing only parts of sentences, so I can't comment on what you spoke.

Lama Sing: Do you wish to comment on anything that you experienced?

Susan: I went through beautiful colors! I've not experienced them like this before. It was a little distracting because it took quite some time to move through those and, by that time, things were already transpiring with the Channel.

Lama Sing: What about the colors did you find beautiful and simultaneously distracting?

Susan: They were so beautiful and changing all the time. I did not expect that... almost like a kaleidoscope.

Lama Sing: Can you conclude anything from this?
[pause]

Let us help you. You mentioned a key... kaleidoscope. The colors weren't rigid, correct?

Susan: Correct.

Lama Sing: There is a level, dimension (whatever suits the discussion), wherein the energies of Color are continually being created, forming, interacting with one another.

Consciousness is that which gives birth to this. The Children of God Know and enjoy expression of Consciousness... the kaleidoscope of dancing, moving, embracing colors. See?

> April 10
>
> In order to understand, through the thinking process, finiteness creates dimension, form, color, specificity, time, space.

[Journey 9 concludes – Lama Sing continues to dialogue with Susan:]

Lama Sing: The Children of God often "contemplate." They Know expressions, and so, you could say that they enjoy the expressions. The result is like the kaleidoscope of magical, dancing, moving, embracing colors. See?

Do you remember soaring?

Susan: Yes.

Lama Sing: But you do not remember any wings or such, true? In fact, can you remember a form?

Susan: No, just the realization of movement.

Lama Sing: Yes. Consciousness soars.

And Consciousness chooses to Know Itself. Consciousness can Know Itself completely. In effect, Consciousness soars upon Itself. And there is no ending. It is continually evolving, changing, because, as Consciousness moves upon Itself and Knows Itself, then there are those things that *are* that come into realization... not into finiteness but *from*   finiteness the perception would be the collage of colors. See?

Is this making sense?

Susan: Until the last statement... From finiteness it would be experienced as a collage of colors?

Lama Sing: That is correct because finiteness wishes to understand and *thinks* and, through the thinking process, finiteness creates dimension, color, resonance, specificity, form, and things such as time and space. See?

You have experienced Consciousness and consciousness of finiteness simultaneously.

> April 11
>
> You can experience the World-Between-Worlds. You would move to it by following a path of light, your lifeline.

Zachary: Time is measured beyond the Earth such that, the further you move from the Earth, the more it differs from the understanding in Earth. I offer this here that, in what is about to be given, if you fall prey to attempting to align things nicely to the time-line as it is in the Earth you may stumble a bit here and there. If that occurs don't concern. Just follow along as best you can and try not to fall back to sheer reliance upon finite logic:

The exploration of the "World-Between-Worlds" mentioned previously is magnificent. It is perhaps of value to you who are reading these words to recognize that the choice to be in the World-Between-Worlds is merely that... a choice. The reluctance to recognize that such is possible is built upon the thinking, teachings that are a part of the history of the Earth.

Movement to the World-Between-Worlds is generally along a path of light. That light is, for those in physical body, the lifeline, as Susahn discovered as she sought in meditation to follow what is called *the silver cord*, the line of life-giving energy between body and Spirit, and came upon this "world." It is an expanse that lies between definitions. Definitions are those areas of consciousness that are decided upon by small groups. (Yes, it can be an expression of an individual, but the sustaining of it would fall solely to the individual.)

This "Realm," the World-Between-Worlds, is wondrous. It is participated in from realms beyond the Earth since "eons" ago. The characteristics of it are: openness, light, and warmth; whatever is anticipated quickly manifests; all that is, is in harmony with itself, thus, there is no separateness and nothing to preserve or to protect; it is incredibly diverse, vast, and constantly in motion, exploring, exchanging, and so harmonious it is grand to experience.

> April 12
>
> There is a Bridge of Light in place now that spans the lesser realms of shadow between the Earth and Beyond.

Zachary: The World-Between Worlds is associated with the Bridge of Light to the extent that the Bridge of Light is now a passable portal for those of us who choose to enter the Earth, but do not choose to enter in finite body.

The Bridge of Light is the work of a group of souls in the Earth who chose to use their power as Children of God to manifest a Bridge to span the realms of shadow between the Earth and the realms beyond. Universal Law was conformed to because the Bridge was built by the choice of the group from within in the Earth. Prior to this Bridge, it was not uncommon for one to become lured off their path of Light into the Shadowlands, the Sea of Faces, and lesser realms. Those leaving Earth in the process you call death can choose to use the Bridge to move more or less unimpeded now, and they give of their energy in thankfulness. So the Bridge is expanding, extending further and further because of this continual flow of gifts.

Because I am a guide and brother to this Channel, I find it quite easy to move to and fro on the Bridge of Light, for I can follow the line of Light that connects he and I eternally. Often, as I pass across the Bridge of Light, by choice I am not perceivable. Other times, I choose to take a form, for this empowers others to interact with me with greater ease, particularly those who are newly crossing over.

So I pause to "chat" with some who are now sort of continually in residence upon the Bridge of Light. We do so using form because this gives us entrée to interact with those who are coming across in the form that is that which leaves the physical. (There is a period of time when an entity departs the Earth where they sustain a form, thought of by some as the astral, a depiction of the body but in energy form. It looks like, feels like, acts like a physical body).

April 13

The Bridge of Light supports those transiting from Earthly incarnation, but those in the shadows continue to try to lure.

Zachary: Crossing the Bridge of Light is very much like crossing a bridge in the Earth, I should think, with the exception that the Bridge has an energy. It was created and is being sustained by the love and prayers and intent of the original creators, and that has been augmented by countless others who have used the Bridge and realized the gift that it offers.

As I move across the Bridge, it is a delight to feel the blessings. They are as gentle breezes that waft across, gently caressing your being. There is often the impact upon you to pause and sort of drink in the awe and joy and thankfulness of one who has crossed the Bridge and found their joy waiting.

Occasionally, I will move over to a side of the Bridge to look upon areas that are places of rest for those who would journey but can go no further, whose spirits are weary.

Here, I see on this side, for example, an expansive beautiful area of greenery with a lovely stream, and flowers that are actually blessings that were placed here. Many are gathered here waiting to assist those who seek from them, and some from the World-Between-Worlds are making the way ready for that time ahead of the Promise.

I can also see on the periphery the dance of the shadows, still trying to call out, strata of ways of thinking and the entities who still choose to dwell in them trying to get the attention of travelers crossing the Bridge. Some days these are more evident than others.

> April 14
>
> Remember as you prepare for sleep to state an intent. It helps to balance the force of limitation struggling to sustain itself.

Zachary: As I cross the Bridge, I find tiny paths of light, which I have noticed are growing in the recent Earth years as the Children have gone here and there. It is like they leave little tracks of light where they have been... very lovely. And, as much as the forces of mass-mind thought would seek to erase these or cloud them over, it is yielding to their purity.

And, over here, I find the path that leads to my brother, the Channel, and to the many others of you who are choosing. It, too, can now be seen for its clarity and its purity. Sometimes I find one or more of you walking along the pathway as you are in contemplation or prayer or meditation.

I would, again, urge you to remember as you prepare for sleep to have an intent. State it. For the struggle here, as I move closer to the consciousness of Earth, is quite dynamic! The struggle is intensifying as the balance scale is supplying thought, energy, to that which would seek to sustain itself. See?

So, from this side, the Earth side, the Bridge becomes quite different.

> April 15
>
> There is a profound sweetness that can be known. It is the gift of God when He created *You*.

[Journey 10 begins:]

It is perhaps curious to consider the experiences for the Channel in this particular journey, for he has begun it such that it is not only into Consciousness but also into the depth and breadth of his own creation.

How does this differ, one might ask, from moving into Creation itself?

The answer is very sweet: It is moving into that part of Creation that is singularly, and solely, you.

Therein is a sweetness that can be known: It is the gift of God to create *You*. And, as one might journey unto such a destination, all those things that might otherwise be as veils unto this beautiful gift must part or fall away.

So it is that these are the events that are transpiring for him. Not too much different than his past journeys unto Consciousness itself but different in the sense that he is knowing it, seeing it.

> **April 16**
>
> Joy arises from living in the Love of God, a joy of Peace and the Freedom that is the gift of the prime Law: Free Will.

[Journey 10 continues:]

We move forward in your time and reach that point where the Channel has come to realize Consciousness again from the perspective that is aligned with his consciousness in Earth, and there is the renewed sense of peace, *the* Peace of God. His reaction to it is soft laughter, laughter of such unlimited nature that joyful freedom rises from within in the descriptive form of laughter.

Now he acknowledges the existence from which he has come and draws upon his intent. For some, it might seem curious that there could be such a separation, but it is so for all. It is most evident to all at the moment of the conclusion of the just-previous Earth-life. For those who are capable of attaining same while yet in finiteness, it is a journey that can be accomplished through meditation, dream, and such.

His movement is gentle now and he has taken form. Because he anticipates the same on the part of those he will meet, his anticipation goes forth as a creative intent and, thus, it is so.

A part of him knows the answers to his questions. Another part seeks answers for him and his mate and perhaps others to know and share while yet in the Earth. So a sort of dialog transpires, commonplace in the Earth but not so in Spirit, for Spirit needs no evaluation but is always in a state of joy. That joy arises from living in the Love of God, which is the Peace and the Freedom that is the gift of the prime Law: Free Will.

The Channel contemplates what we are sharing with you and smiles, turning to look at Lama Sing and all of us. This is a curious experience as we are communicating to you and being one with him here.

April 17

> All thought sends an energy that resonates in Consciousness, where its "song" unfolds and is borne back to its source.

[Journey 10 continues:]

The Channel asks the Child of God, "Would you explain what I think I understood... that you came from where the Colors are born? Was your meaning that they are *born* as being created, or *borne* as being carried by you and others? And could you also expand upon the Brotherhood, as I believe it was referred to."

It is curious to look upon the entity who has taken form based upon the Channel's expectation of it. The Channel knows the true nature of his friend, but he finds ease in expressing himself in a form.

"The Color of Creation is based upon that which is (as we would call it) the *song* present," responds the Child of God. "The *song* is just another term for what you call intent, or wish.

"Whatsoever is thought in the Earth sends forth an emanation, an energy. And that energy creates a resonance that is expressed in vibratory sound, color, energy, and variations, many not defined in Earth but merely called levels of energy. These energies are neither wave nor particle. They are moreso undulations in the fabric of existence as that existence is defined wherein the intent or thought is created.

"Here, in Consciousness, there is the unfolding that resonates with that and, thus, it is born in creation by the intent or song and, thereafter, is borne into the source of the creation."

> April 18
>
> One's intent is creative, for it is Known by all of Consciousness and Consciousness immediately responds.

[Journey 10 continues:]

"How wonderful!" the Channel exclaims. "Let me inquire further in order that, when I return to my finiteness, I might be able to grasp this clearly. A group of people gathering to a specific intent that they all agree upon could then create an energized intent that goes forward and is thereafter a "song?" And Consciousness immediately responds and creates correspondingly, which you and your colleagues bear to the Earth?"

"You are correct."

"Why would you need to create color and why would you, as an individual or as a group, bring those colors to the Earth?"

"We do this because it is our choice. In Consciousness, as you well know, you can *Know*. And according to what brings you, individually, the greatest joy, when those resonances occur they are like subtle stimuli to you."

The Channel inserts, "In a symphony, there might be certain tones or certain chords that bring one a sense of joy in hearing them. Is it similar to that?"

"Yes, very similar to that but without limitation... an array of choices each Child of God has made that is, therefore, their intent. The *intent* of a Child of God is also creative. Your intent, for example, was to be pure in Consciousness. Your definition of being pure in Consciousness was to be, as you call it, alone, yet you full know that you are never alone. It is similar to this. If you have an intent and something stimulates a contemplation, that stimulation is sufficient to arise other flows of energy."

> April 19
>
> During prayer the individual is often most open and receptive, and the creative Colors, energies, are brought to them.

As we make choices in harmony with ourselves and with our brethren and we create a greater intent, that act begins to manifest harmonics (as you would understand it in the Earth).

It is natural while in physical body to think in terms of breadth and depth and linear progression, time, alignments with measurements, and such. But set that aside for just a moment and contemplate this:

Consciousness creates upon and within itself Consciousness. In other words, Consciousness *births* Consciousness, and *it* births, and *it* births, and so forth.

Sometimes it would seem that Consciousness is birthing or creating anew within itself. Other times (using Earthly terms), Consciousness creates beyond itself.

When Consciousness sees and knows Itself and knows that within Itself there is a void, Consciousness can choose or intend to fill the void, and do so with an expansion of the void to include depth and perspective, harmonics, and all sorts of things that could be seen, felt, known in all of the sensory perceptive mechanisms of the Earth, and far beyond.

We here choose to bring forth the Color that is the creative means for thought to manifest, and this most frequently is in answer to prayer. The reason for this (as you would call it in the Earth) is very simple: It is during prayer that the individual is often most open and receptive and, thus, the creative Colors, energies, are brought to them. Those who see the "answer" to the prayer accept the Colors and create and move into the Peace of Creation. Those who cannot simply conclude the prayer or repeat it again and again and again and, all the while, the answer has been there from the onset.

> **April 20**
>
> Fear, hatred, and such as this are a call to your song. We are in harmony with you, offering our song and receiving yours.

The World-Between-Worlds is Consciousness expressing itself. Remembering and defining for the record in Earth: A realm is simply a location (so to say) that is comprised of those of like-intent, those of like-thinking.

The World-Between-Worlds is like a Neutral Zone, the place of the free-flowing Will of God. It is, in essence, embracing the finite expressions that are the array of the Earth realm. (We are using the term *realm* to differentiate from the Earth as a planet, as a place for those who are focused in physical form, and beyond the specific sphere of Earth to those dimensions or realms that embrace and surround the Earth, such as you have called the Sea of Faces, the Shadowland, and many others that suit those who chose them or have created them. We are, in a manner of speaking, embracing these because they are about to change.)

So the World-Between-Worlds is a sort of gathering place. It would be like in Earth where you might have a musician over here, and another several city blocks down there, and two more a mile away, each playing individually, and one morning they arise and feel guided to go to some central little music hall. And they find one another there, all guided by some mysterious inner voice. So they embrace, laugh, and decide to create music together. The beauty of harmonics that come from them is directly relevant to their intention to produce it. That is the World-Between-Worlds. That is why we are here, offering our song to those who would have it and receiving theirs, as they are willing to give it.

When you see fear, hatred, and such as these, know them to be a call to your own song. And remember that we here are in harmony with you as we prepare for those times.

> ## April 21
>
> Apply all that you know that can fulfill that which you might discern as yet needed, in order that you can *be* complete.

How would you color faithfulness? From the rainbow of colors known and accepted in the Earth, what would be the choice to portray faith and faithfulness?

Here is our Brother, whom the Channel refers to as the Master. What color would you place around Him? In your answer, ask yourself: Would this color suit *you*?

A journey into Oneness with God begins with the discovery of the faith that enables that journey to be passable. Those who would seek to know and understand the nature of our Brother's coming return to the Earth are also then certainly asking, "What is *my* nature in that regard?" For if you perceive yourself distant from Him or even that you and He are not of the same God, then there is something to discover. Perhaps that is the color of your own faith and the color that would be placed about you.

It is not intended to be a comparative analysis, judgmental in its nature, but moreso that of a joyful quest to discover what feels beautiful and good.

The passage of the sacred Truth through the colors brings understanding. It is the movement of Consciousness that can awaken the discovery of all that is but only insofar as one who is in that, journeying with it, is willing to seek according to that which is within them. And upon the discovery of the nature of that, to apply all that they know to bring this into a pathway – a way of thinking, a way of believing – that can fulfill that which might be discerned as yet needed in order that self can *be* complete.

> April 22
>
> To comprehend the seeming incomprehensible take your Consciousness with you wherever you are. Don't be without it.

[Journey 10 continues:]

The Channel is presently in Consciousness and the sweetness of its embrace. We find that others are moving towards him slowly awaiting his choice, as are we.

Many of the Children of God are encircling him, as they know him to be in contemplation.

One comes a bit forward and offers the song that is hers to give, and he becomes illuminated and answers. She is now in close proximity to him though yet a bit distant, recognizing that there is something that he is seeking. Thus, this is being honored.
[Pause]

"Why are you all here?" he inquires.
"Because we love you."

There are energies of contemplation that are seen moving in and through the position of the Channel here in Consciousness and, as this is occurring, the entire group is... you would call it, *drifting*.
[Pause]

"I am seeking something that I cannot identify."
"We can assist you in your quest."
"Will it be mine then or merely something I know of?"
"If you know something, is it not then yours?"
"There are aspects here that are incomprehensible in the Earth. How would you suggest I deal with those?"
"Do not be without your Consciousness. Take your Consciousness with you wherever you are. Just as you do so here, do so there. Do so everywhere you are."

> April 23
>
> The Channel discovered what he called a void at the edge of Creation, beautiful because he felt the utter sweetness of God.

[Journey 10 continues:]

The Children of God are surrounding the Channel in one very large beautiful sphere of energy. The Channel is in oneness with them. They commune with him as they move him. Instantly, they are before the edge of Creation and they separate so that the individuality of the Channel can come forth, in order that he can fulfill his quest.

He closely "examines" Consciousness. Just a very brief distance beyond Consciousness is what he would call a void. Slowly, he begins to move, realizing only he and the Child of God who has been communing with him are moving.

"Do you intend to move into the void?"

"Yes," he responds.

"Do you wish to not be?"

"I believe it's impossible for me to not be."

"Then what is your quest by moving into the void?"

"I wish to Know it."

[pause]

She is silent, moving with him in tandem, yet separate.

The Channel is awed. "This is incredibly beautiful"

"It is. What of it brings to you the thought of its beauty?"

"I think it's the purity, the utter sweetness of God going forth. My gratitude to you for journeying with me."

"Why does my presence invoke gratitude from you?"

Instantly, the Channel understands that, with her present beside him, it is not a void.

"Some seek this and no more than this," she offers softly.

"Why do you say, no more than this?"

"Why not answer your own question?" She responds with her gift of laughter.

> April 24
>
> Love is the prime gift of God; but Love needs a reflection, something to interact with, in order to be truly Known.

[Journey 10 continues:]

The Channel reaches out to expand himself and realizes that there is no definition, only the feeling of immensity. "It is, then, as one of the primal discoveries or thoughts. I don't know the nomenclature, but it is one of the primal..."

Instantly, the Child of God, with some curious force, sweeps the Channel up and they are back among the group of the other Children of God who had been participating with the Channel. They become one again, and others come to join them as their laughter reaches out to all of Consciousness.

Off they go, soaring about, passing through one color and another, and through this veil and that. To the wonder of the Channel, they even pass above the Earth, swooping down over cities, lush hills and valleys, sparse areas, and up again through the veils and into realms and back into Consciousness. And they pause.

"What you were speaking of when we were in the void is Love. Love needs (using your word *need*) a reflection in order to be known. It needs something to interact with. In the void is the potential of creation, the colors reaching out into the void birthing themselves and knowing themselves, wondrous gifts of God, but they are only potentials, elemental tools.

"The prime gift of God is Love. To have journeyed alone in the void would give you naught to know from. You would seek to know. Yet without their expression it is difficult (as you said at the onset) to truly know them, to make them your own.

> ## April 25
>
> Love does not need. Love is full, rich, complete. Love is that which gives as one serves.

[Journey 10 concludes:]

Child of God: You consider Consciousness different than consciousness in your expression in finiteness. That array of choices has made manifest a structure which is in accordance with that structure's law, perfect until it is changed from within. We can pass through it, as we just have done. We can *walk* upon the Earth (as you would call it) and yet, not be of it.

So in the times past, as you have asked of us, do we *know* it? Yes, we know it. Is it ours? No, for if it were ours, then we would have to sustain it. If it were our creation, then we would have to nourish it. But here, Consciousness is ours, for we are not separate but one with it, not independently creating but in a state of oneness, *being* as we choose to be.

We know your contemplation, because you have placed it into Consciousness. We know it as we know Consciousness, but you have the power to create and to isolate creation. And we are one with you, and that oneness permits us as you will it, see, to know. It is not to imply limitation. It is to point out qualities of what you call love.

Love does not need, in the sense often equated with that term in the Earth.

Love is full, rich, complete.

Love is that which gives as one serves. It is Love that is a gift from our sweet Brother, and it is what you call compassion that empowers Him to know where to give it.

So, do we know these things of which you speak? We know them. We do not choose to *be* them.

We know finiteness, but but we do not choose to be finite. You know a tree, a rock, but you do not choose to *be* them. We are not one with them as you mean it but, as the air surrounds and caresses them, we know them.

April 26

> The greater work for others is by example, and through that claiming that empowers them.

[Note: These questions were submitted from a group who were following the "Consciousness" readings:]

Question: Claiming one's truth is so important, but claiming is foreign to so many. The word 'claim' turns off so many. How do we bring this into the mainstream?"

Lama Sing: To bring this into the mainstream would require that the mainstream is seeking it. It would be better that we respond as individuals come forward asking, open to receive it.

The greater work can be done by the example and through that claiming that so empowers them that, through this power, all manner of works can be accomplished.

Question: Is it on track for the Master to come in 2007?

Lama Sing: There are those who will recognize His presence in the year 2007. His actual "return" is not ours to give. He will come unto those who are of that faith so as to receive Him as the Way is open and passable. Then yes, it is as you said: on track.

Question: Will the Master manifest physically?

Lama Sing: Yes. As He left, so shall He return.

Question: Will His presence be evidential?

Lama Sing: If the Master comes to one and states, "I am He for whom you have been waiting," they have the choice to believe or not. The Master might ask, "If I make the sun rise in the midst of the night you will believe it insofar as you can see it. And, when it is gone, shall you still believe?"

In the heart and mind of each who shall behold Him, they will decide. We cannot here.

> April 27
>
> If you are capable of giving love and giving compassion, then you can receive love and compassion.

[Q&A continues:]

Question: The Bible warns of false prophets claiming to be the returning Christ. Will the deception be so clever as to fool even the best intentioned?

Lama Sing: Is there willingness to celebrate His return? Is there the willingness to see, "Here comes that One who bears only love, only compassion," and that He would seek to give it unto all who would receive it? Can this be imitated? Can, in truth, there be that which is an illusion when pure Love is the offering? We think it not so.

We find the Master to be unquestionable. The questions, then, would arise within those who are not ready to receive Him.

Will you know Him? This depends on that one who views Him. Can you receive Love? Can you know Compassion? Yes, if you are capable of giving Love and giving Compassion.

It is not to play tricks here. It is not to offer pretense as an answer to questions that are sincere in nature. It is to point out that each heart, each mind, must open and prepare the Way to receive that which is to be offered.

One can perceive a sunrise and see in it the ending of night or the beginning of day. Which is truth? See?

> **April 28**
>
> You are the composite of your experiences.
> You are not any one of these; you are all of them.

Lama Sing: An addendum to the questions and answers:

- To know a true prophet of God, perhaps the most outstanding point is do they seek to set you free? Those who seek to take from you or take command of you are not true to the Sacred Truth. The Master seeks to *give* to you utterly, and to lift you up so as you are seeking to be lifted up. That is how to tell the difference. You can seek counsel in words that are recorded and listen to the wise insights. But that which you seek is within you, in the temple of the One God: that Truth that shall endure all. Let all that is without reflect that Truth back to you, in order that your beauty is constantly growing.

- So you have sought, brothers and sisters, "Who am I?" In your search did you find something of profound beauty? Did you stray off to explore some error, some fault, some decision that you, in retrospect, might have done otherwise? Or have you passed through these things to see and *rejoice* over them? For that is *why* you are, that is *what* you are. You are the composite of your experiences. You are not any one of these; you are all of them.

- Each journey has a beginning and an ending. Just so, each life in the Earth plane has a beginning and an ending. What transpires between those two points is based upon an array of choices. Some of these choices may appear to be outside of the control of the individual who is on that particular journey and, yet with some contemplation one can understand that this journey was the choice of that traveler, perhaps with the intent to awaken another who is dearly loved and who remains continually walking upon that or a similar journey.

> April 29
>
> As one holds an intent, it becomes the path, the power. The greatest potential in an intent is that you have chosen.

The Channel asks questions in the journeys not so much to know them here, for he knows the answers. He is trying to gain record of the questions and answers for himself upon return to finiteness, and for others who might read or hear these works.

He is greatly interested in the Children of God because they have never taken on incarnations, physical bodies. The attentiveness by the Children of God to the Channel is relevant to his intent, his state of consciousness.

In the latest journey, the Channel noticed a number of Children coming. It was because he was activating his oneness with them in a different way. He was actively seeking oneness with them by questioning his oneness with them.

If one approaches as a questioner, the reaction might be different than if the approach is as one seeking oneness.

Consciousness gives life to the World-Between-Worlds because it is *chosen*, and the choosing came from a Child of God supported by the love and presence of other Children of God. Consciousness and the World-Between-Worlds are as one, but they are on the periphery of what the Channel calls *pure* Consciousness because there are choices involved, choices to manifest, or act, or react.

Within the body of Consciousness there are those things that are relevant that have to do with expressions of intent.

As one holds an intent it becomes the path. It becomes the power. The greatest power and potential that comes forth from putting before you an intent is that you have chosen.

> April 30
>
> There are forces at the ready that can be called. One must know the nature of *themselves* in order to issue that call.

[Journey 11 begins:]
Their approach, as you would call it, is like two spheres of light that merge and then disengage, and merge and go soaring across the nothingness, which is the approach to the World-Between-Worlds. It is like flying, like becoming boundless.

There are those forces that are always at the ready that can be "called." One must know the nature of *themselves* in order to issue that call.

The relationship between self and those forces is eternal; the memory of them is often not so clear.

> **May 1**
>
> What you can do to assist in that which lies ahead, in the Promise, is within you. The outer becomes the evidence.

[Journey 11 continues:]

Zachary: The Channel and I move with great ease and joy. We find many greeting us with warmth and joy and as we move now into the World-Between-Worlds.

It is very beautiful, what someone has created here, and we move into definable form to stroll about this vast, beautiful garden of lush green. There is a sky with lovely clouds, and water.

"This is beautiful. Who put this here?" the Channel asks.

"You didn't?" Zachary coyly responds. "Someone has intended this as a gift. Others who are coming here from finiteness, namely from the Earth, see it to be appropriate."

"Others are coming here from the Earth?"

"Indeed. Some you consciously know, others you do not."

"What is their intent?"

"To help, as you are intending to help."

"I am having a wonderful time."

"Then that is the gift you bear. In part, it's why the Children of God gather with you. Joy is an essence very special among those who have not followed the path of definition. When someone, such as yourself who has managed to reclaim the path of oneness with them, expresses concentrated joy, it is magnetic. It brings the Children of God together. Very much like in finiteness on the Earth, when you and your colleagues gather and there is joy, others wish to participate.

And, by the way, regarding the Promise, which comes, it isn't so much what you can do to help. It is what you can do within yourself to help yourself. What you can do to assist in that which lies ahead, in the Promise, is within you, not so much without. The outer becomes the evidence.

> **May 2**
>
> As prayer of the faithful is blessed it grows, spreads, and becomes known, and others will seek to do the same.

[Journey 11 concludes:]

The Channel is joined now by the Master. As they begin to move, the Channel recognizes the path as his own, that which he uses for the readings. They continue along the path until they are upon the Earth.

Gazing about, the Channel recognizes this as a place of focus in Our Lady's current prayer work. Here and there, he sees shimmering figures waving to them. The Master points to them, and places His hand over His heart and gestures to them with out-stretched hand.

The Channel does the same. "Tell me, Master, what do they do here?"

"It is the fulfillment of the Law. Insofar as they were asked to come, through prayer, so is the Law perfect and they can be here with their presence. The faith of those who have sent this prayer forth will be enriched, blessed, and it will grow. As it grows, the faithful will come forward and their faith will grow, and their works will become known, and no doubt others will know of it and the blessings will spread. For as one tastes of the Bread of Life, others will seek to do the same."

The Master turns the Channel and are immediately back in the World-Between-Worlds. He embraces the Channel, turns, and is gone.

The Channel stares for a moment at the void, precisely where the Master was only a moment ago. His consciousness reaches out and he finds joy in seeing the Master moving towards a gathering of light... moving, moving. And he releases it and smiles.

> ## May 3
>
> Intense contemplation can move you into that contemplation.

Do not contemplate too deeply. If you become too intensely focused, that intense contemplation can create, and you are the creator creating a scenario for yourself.

To contemplate something is very good. It helps you broaden, to reach beyond habit or traditional thinking. But contemplating with intensity can move you into that contemplation.

If you are contemplating oneness with God then, of course, the end result is desirable; if you are contemplating from (capital C) Consciousness what it would be like in some aspect of (small c) consciousness, then that is where you could find yourself. See?

You can real-ize (make real) yourself here, in a manner of speaking. If you can reclaim Oneness while in physical body on Earth, then that is the first step. Then the intent would come after this.

> **May 4**
>
> What is my nature? Who am I? What is my source of joy that contributes to my journey and direction in daily life?

It is good for all to consider during these times:
What is my nature?
Who am I?
Where is my direction? Is my direction unto that which I find present in the daily influences borne unto me? Or does it flow from something within me not so much defined in terms of the material but moreso as an ideal that springs forth joy from my heart as I contemplate it?

Then think on these things, and know them. For in the knowing of them, can you claim dominion.

It is not to suggest that *this is good* and *that is bad*, only that you should look within self to see: *Is this contributing to my journey, or is it added baggage as I travel?*

It is good also to consider: *What is my source of joy?*

And, first and foremost: *Do I have a source of joy?*

As odd as that might sound, many of you may find at first glance that you cannot identify a single source of joy. You might offer an array of *things* but no sense of a direction that brings joy in the doing, in the being, in daily life.

These things we offer to you as gifts, guidance, if you will, not mandates. For the greatest of all guidance always comes from within you. Therein is that temple in which the Spirit of God is always awaiting you.

> May 5
>
> When you truly realize that there is naught between you and the Love of God, you will know who You are.

    What is the song you sing when you come into close oneness with the Spirit of God?

    What is that dance you would do from the joy within you in the presence of God?

    Who do you become when you realize that you are forgiven, that there is naught between you and the Heart of God, the Love of God? What are you in that moment?

    That is the first work that we would encourage each to be about and, when it is accomplished, then you will know your Self. You will know who You are, what You are, and what works lie before You. It is the standard by which you can measure all else and, if there is that experience, that force, or energy that comes to you and, as a causal effect, strives to minimize this, then give to it of Self in the mind, in the heart, in the Spirit. And it will either be purified or depart.

> **May 6**
>
> Let there always be that state between you and God, always the awakened state of being.

In the course of a day's activity on Earth, even though it is known that the sun does not move, it is a believed standard that the sun rises and the sun sets, and between those two events is the consciousness of the wake state.

Let there always be that state between you and God. Never let there be the setting of that consciousness, always the awakened state of being.

Just as you know intellectually that the sun is not measurably moving, that it is the Earth, then ask, *Am I moving and God is stationary? How is my relationship with God to be measured?*

The answer is you cannot measure that which always is. Therefore you must conclude that you, as well, always are.

> **May 7**
>
> Prayer is the instilling of hope, the calling forth of the Perfection within, and the willfulness to know, through faith, it is so.

What is conditionalized prayer? It is a prayer that has hesitations. It is a prayer that is uncertain of its own potential. It is a prayer that goes forth moreso questioning than answering. It is a prayer that comes from the good intent but the incomplete belief.

It is not the limitation of a prayer that should go forth. It is the instilling of hope, the calling forth of the perfection within and the willfulness to know, through absolute faith, that it is so.

Prayer is a living gift. And, no matter what, no matter where, the gift of prayer is also always a gift to self.

> ## May 8
>
> Never stop long before you renew the dream that is greatest of all dreams: that you awaken to the full potential of your Being.

    You may find at times that it seems quite difficult to build a dream. You may find at times that where you are and who you are and what is involved with you in your life lacks a certain vibrancy or beauty that was the epitome of your dreams in years before.

    If this is so for you, consider for a moment, is this the dream that you always sought? That, now in the realization of it, the sweetness, the luster, is not as you had anticipated?

    It is of great importance to always renew and rejoice in your dreams each and every day, for so doing gives life to them. Even though it may appear that you have gained all that you have sought or reached the accomplishment of those things you set out to do, ever are the greater just beyond where you are.

    In the teachings that are held sacred all throughout the Earth you will find that the journey is an eternal one. Thus, see this and know it to indicate to you not to become lost in an accomplishment but inspired by it. Realize that, as there has been an accomplishment, whether great or small, this evidences to you that building the dream, the intent, the hopeful anticipation, is the first step to bringing it into reality.

    Never stop too long before you renew the dream that is greatest of all: that you awaken to that which is the full potential of your Being.

> ## May 9
>
> You are favored Children of God. Do not let challenges limit this. Know it. Feel it. Live it. And allow yourself to become it.

You are favored Children of God.

So many, so very many, deny it. The habit guides them to believe in those things that are of a life that lacks the realization of God's presence in them and in their life.

I am a favored Child of God.

Do not let challenges of ego and other such limit this.

Know it, feel it, live it.

And then allow yourself to become that.

May 10

> How many times do you believe yourself to be alone, when all the while, we seeking are to walk with you? You must allow it.

The Earth is a beautiful place. It is an opportunity that so many clamor to have: to enter the Earth. But often, upon arriving, they don't know what to do with the opportunity.

If you cannot find your own Spirit, if you cannot find the source of joy for you, what shall you do? It is a simple thing for us to say, simply pause and reach out and we are one with you. But how are you to know this and believe in it? Well curiously, you control that. We cannot control it for you.

It is not the quest of something. It is not the search for meaning for each day in the Earthly sense. It is the search that brings meaning to the heart, to the Spirit, enriched by realizing that you are not alone in the journey. And the greater you open yourself to bring into your realization others who walk side by side with you, the greater joy shall become yours in your day-to-day living.

Walking about and pausing before a scene of beauty, listening to the laughter of a child, the sound of water caressing the rocks as it moves in its journey, the wind in the trees, the change of the sky from moment to moment, hour to hour throughout the Earth day, how many times do you pause in all this and believe yourself to be alone, when all the while, we are with you, seeking to walk with you?

Actually, we can do this for you, but you must allow it. You must open the door and keep it open, provide space in your mind and heart and consciousness, that you can know we are with you, seeking to bring you joy and happiness, ease and hope.

May 11

> In prayer, think of yourself as that one *chosen by God* to answer that call. You are the vessel. Believe it.

Don't just think about those who have asked for your prayer. Don't just read the names and say a silent prayer.

Think of yourself as that one chosen by God to answer that prayer!

Pause and make a space in your life – literally and figuratively, spiritually and actually – and in that space, create holiness where you reclaim your oneness with God. And listen...

Hear God saying to you, "I am gladdened that you are in service here my son, my daughter. I am using you. You are my pathway that honors my Word and my Law that opens the way that I might gift one who has asked for this gift. You are the vessel, the cup, in which the Wine of Life is given."

And, when the day ends, pause to reaffirm this. Affirm in prayer that you are resting your body as a vehicle that has served you well that day. Affirm that you return to join your Spirit in glad celebration with other children of God that you might soar and journey with in unbelievable ways. Look to them with anticipation. They come to you. Enter into your sleep in the Peace of God and rejoice and celebrate in that Peace, letting all else takes its proper position as those foundational building stones and thoughts upon which the future shall rest. And when you awaken, do the same. See the light of a new day and rejoice and celebrate that.

Again, the opportunity is yours to bring the hope of God, the love of God, to just one more soul, one more brother, one more sister.

Believe in that and do it as though you know it to be true. And it shall be.

May 12

> What limits you? Your doubt, your fondness for the familiar, your wish to have done for you that which is only yours to do.

What limits you? Your own doubt, your own fondness for the familiar, your own wish to have done for you that which is only yours to do.

If you seek to know your purpose, begin by seeking to know your Self, for you are the instrument through which the purpose shall be fulfilled.

Reclaim that instrument with the authority of a Child of God who is celebrating that, who is calling out in silent wonder and love, that those who have ears to hear or needs to be fulfilled can join in with you and partake of these, from you and with you.

Let not one day pass you by without affirming these things. Let not one day pass you by without building the potential for your own belief. Build it. Claim it. And live it.

When you pause and seek the silence within self, you are placing yourself in the Spirit of God and in the flow of that which can become the substance from which you can build anything! Believe unto It. And choose those things that will fashion a pathway of that belief and, one day, you will awaken and it will be yours.

The spaces are those times and places of listening, for the Word of God has never stopped. It flows. It can be heard in the spaces.

> ## May 13
>
> There are opportunities to celebrate, and those events that seem to lack that opportunity. Learn to celebrate in both.

    In the journey that you are all upon, there are those opportunities to celebrate and those that seem to lack the opportunity to celebrate. If you learn to celebrate through both, you will find less and less opportunities that are not filled with that same joy. In other words, like attracts.

    Wheresoever a soul has chosen to sojourn, which is the better, that they shall lament their choice and that place wherein they are sojourning, or that they might rejoice and celebrate it. See? Which makes for the better journey?

> **May 14**
>
> You are bearing the Color of your choice. Your choices are what manifest who you are and what you experience.

It is often thought that there are two opposite polarities, two balancing forces. One is generally called light and the other called darkness. If you think of light in its purest form, what can you perceive within it? Contrastingly, if you think of darkness in its purest form, what can you perceive within it?

In the darkness, it would be difficult to perceive color. In the light, even though color is present, it is difficult to be seen because the light is absolute. Therefore, one might find that there must be a point between these two beautiful polarities, each giving along with the other to that median point that which they have to give.

The children of God pass through these median points, perceive them and experience them. Often, this experiencing is done in a finite expression such as is known on Earth. So, as we look upon the Earth, using it for an example, we can see that your world is comprised of what is called color. Yet Color is so much more than this. It is a representation of energy, a signet of how one is feeling, or thinking, or being, whether on the Earth or elsewhere.

Color has a source of origin, which is God. That Color flows from the creative potential of God in pure form that is beyond definition, expression, or understanding in the Earth plane as a level of consciousness.

You are bearing the Color of your choice to the Earth. Your choices are what manifest who and what you are and what you experience. It begins with the choices that you make as an individual, that you would see in your meditation, or prayer, or in your sleep, those times when you are pausing to set aside the influence of finiteness and seeking to know yourself in broader more eternal level.

> **May 15**
>
> You command the criterion for determining your day. Either you create your day, or you allow it to be created for you.

Colors are thought of as reflections, pigment, light. Relatively little consideration is given them except by those who are seeking to manipulate you, for instance to influence you to consider products, or ways of living, or any such. But it is not the color you see as is portrayed in an advertisement that is influencing you. It is your feeling about those colors.

Some colors are known to remind you of a state of comfort. Other colors are known to stimulate an emotional response in ways that are directed towards that particular intent, or product, or advertisement.

So color is more than just the color charts and such. It is representative of states of consciousness, states of being, levels of expression, for emotion is the substance from which mind builds, and emotion uses color energy.

So how do you live with this and discover it to be useful as a tool? You first begin within yourself. You come to realize that you are encountering energies that are sustaining various ways of manifestation, thoughtforms, light, all that sort. In your daily life there are emotions that surround you as you begin the day. Do these ever change? How do they change? Are some days "better" than others? What is the criterion for determining the "better-ness"?

Consider now that you are in command of all of this. Does that seem plausible to you? Does it seem attainable? Then why do you not do it?

Do you see how you create your day, or how you allow your day to be created for you?

> **May 16**
>
> It is *impossible* for the Universe or the day to be the master over you. That is not possible. That is an illusion.

Consider waking up and thinking, as one of your first thoughts, *I am in command. I am in control. I have the power of God to take Color and, in effect, paint my day.*

You are akin to an artist who looks at a pallet of beautiful color, and the artist considers, *What should I do with this day? What should I create?*

The day is nothing but thoughtform manifesting color that is the substance of your intent, the body of your emotional self. This is a major thoughtform we are offering to you. You can do this before you step out of the bed. You can do this as you are trying to arrange your hair where you have the opportunity to pause. Does it take a great deal of time? Would your schedule for the day miss three or four seconds? If it would, you're too busy. See? Pause and think about the Color that is in your day.

Some would argue that there are others who will try to take the color away from you or give you some color that is... well, not pleasant. Some would say that, when they pause to assume the day or choose a color for the day, that it's almost as though the Universe feels challenged, and that the day seems the total opposite of what was intended or expected. That is an illusion. It is *impossible* for the Universe or the day to be the master over you. That is not possible!

So, when the day begins, before you open your eyes, feel the Color and take dominion. Choose it. Pause before you arise and fill any sense of a lack in you. Think of yourself for a moment first, and *then* the schedule. See? Better to arrive late than to arrive on time incomplete.

The quality and joy of a day is not measured alone by its Color. It is measured by that which is in the heart of the bearer of the Color.

> May 17
>
> There is nothing that you are powerless over.

It is irreversible, *irreversible*, that you will experience what you call challenge, sadness, losses, and all those things as they are known to all of you. You cannot avoid this. It is part of the journey. You are learning to accept the gifts, and to release them when it is time to make room for something new. See?

You want to begin your day receiving that Color from God. And so you change the day, not by avoiding what you feel because that is a part of your journey, but you do not let that feeling change you. You let it lift you up.

There is nothing that is in your life that you are powerless over. That is an illusion. It is possible that life can bring to you things that are indeed a challenge, or are indeed something of sadness, or of limitation, and these things can even impact the temple in which you dwell to a point. Once you cross the threshold of being one with yourself – in other words, not the inner self and the outer self, but the one Self with a capital S – then you control who and what you are and what experiences you have.

But in the wisdom of your oneness, you recognize the right of others to choose. So you do not go about putting a color on this one and another color on that one and changing their lives because, once you have that Oneness, you can also See and, in the Seeing, comes the realization that they are not alone, they are not helpless. They are where they are because, believe it or not, this is something that will contribute to them. Maybe not in this lifetime, or in the next, or in twenty lifetimes, but it will contribute to them once they release it and see it for what it is and ask for something better. See?

> **May 18**
>
> Two or more gathered in the Earth realm can build a "realm" that is not bound by the limitations of Earth.

Where two or more who are incarnate in the Earth realm are gathered, these two can build a "realm" and they are not bound by the limitations of the realm that is Earth because they have reached Oneness. Together, they have conformed to Universal Law, which cannot deny them the right to create Consciousness. See? From within Consciousness, now, the subject who, let us say in this case sought healing, has granted these two or more who are creating this realm, this Consciousness, the right to let them heal the subject. See? So again, another Law is fulfilled, is it not: If you ask, it is given. This one asked.

Now we have an environment of these two or more practitioners (preferably enough in number to surround the entity from all of the holy points). Here, the dis-ease is seen for what it is: a condition that lacks ease, nothing more. It is not a tumor that is comprised of... well, all of the conditions or definition of dis-ease. They immediately see this as something that is not in harmony with the realm they are creating and it is a simple matter, then, to speak a word, to chant a mantra, to touch that entity, or to visualize (which is creating, see) that body as perfect.

Here is another Law agreed upon: What truly is, is the person who is dis-eased is a child of God. The child of God is not imperfect. He or she is perfect. Therefore, the dis-ease must be something that is not of their conscious choice.

So it is a simple matter here to say, in effect, "Do not choose it" and, having been given the power, they give their love to the dis-ease. In effect, they surround it with love. This could be a Color that is missing in the subject. It could be a combination of thoughtforms that the entity has accepted, knowingly or unknowingly, subjectively or consciously.

> **May 19**
>
> Believe *from the perfection of your Being*, and it must manifest. There can be no belief in an inner Self and an outer self.

So they have before them an entity who is now as they are meant to be – perfect, in their realm. The entity who has asked for healing is perfect in this created realm but may or may not be "perfect" in the Earth. So how do these who have created this realm give this entity back to Earth consciousness and not have that tumor, or whatever it is, simply return? They change the entity's consciousness. They can do this from their new realm, for in their new realm, they control the consciousness. So the entity is awakened. They return a call, so to say, to the dis-eased entity, and call forth the perfection.

Now, another Law comes into play here. It is the Law of Faith: If one believes *from the perfection of their Being*, then it must be so. So they call upon the entity to believe, just as the Master did: *"Do you believe?"* See? Within that reality the practitioners, the shamans, or howsoever you might title them, would then ask the subject to build with their own belief of their perfection (and some variations on this… quite a number are known to us), but they basically ask the subject to now *Be whole*. In other words: *Be* what we have given you.

The closing of the entity so that they can return to Earth is a very sacred work and it is highly variable depending upon the position of the practitioners in the Universal Forces and in Consciousness. Many of these practitioners are not bearing capital C Consciousness while in the Earth. They know of it, but what they are masters of is Universal Law, which enables their mastery to function in finiteness, in "reality." See?

But *you* must, each of you who are creating this new realm of Consciousness, be in your own Oneness. You can't be separate. In other words, you cannot have an inner Self and an outer self. If that sounds difficult, then begin by deciding who you are and what you are.

> **May 20**
>
> Creation is not normally manifested from the level of three-dimensional finiteness. It is created in the Beyond.

You decide what has power in your day. See? That is the starting point.

As you consider combining forces to create a new realm, a new Consciousness, it is good to recall that the Uniqueness of each individual adds strength to that intention.

Also, so that there is no violation of the Law Universal as it is expressed in the dimensions of finiteness, you can move here to this new realm and do your creating. It is very wise to move out to do your work, to begin your work and to connect in that which is not bound to the finite.

To do a work, there would be a focal point. Not to imply that a literal work must be in the center of your group but an intention. See? You might well, for example, choose that this week's intention is to place joy in midst of your realm that you are creating. So, when you reach a meditative state prior to leaving your bed you would think of putting joy in the center of yourselves with each of you and the joy is in the center. See? This gives definition. It also begins the process of creation, does it not?

For example, the counterpoint would be to create nothing. To create a realm, you would not logically choose to create a realm of nothing because "nothing" already exists.

Actual creation is not normally manifested from the level of three-dimensional finiteness. It is created *beyond*... here, see, in the "Beyond." The logic being, you do not have forces of opposition as you begin your creation, sort of warding off opposing forces with one hand and creating with the other.

> **May 21**
>
> Seek Consciousness. Flaws, areas that are out of harmony, are impossible in Consciousness.

Practice being outside of the finite, where your thought is not an active part of your experiencing. Seek Consciousness. Seek to *be* that which can experience, that which can Know.

Recognize that, as you would see flaws, as you would see areas that are out of harmony, that in and of itself is impossible. So, if you see someone with dis-ease, they are experiencing an impossibility, but because they are children of God, they have the power to create a lifetime wherein the impossible becomes possible and manifests. But here, beyond the finite, such a thing cannot be found. You cannot find something that is "imperfect" such as dis-ease implies. So, when we say it is impossible, we are striving to tell you that this is a well person who is accepting the illusion of not being well. Mass-mind thought nourishes the claiming of a lack of perfection.

So, as you are focusing upon building a realm of Consciousness, recognize that in the first place it is already perfect; you do not have to labor to make it perfect. Do not come into that work believing that you have to create perfection. This is most important, do you see!

Here is a question for you from several of the Elders: Where would you create this realm?

If you are creating from within the finiteness, then you are creating, in a manner of speaking, subject to Universal Law. If you would empower one another to create it *within yourself*, then you are beginning to walk upon the path of mastery in that single thought.

So it is very important that you recognize where you are creating.

> **May 22**
>
> Whenever energies are called, all of Consciousness is aware that someone is calling, including the forces of opposition.

By agreement, then, this realm of Consciousness would be a domain subject only to the "Laws" of this domain. For instance, Law #1 could be: this is a realm of joy. Law #2: this is a realm of compassion. Law #3: this is a realm of truth. You see? The laws here would be similar to the Universal Laws of finiteness, and they become mandates. They become the force that is being created and that will then be the dominating force.

Let us take a scenario. We have this realm, this domain, that has been created through agreement of a group of Children of God. It consists of "laws" that define its structure. These will be drawn from the creators, and the creators will be the sustaining forces of this. If only two of you remain, that is sufficient under the Law to sustain your realm. The more the realm is loved, the greater is its brilliance.

Whenever energies are called – and they *are* called – the entire expression of Consciousness is aware that someone is calling the energies. See? Because the universe is perfect and in harmony, Consciousness will immediately bring to you everything that you call for, practically instantly if you have no hesitation. In the same instant, all of Consciousness has the right to inquire, *What is your intent?* Note that we used the word *all* of Consciousness. Therefore, that means that those forces that are in opposition to change in the Earth also have an opportunity to ask you, *What is your intent?* And they will probably seek to ask you individually if they can separate you.

> **May 23**
>
> Consciousness is like a blank canvas. You choose what you will paint.

    If you have a blank canvas you contemplate what you're going to paint on it and, once you decide, you begin to put the underlayment on the canvas. This will probably not have much defined form, but it will be the foundation for the remainder of the painting. As you begin the process of choosing all the other colors, you are becoming more and more and more defined.

    Now, go back to the blank canvas – that is Consciousness.

    Now, go to the underlayment – that is a step or two away from pure Consciousness.

    And on, and on, and on. See? Something to think about.

> **May 24**
>
> One can create a realm, but it nearly always requires two or more to sustain it.

You alone can create a realm.

You would have a scenario something like this: You are in meditation and you realize that you would like to see the manifestation of a certain realm of consciousness. You decide that, and you have succeeded... You *are* that realm. See?

You sustain it by your continued belief in it, your continued filling of it.

You create a realm, and you succeed in believing in it. You believe in it, and you intend it. You intend it in your day all throughout. You never are in an occasion where you are not aware of your realm. You are always giving life to it.

What happens if you do not?

You see, to keep that realm, that consciousness, in manifestation you need to continually be energizing it.

[The readings on creating and manifesting conclude.]

> May 25
>
> You are awakening, choosing to know of your Source and that you are unique. This is a primary power for you.

On the Earth, God is imagined to be something so grand, so wise, so perfect that it – God – must be distant from this "mess." But it is not so. The "mess" couldn't exist without God. God is the life-force and all that is, is of God. It is of God as the children of God choose to manifest it. It is like you as parents might allow children to manifest something even though you would have no consciousness of what that is or what its purpose is. See?

Individual souls expressed in Consciousness, and then expressed in defined consciousness and, then dwelling within the experience of that defined consciousness, may find themselves interacting with other defined consciousnesses. This may become something that is sought after as the feeling of being separate and independent and all-powerful becomes more evident, and as the realization comes about that doing certain things can gain other things over here and doing certain things here can gain things over there, and on and on. What is so often forgotten is where the journey began. See?

Light and darkness are brethren – brothers, sisters – there is unlimited love between them. The fashioning of them is the choice of the Children of God within the opportunity of the flow of life, of God.

You are now reawakening yourselves. You are choosing to know of the Source of who and what you are, and the realization that you are unique and intended to be so. This is a foundational power for you. And the colors you have experienced are given to you because they will lift you up even further.

> **May 26**
>
> It is possible to discover in each and every moment that you are reborn. But nothing is *beyond* self that is not also *within*.

It is possible to discover – in each and every moment – that you are reborn. It is possible to discover that, each day, you are reborn, and on and on with every measurement of time, indeed, throughout eternity: *Now* I am reborn. *Now* I am renewed. *Now* my journey is one of wisdom and enlightenment.

But there is nothing out there *beyond* self that is not also to be found *within* you, for the gifts of God are given with equality all throughout and with no judgment.

> May 27
>
> There comes a point where the basis for understanding is set aside, that the greater Consciousness present can come forth.

[Journey 12 begins:]

Our brother has been taken to journey upon the uniqueness and beauty of the sounds within Consciousness, difficult to define in terms understandable to those of consciousness on Earth, yet we offer these comments that you might awaken that knowledge that lies within you, already complete:

At the onset was the playing of the music on the recording device. These voices lifted up with an intent that was seen and felt as oneness. That oneness prepared a pathway. That pathway can be traveled. Their voices in union did not fill only the holy chamber in which this music was produced, for that which is given of Children of God is something that continues on; they do not perish but go forth from level of expression to level of expression.

The more rarified the atmosphere would become, as one journeys outward from the surface of the Earth, the more rarified the vibrations become. The rarefication is not the obliteration of them but the transformation, that these come into the greater harmony with that which is, and the potential is increased.

At first, the movement was with peace and joy, until a point wherein the consciousness as it is known in embodiment on Earth could no longer grasp the elementals of the rarefication, you might call it, of this journey's progression.

So there comes a subtle shift in the capacity to recognize and understand, where the basis for understanding is not drawn singularly from that as has been the experience and knowledge gained in a lifetime on Earth. Rather, this is set to the side, and the greater Consciousness comes forth that remembers and acknowledges that the Greater is always present. In the acknowledgement of this, the Greater becomes manifest.

> May 28
>
> The continued Knowing and choice of loving neutrality offers the potential to be in oneness with *absolute* Consciousness.

[Journey 12 continues:]
There are many practices, teachings, religions and quasi-religions that use methods of intonation and mantra of the sacred sounds and all such, but the truth is that you can capture much more than this by recognizing these simple things that are being revealed in our brother's journey:

There was that shift wherein he was neither physical nor Spiritual. You call it the World-Between-Worlds… neither in finite form nor infinite form. He was in a state of neutrality, choosing to *not choose*, choosing to *not be*, believing that to be perfection and that the harmony that can be gained through such could be implemented for the Greater Consciousness. (Using that term to give reference or gradient of movement.)

Here, then, was the opportunity to question. Many *would* question and discontinue the journey. They might, for example, choose to simply fall into a sleep. So what is the differentiating point here? It is Knowing. It is the Knowing that the loving neutrality is an empowering tool in terms of what you are seeking. Being in that state can empower those Forces of God oft called Universal to enable you to answer a call that is not spoken, an invitation that is not given. It is the willingness to submit unto Oneness with God.

From this point, there is the realization that consciousness, time, form, dimension respond to the seeker, that the continued choice of loving neutrality, empowered by the Knowing of it, gains one the potential to be in a state of Oneness with utter Consciousness, *absolute* Consciousness.

The gaining of this is not the relinquishing of the other. It is the positioning of it as a part of that which is righteous. The one does not deny nor diminish the other. Each gives honor, as though portions of one body seeking to build wellbeing.

> **May 29**
>
> In Consciousness, when a gift is received, welcomed – indeed, is loved – that which is given is returned many-fold over.

[Journey 12 continues:]

The Channel is not so much following the sound but moving within it, *being* the sound. This, of course, is a "statement" to Consciousness. As a statement to Consciousness, it can be answered and most always is. The answer here is in the form of those whom he had called to join with us. So there is the addition of greater reverberation, expressions that are in simpatico at levels that are impossible to know from a limited form and ecstatic to experience here.

Just as you hear music rise and fall, swell and diminish, other voices coming and going and intermingling with one another, here, it is motion. It is the motion of this movement that is being gifted to him and, because he is receiving it, welcoming it – indeed, is loving it – that which is given is returned many-fold over. The movement continues for a beautiful journey that increases in its rapidity, its motion, building, until it comes to a pinnacle of sweetness and harmony that also builds gradually, gently, to a single clear tone. As this tone goes forth, it is answered over there, and over here, up there, and far and away:

The Child of God known to this, our Channel, speaks. Others gather about him, a great number of them surrounding our brother, as he moves off ever so slowly seeking out universes and galactic formations in the known universe to see them for the beauty that he has so oft admired.

Finally, he moves again to a state of stillness, surrounded by the Children of God. Slowly, he reaches his Consciousness into the void that lies at the edge of creation and begins to laugh softly. For a moment, there is the stillness, the wonder, and then we hear a single laugh, then another, and another, and they go careening about like so many beautiful spheres of light, streaming dazzling creations behind them.

> May 30
>
> You are always creating something within yourself. It is you who decides what that creation will be.

[Journey 12 continues:]

Slowly, the laughter and careening begins to diminish and focuses into a sphere of smaller spheres, very brilliant, moving, undulating.

And we hear the tone again, the single tone. With beautiful delicacy, the individual spheres move out and join into one large concentric circle, and then they majestically soar off in different directions.

Gently, softly, their tone can be heard, increasing again and again, until now it is a river of sound, moving and undulating. One voice calls and twenty answer it, and another here and two over there, always alive and vibrant. Now the colors come to embrace the sound and the river of life moves throughout Consciousness.

You see? You are creating. You are creating this within you.

Our brother returns slowly, in a large curving arc, back towards definition, where the Consciousness begins to form itself into that which can embrace finiteness and nurture it.

Just as the fruit might embrace the seed that is the hope of the future, so is there that embrace in finiteness. It is soft and malleable and sweet, and life is continually poured into it from that which is the Eternal Life.

It doesn't matter who believes and who does not. It remains for them, for they are gifted with that choice, first and foremost. Then who, if not you, can gift self in just such a similar way?

> May 31
>
> If you can believe it, it is done; if you doubt it, it remains where the power is.

[Journey 12 concludes:]

You take a journey from finite expression, which is the definition of your physical body. How do you measure the journey? You measure it by the gladness in your heart. Your measure is the peace it endows you with for doing it, the faith, the hope, and the promise that you hold within that continually inspires you to keep a steady course.

If you can believe it, it is done; if you doubt it, it remains where the power is. There is the continuity of Consciousness that is woven all throughout all existence. It cannot be broken. It cannot be severed. It cannot be bent, tied, warped, nothing. It is a perfect continuity of Consciousness.

So, in answering what you discern to be a call, it is your choice, your decision, always, each of you, what the degree is to which you will respond. Do you believe sufficiently that the continuum of Consciousness is real, is true, and is functional for you and perhaps the one in need? If you do realize this and it is your choice, then you are following in the path of our Brother, the Master, the Christ.

The Master sees not the expression, the form of definition in finiteness, as that which is. They are not that which is before Him, not just the step that has been taken. His perception of them is as an eternal creation of God.

> June 1
>
> Return a blessing to yourself for a blessing you have given to another. Open the pathway, that *you* can receive.

    As our brother called out a single tone, there were moments of pause, that all those might hear it and know it and feel its goodness and its sweetness, and it would so inspire them that they could not resist reaching within themselves to bring their note to offer as a gift in return to a gift received.

    Do this for yourselves in your journey through life: In this day and the next and all of them, return a tone to yourself for a tone given. Return a blessing to yourself for a blessing you have given to others. Open the pathway, that *you* can receive, that the greater can be given.

> ### June 2
>
> The path is a Circle of Light back to oneness with God, bearing the gifts of experience and the harvest of wisdom.

Yours is not a quest for something you do not have; it is a quest to be free of that which veils or limits that which you have always had.

The word *power* rises to the forefront in most all quests that are a part of the journeys of those seeking to know themselves. The word power connotes variations of meanings. Power, in its truth, begins by knowing the Peace of God. From the Peace of God, one can have the wisdom and the knowing that the power, which is ever one with God, can easily flow through and be directed by that one.

Whenever challenges are met upon a pathway in the definition called finiteness it is good to realize them as stepping-stones, as opportunities. But often, these statements fall short of the understanding one seeks on the pathway of mastery. The early stages of one meeting a challenge can be disruptive, to say the least. Yet so oft it is important that the power you seek and claim be expressed in those very initial moments.

It is also well to recognize that, in the journey through life, there was the agreement to hold sacred the choices and collective beliefs of those who have gone before you, who are present in the current, and who shall follow. For theirs are the intentions to use finiteness to build the depth and knowledge of understanding in order that the eternal nature can be better understood.

There are those who have gone through these portals of flesh and have discovered that the path is a great Circle of Light that brings one back unto oneness with God. But in the return, they bear the gifts of experience, having gathered the harvest of their labors, which is wisdom.

So it is difficult to judge a portion of the Circle of Light as greater than or less than another. For, in truth, it is one circle, providing the soul a unique and different perspective.

> June 3
>
> What manifestations on the path would be acceptable for one attaining mastery? Your *Spirit* finds joy in *every* step.

You have explored the Colors and, in the knowing of them, you have known aspects of definition associated with them. You have simultaneously called to the understanding and emotion associated with those Colors that are not only within self but also within those who are about you. All of your senses are enhanced by the Color of that day, fine-tuned, so that at the conclusion of the Earth day. You not only have an understanding of that particular Color, but perhaps you have discovered some aspects of self, of definition, and of others, that will be contributive to you on your path to mastery.

But what is the measure of your accomplishment? What would be the manifestations that would be acceptable or not for one who is attaining mastery?

Let us consider your *Spirits* contemplating these things, celebrating them, finding joy in them in every step of the way, *every* step...

Spirit is the pattern. It is the way, the Light, the power. The manifestation of Spirit so oft passes through the mind and the emotion. Spirit reaches out to touch its own expression. You are the expression of God that has created this form. Without God, there would be naught in existence, and without your Spirit, your temple of flesh would not be.

Certainly in some manner here and there this has been considered. But as a master, you would not just consider it. You would know it. You would know it to the degree that the filters of thought and emotion and the Colors and all of the sensory perceptions that are associated with the journeys, including the current one, would become tools, those implements that one can choose and master the usage of to make the way more open, more passable, more peaceful.

> June 4
>
> Your Book of Life is controlled by no one but you. Write each page with your hand of love, which is the hand of God.

You are seated under a tree reading a very fine book. Its binding is handcrafted. You can feel the artistry. As you turn page after page you can know the delicacy with which each page has been made. The print on the page seems to long for you to touch it with your eyes and mind, and as you progress through the book you learn and feel from it those thoughts the author wished you to feel and know. The greater you can feel and know them, the more skilled the author is considered.

Pause from that image. That book could be representative of your journey in this lifetime to the current. Look at that book now as though it represents your life. Can you feel the dedication that went into fashioning the cover of this precious book? Do you sense a reverence, that the preparation of each page was done with loving intent, and a skill and patience unexcelled by any? Again, look at the print. Does it speak to you as the earlier book did? Scan back through the pages. Is the writing clear, with thought and reverence for the experiences being recorded? Are some chapters less than others? Are some pages not as grand as others?

Your life and that book, as a master, are under control of no one but you unless you do not choose, do not believe in your worthiness to choose, unless you regard yourself as the author as shadowed here and there with despair or remorse for that which was not done or that which was done in error by the judgment of others or self.

You carry the book within. It is you. Wherever you are and whatever you do, the book is with you. The you that is before us right now is the one who takes pen to hand. And now the work begins from here. Look at *each* page with love and reverence. Where there was an "error" place upon it your hand of forgiveness and love, which can wipe it away, for the hand that does so is the hand of God through you.

> June 5
>
> The belief is that, once a thing is defined, once something has happened, it simply is. But the "definition" can be controlled.

As challenge is encountered, it is not through error in self. It is not through the lack of righteousness or because of some inappropriate action or behavior. It is, perhaps, the way that story was written.

So it is not that you would begin from this point forward and write with perfection. It is, rather, that you must be able to, as given, look down upon your book anywhere, everywhere within it, and do so with the Peace of God all about you.

The Peace of God is not static. It is not like a frozen cube of water. The Peace of God is alive and vibrant. Within the Peace of God are all the Colors... all the expressions, all the scents, all of the sensations and feelings, and so much more.

You have the choice to set yourself Free and flow into these wondrous, majestic manifestations or opportunities to manifest, or you can simply dwell in the Peace of God as one would dwell in the peace of a warm sunlit day. If you journey upon those waves of definition and perhaps find yourself incarnate in physical form in Earth, then the influences and forces that have been collectively focused within and about the Earth are surely going to be experienced if you have chosen to be there. When you do experience these forces, see them as the movement of the contrast.

The parable or analogy of the book is offered to support you in your quest for understanding. Where you are at this point, you have written a good bit of that book, and you, as the author, have written it in a certain style or expression or characteristic. Now, in this chapter, you are changing all that.

It is believed in finiteness that, once defined, it simply is. Now you are learning that you control the "definition." This is a major change in the tone of the book. See? You are transforming it.

> June 6
>
> In the process of creating: Shift the focus to beyond finiteness, be "vanilla," call the forces, hold the faith, and hold the intent.

In the process of creating, one would first reach that state that is, for the most part, vanilla, where you don't have flavor, you don't have errant energies. You just are. Then you re-focus on that choice.

Let's say that your choice is to create some abundance. So agree upon the creation, agree upon times when you will drop everything and do this:

Make your body comfortable.

Then shift all of your consciousness to here with us. Take a position that is balanced, so that you feel that the flow of energy is harmonized. (Do you understand that? Here, you are not working with the limitations of finiteness; you are working in an environment in which you are the creators.)

Call upon those forces to create the intent, and let those energies, tones, sounds, and colors, come to the center.

Don't do anything but hold your faith, hold your vanilla and remember the intent. See?

You do not, at least in the first number of such times, have to expect it to actually make a form. And here's the obvious reason... You haven't defined the form of abundance. Abundance has many different forms, so you need to choose. Not so much so that you limit God to bring this to you but that you can define it in a clearer sense. You might wish to have abundance in terms of health. See?

You must first make room within the consciousness, that the consciousness becomes malleable.

> **June 7**
>
> Work from the infinite side of the veil. You would be removed from the forces in the Earth that seek to challenge your intent.

When you begin to extend your area of dominion to where it engages the choices and dominion of others – and because you have an expression in the Earth realm, you are within the Law to do this – you must assure your rightness in this. Remembering, as was given previously, if you issue a call, that call to the Universe can be questioned and can be responded to by *all*.

If you bring your intent here with us and work from this "side of the veil" you would be removed from those forces in the Earth that seek to challenge your intent. You are only subject to a "Law" as you bring the work to that level where those Laws apply. See? By creating *here*, you will supersede that, in a manner of speaking. Then the only thing that remains for you to do is believe in it.

> June 8
>
> The Peace of God is the state of being in which *all* is experienced as good, its Presence waiting only for you to take of it.

What is peace? How do you differentiate peace from what we would call *the Peace of God?"*

We here would define peace of one who journeys in definition or finiteness having attained a state of balance. Generally speaking in definition, or incarnation, it is having attained those things expected of one, those things that are implied as necessities, and having reached a state of peaceful existence.

The Peace of God is the state of being in which all is experienced as good.

There are no requirements in the latter. There are no expectations. There is only its Presence awaiting you, each of you, to reach out and partake of same. See?

> **June 9**
>
> Who am I? What am I? Why am I expressed here? To what journey shall I travel? What shall await me at the end?

    The expressed universe might ask of itself many questions. These questions from the universe lie within the hearts and minds of all who dwell in finiteness in Earth and in those levels of expression adjacent to same. These are questions that are known by many who have come to a pathway of seeking.

    In brief, once one in finiteness has lived and tasted of the fruit of Life, they come to consciousness, and consciousness provides them with sufficiency to know, to discern, to define, to qualify, to equate, and to assess and, from the assessing, to Know. The questions are supported by the living light of the universe called Universal Law and expressed differently by each one who perceives them, who experiences them, who comes to know them and call them their own.

    But we could paraphrase or summate these in just these several ways: Who am I? What am I? Why am I expressed? Why am I expressed here? To what journey shall I travel? What shall await me at the end of that journey? And, at the journey's end, shall I or some aspect of me that I know not continue on?

    These and other derivations are within each child of God as seeds. As these are harvested, some gain the greater, some the lesser and repeat the process again and again. But all are given the opportunity to ask and to receive, to seek and to have it given to them.

    The key in this lies in the willingness of the seeker to ask, to receive, to explore, and to Know – not on the basis of that which has been experienced or known but as reflections upon the questions of Consciousness within Self.

June 10

> The mind is the tool of the Spirit, a path of exchange between the potential and the manifest, that the potential can grow.

What is the relationship between the mind and the Spirit? Is the mind an eternal part of the Spirit or is the mind, as it is known in Earth, merely a byproduct of the Spiritual self that is seeking to gain or to contribute (or both) in that journey?

It is the tool of the Spirit that is intended to be a stepping-stone, that the eternal Consciousness and wisdom of Spirit can be brought to the level of expression in the definition called finiteness, and that the accomplishments in finiteness can be delivered to the Spirit.

Mind is a pathway of exchange between the potential and the manifest, and from the manifest to the potential, in order that the potential can grow. And, through the growth of the potential, what is called *the Universe* thusly continues its expansion and acceleration. It is the pulse of Creation. It is the intent that that which is given is received and, in the receipt, is multiplied and, in the multiplication, becomes manifest as Consciousness, that that Consciousness, then, can know itself.

> **June 11**
>
> The Children of God are the Consciousness of God set free to quest, that the glory and wonder of all might be known.

As given, in the beginning was the Word and the Word was with God. And the presence of God was known only by the presence of the Darkness, and the Darkness was known to be good and rich and all-fulfilling and there was not a want or question or doubt.

And when God spoke the Word forth, Consciousness saw Itself and awakened, embraced by the loving Darkness and empowered to see itself in the contrast. So the Way was opened, and the Word continues forth.

The Word of God is in all things, in all creation, and in all of the Children of God, and remains ever as that small spark of life waiting to be nourished, that its flame might glow brightly and that they would know from whence they have come and whom they are. That flame is called the Peace of God.

In the turning of the Light to seek and know Itself, there was the contrast against the Darkness, and the Darkness reached out. But the Light, in its new birth, knew only Itself as light might know light and, thus, it journeyed forth within and a part of Itself... not with that called emotion but in the joy and curiosity such as you would know in the newborn babe. Hence, there was, from this time forward, the title *the Children of God*.

The Children of God are the Consciousness of God set free and given the greatest gifts of all: that, as a living part of God, such independence might envelop them in a state wherein they would quest to build the foundations upon which the glory of God and the wonder of all might have its foundation and be known.

> June 12
>
> In the process of freeing and forgiving, you forgive and free yourself. In the process of loving, you find yourself loved.

Do not cling to one step, one teaching, one methodology, one technique, one mantra, one prayer. For though these might call out vigorously with their beauty and their preciousness, greater than this lies beyond, such that words have no manner of expression to define them.

Yet as you come to know the Peace of God, your perception is freed from the little calls, the tiny voices, the habits of your own creation that expect you to perpetuate them. These are relevant to self and, therefore, you are their creator. You can choose to support them and give them sustenance, or you can use that within you that He has gifted you with to, in turn, gift them by setting them free.

It may be difficult from the Earth to think of *setting something free* but, whatever you have placed within a creation, in a sense, fills that thoughtform with the power of God to give it life. To set it free is to say to it, *I have given you form, and now I release you.*

In the process of freeing, you free yourself.

In the process of forgiving, you forgive and free yourself.

In the process of loving, you find yourself loved.

These and the greater are the simple truths our Brother brought to the Earth as the Master called Christ.

As you have pondered that He said unto you that you would do even greater, He stands with you, that this truth as He gave it shall manifest good fruit more abundant than ever imagined. And that whatever you take within becomes a part of you, nourished with the fruits of your labor, your gifts, and thus, *the greater*, you see, will have been given. Thus, the truth: *Greater than these shall ye do.*

> **June 13**
>
> It is good to know that you are retracing footsteps: So, as you descended into Earth consciousness, so can you ascend.

The nature of each step on the path is as much a recovery of Consciousness as it is a discovery. It is good to know this because it will remind you that you are retracing paths, footsteps: So, as you descended into Earth consciousness, so can you ascend from Earth consciousness.

As you make the way open and passable for yourself, that path remains and others who find it will desire to walk upon it, and the greater is your joy and glory of your discoveries on the pathway, the greater shall those be for those who will follow you.

> **June 14**
>
> Accomplishments come in the willingness to move from the familiar to that which is unknown. It is always a test of faith.

The experiences of one who journeys to Consciousness begin at a point of acceptance. From that point on, the acceptance grows through the familiarity and the comfort that comes about through the exchange. As that exchange grows, the expansion of that comfort includes other dimensions, other realms, other entities, until the growth of the expansion meets itself, at which point there is the Oneness.

In the transition of steps, there are accomplishments. These come about as the willingness to move forward from the familiar to that which is unknown but soon to be discovered. The requirement is, as always, a test of faith. Every step in such a journey one is asked to prove themselves to themselves, that they would believe such that would lift them up and carry them beyond.

The intention of your works goes before all that you do. After that, there comes the actualizing of what you perceive and what you believe shall be the destination. But the intent is always first and foremost.

> **June 15**
>
> It is always good to precede your works with a prayer that is sincere.

When one journeys upon a pathway there is normally the desire to share, and that desire brings about a spreading out of consciousness. This process would be one well to be considered at the physical level as well as the Spiritual level. The spreading out of consciousness takes on a different interaction with the forces that are around you and, thus,.

With our brother, the Channel, there is a certain part of the journey of "spreading out" wherein he must submit. He must yield based upon faith to complete a part of the journey.

It is at that part of the journey that so many cannot find the capacity to proceed. It is this faith that completes the journey.

In this particular instance, the journey is involving an intent to create a pathway. This would require that Michael, Lord of the Way, would either remain passive or that he would simply create that which would obscure the pathway, or rarely – see, very rarely – that he might participate in it. In this instance, he chose the latter.

He has interacted with our Channel in past and recognizes the intent is of a certain nature that he chooses to continue to prevail around and over. In brief, he is protecting the Channel's pathway.

The movement to permit a journey wherein the Channel moves from definition to the infinite creates an opening, a pathway. As just given, Our Lord prevails over it and protects and preserves it. In this, then, wherein Universal Law is honored because this Channel has chosen from within finiteness to open a path, a way, many here are moving to the Earth without violating Universal Law and doing works therein, and setting in place those things which are to be answers to prayers or changes in consciousness in those times ahead.

> June 16
>
> Feel the joy of the freedom of your work. Expanding the gifts of God is part of the reason you are there.

It is important to be willing to discover aspects of self and to find that such discoveries are gifts, not judgments assessed as good or bad.

Recognize that you are coming to that point of power that you are seeking, from within a definition that does not (except in minimal states) believe in. Disbelief creates barriers to belief, see, perhaps not literal barriers but limiting thoughtforms.

Thus, when you go to a place of power, ascertain that you are not already working against yourself, so to say. Feel the joy of the freedom of your work. It is not relevant to you what has been or what shall be. What is relevant is the joy and glory of what you are doing now.

Remember that your Father loves you, loves all of you, loves all of existence. True love does not limit, does not command nor demand. True love is open and passive.

You can expand the gifts of God. You can because you are in that domain wherein you have complied with Universal Law. That is part of the reason you are there. You chose this.

> **June 17**
>
> Universal Consciousness is based upon Oneness. If you choose, you can re-member it.

Make yourself comfortable.

Let yourself feel the energies swirling about you, perhaps warm or tingling. Take the energies within you. You will feel a rush of something. Then wait for the peace that follows.

In the peace, let yourself feel, sense, know, perceive something that is like a very sweet vibration. You might feel this as though it is a hum or a tone.

Then, as you become a part of Universal Consciousness, feel as though you are reaching out beyond yourself in every direction. It is very pleasant, very peaceful. There is nothing but peace, yet you are conscious of it. It is as though you can be aware anywhere, everywhere, yet you know where and how you have positioned yourself for this exercise.

Just know it. Become familiar with it. Feel the curious sensation that it seems to invoke from within your being.

When you have completed this little exercise, celebrate. It is the bringing, through agreement, the state of Oneness that can make a pathway for Universal Consciousness.

It is curious to recognize that there is a point of acceptance, a place of beauty, honor, and of Universal Law between meditation and consciousness, the awake state and sleep.

Universal Consciousness is based upon Oneness. The Master, the Christ, knows Oneness. He *is* Oneness. If you choose, you can reclaim this to a degree and re-member it upon conclusion here when you return to definition.

> June 18
>
> Those who believe shall find, for unto the believers shall it be opened and given.

If ever you find yourself in that darkness that is fear, do not turn away from it but confront it. For it is in the willingness of self to face all things that can truly come the actualization that you are a Child of God. When there is that task that overwhelms, that need that seems excessive, reach out to those who journey with you, seen and unseen, and gather up the greater unto that need, that task.

Thus is the way of preparation. It is the manner in which those who are the faithful would work together that the burden is not great but moderate because it is shared, that the work is not heavy and toilsome but light and gay to behold because it is endured by all.

Who among you can find the Silence? Who among you can speak to the Silence and then truly hear, can look to the Silence with a sense of peaceful joy and anticipation and truly listen?

It is you, each one of you, who shall become aware of these words. *Know* that it is you! It is only for you to believe and reclaim and then enact that, that it shall truly come to pass. If you try and find it not possible and try again and also it is not possible, then try again and it will become possible. For those who believe shall find; unto the believers shall it be opened and given.

The "veil" is most often and most likely comprised of some aspects that are called fear. Whether these are the more gentle fears of the unknown or the unanticipated, or the more substantial fears that something might grasp you up and take you away or that you might not find your way back from that journey. It isn't the measure of the depth and breadth and intensity. It is how one deals with it that shall matter. But be light and gentle with self. Little by little as you walk along, turn slowly and look behind you.

> **June 19**
>
> There comes that time for everyone that all that is needed, all that is fulfilling, must be recognized to be within self.

It came to pass recently that the symbols that the Channel had always sought prior to taking a journey here (a "reading," as it is called) that were so compelling to him because they signaled to him that the way was open and that he was fully prepared do be a clear and open channel, no longer appeared to him. Instead, in "going out" when he does the reading, he now sees only the vast darkness. When he spoke of this this morning to his mate, he wept.

As illustrated by the Master, the Christ, as one meets that hour wherein the knowing gives way to that which is the prophesy, then there is that which is met in such a way where the known becomes the unknown, where that which is called upon must be summoned from within self.

Where is that which is within self that can answer this call?

So it was given in this journey that his meeting was with himself.

It is to be understood that, as one grows in tenure and service, and that service is recognized by a certain procedure, that procedure becomes symbolic of that one's love and faith in their God. Then, as this is taken away, there is a sense of loss. There is that which is now absent. And then there comes that position in the journey for everyone, that that which was reflected to you must be found at its source that all that is needed, all that is fulfilling, is recognized to be within self.

The reason this experience so impacted him is that you approach a time of great importance. This and the position on the path of this Channel's "work," or awakening, are all coinciding, thus the impact.

June 20

> Often it is thought that the destination is the work.
> The Pathway is the work. See?

You have recently intended to assist a brother in the area of financial abundance, or what is perceived as the lack thereof. Outwardly it may seem that such work is good and, therefore, in harmony with all things, yet the interaction of those intentions do have some abrasive action to those forces that seek to sustain what is.

Theirs has been the status quo, the state of being, for (by your measure, their measure) millennia. See? They have come to know it as all there is. Thus, such works that are acted upon are felt by them as something to be feared, even though they are not literally in opposition to you. The simplicity of your work is very pure, and certainly not with the intent of creating fear but to bring gifts to one in need. But the very elements that you are addressing and seeking to offer, these gifts are *curiously* opposing them. What you call money has no consciousness, no life force. Money itself, does not have difficulty. It is those forces we have spoken of in the form of resistance or reluctance in the giving up of something, whether this comes from a bank, a country, or those pathways that lead to our brother. See? Then these might also be given your love, that *all* forces that are involved would be blessed.

What is your purpose? You are making the way open and passable. You are not going to succeed if you are in opposition to that which is to be made passable. Its force is its domain. Its literal expression is that path. Thus, there must be the pathway of grace, compassion, and love... a path of loving neutrality first, that there is the opening. Then come the love and the compassion.

Those who are perhaps in the greatest need are those who are along the pathway. Often it is thought that the destination is the work... *I must get to the destination that I can do the work.* The pathway is the work. You see?

> **June 21**
>
> There is often that part of self that sees accomplishment as the end, or even a burden, sometimes called the fear of success.

If you have a lamp, and you rotate its switch, it will turn on. If you continue to rotate it, it turns off and then again on.

It is not to say that you cannot lovingly continue to supply what you call a flow of energy, but it is a demonstration of faith to do a work and then, after a time, to smile and say this work is done. Now you can shift to focus directly upon the path. You are still empowering, but now you are simply saying, "This portion has been completed. Now I will move before it and clean the path, bless it, love the pathway and thank it. And I will bless my brother, surround him with light and, then I will see the pathway *from* him."

Then rest. Think of it just as your Brother, where you pause and go to the mountain and be one with your Father, where you bless yourself in the presence of our Father's Light.

You may, on occasion, feel that you should return to a certain prayer or a certain work, not necessarily because you haven't done that work but because you would like to dwell in the creation of it a bit longer. Not out of need but because it speaks to you, it calls to you, it is a joyful thing to do. Recognize the energy rising and rising and reaching a beautiful point, like a symphonic crescendo and then beginning to diminish gently. At this point, you know the best that can be given has been given.

And remember this: that often there is the longing for a certain thing and, simultaneously, the fear of being worthy of having it. So there must be the recognition of this and the intent to *love it to him*. This applies to you all. There is sometimes that part of self that sees accomplishment as the end, a burden, some new responsibility, sometimes called the fear of success. (Some would deny it, and their face would become filled with blood flow.)

> June 22
>
> Knowing the energies continually creating after themselves and being in control of your participation in that has value.

There is no need to labor over the topic of Color. It is intended as a gift, not a labor.

Neither is there the benefit to anyone denying that they are a part of the Colors. Everyone is a part of the Colors because the Colors represent the energies that comprise the construction of finiteness.

Colors are continually being birthed at the "edge of Creation." Incredible. Awesome. Pure.

When turning to look at the Colors as they are manifest in the Earth, they do not speak. They do not call. They seem to be muted.

The joy is in the Colors at the edge of Creation, the energies that are continually moving and creating after themselves. Knowing these energies and becoming in control of your own participation in that does have value.

> June 23
>
> Are you certain that you wish the veil to thin for you... to see two worlds at once? Or would you like "selective thinning"?

    Are you certain?
    Are you *certain* that you wish the veil to thin for you?
    Are you truly willing to see two worlds at once, or perhaps three worlds, or thirty?
    Or would you like "selective thinning"?

> June 24
>
> We – collectively, not of one singular nature but collectively – walk with you, no further away than your outstretched hand.

    We have come from a distance to be with you but not so far that you cannot reach us.
    If you can reach beyond the end of your outstretched arm, just a bit further than that you'll touch us.
    We are those – collectively, not of one singular nature but collectively – who walk with you.

> **June 25**
>
> Sometimes there comes such a sweet stillness that it gives cause to weep, but what comes after the rain is the joy.

There are those times (many of us here know them, see them, share them with you) when the Spirit in your body grieves, not so much so for itself but for something that seems so often just beyond definition, just beyond understanding.

Perhaps it is instigated by a remembrance of your love. Perhaps it is nourished by a feeling that you would like to do more, that you would seek to contribute more, that you would like to look upon your Brother and know that you have done all that you could in His Name.

All of this comes from within the your body, your "friend" (as the Channel and Susahn have begun referring to it), the aspect of you who is expressed in Earth consciousness who might look down at their hands and ask, "How might I, O Lord, use these as instruments? O Brother, make my hands yours."

Sometimes after such, comes a sweet stillness that could give cause to weep a bit, not even knowing the why of it.

But what comes after the rain?

Yes. And so it is with self... A little tear, a little sorrow, is followed by joy and a good bright tomorrow.

June 26

Sometimes the shadows seek to close our Channel's path, that it cannot be found and he cannot return. They cannot succeed.

There are those times for our Channel when returning to the Earth is similar to looking into a fully moonless night sky and looking for that one certain little star that is yours to return to.

Sometimes there are those who seek to close the pathway that it cannot be found and he cannot return. Yet all the while, it is guarded by our brother, Lord of the Way, for this is also the Way and he is also lord of the Channel's path.

The shadows seek to fool, but of course they cannot. The Light he brings does not fit in the pathway (with a note of loving humor).

> June 27
>
> No matter what befalls you, that One who has given you life is within you, continually giving you life, answering as you call.

[Journey 13 begins:]
    There's a certain degree of beauty and joy to be had in realizing that, as one comes to *Know* a thing, it is theirs; that, as one comes to understand and to know the unknown, they are free to journey within it. It is the, we might call it, "failure to believe" that prevents the journey.
    And so as we begin this work with you here this day, our prayer that goes before this work is that you will come to Know, and that the Knowing shall free you.
    Our Channel has begun his journey once again (so it would appear) alone in the Darkness, the Darkness of creation that has no expression. At first, there was that wave of the unfamiliar, quickly followed by the knowing that he controls the destination. Thus, he began by soaring about, lifted up by the Darkness, embraced by it, knowing not whether he would consider his position to be upside down or whatnot, for it mattered not to him.
    So it is a valuable lesson and, thus, we recount it here that, though he still soars, he knows that, at any moment, he can pause and turn inward to become complete with himself and God, and that Completeness, that Oneness, creates the beautiful sound that is likened unto a call near to irresistible in its beauty.
    So is it for each of you: The believing, the faith, the release of fear, the recognition that no matter what befalls you, no matter what is about you, that One who has given you life is within you, not as one who would step before you but as One continually giving you life and answering as you call.
    It is about Knowing.

> June 28
>
> It is impossible to see a brutal act and see it without the definition. Yet each is beyond the limitation of definition.

[Journey 13 continues:]

There was a recent recounting of the Master in the form of a young girl child allowing herself to be repeatedly brutalized by a man, until the man could take it no more and broke down sobbing; whereupon, the young girl revealed herself to be the Master, who instantly lifted the man into the Light.

The question has been asked after that recounting, how it was that the Master deemed His a righteous act, when the man had not called out for help?

This is a point that is of such a capacity as to reveal something that has been hidden for some considerable Earth measure: One of righteousness can respond to *any* call. The man called out in the agony of his own desire. The Master heard and answered that call.

The Master did not become the child that was abused. He *created* the child, and he stood by them both. But as the man wept, his words were, "Oh, my God! What have I done? Please! Help me. Please, forgive me." Thus, he was forgiven, and he was lifted up. And he has realized now his own beauty. He was seeking to know himself in a certain way that could not be fulfilled. It was as one looking in a mirror that was manufactured in a distorted way: no matter what he did, he saw only a distortion. And it was through this – yes, in the Earth, barbaric, heinous – that he was seeking something that he could not understand.

Now he is one of those who does our Brother's works. Who better to help those who have so erred in past? Who better to forgive one of such a nature than one who has been forgiven? We love him dearly. See?

It is impossible to look at an action in the sea of definition and see it without the definition. Yet each of you is beyond the limitation of that called definition. See?

> June 29
>
> The Way is being made open for many souls who had dwelled in fear, unable to find forgiveness, to believe and then to ask.

[Journey 13 continues:]

We can look upon another recent question... that of Jude, who was within the Shadowland.

One of the gifts he has given to humankind is that he placed himself within the domain of the Shadowland where the energy of anger, hatred, sorrow, and all such could be directed towards a domain that was already representing all such thoughts and emotion, thus, deflecting such energy, drawing it off and away, from the Earth proper.

There is perhaps some value in understanding that the "Shadowland" was not created in "balance" to the Earth or as a shelter to it. The Shadowland was, in effect, created as an embrace to the Earth... in other words, as that meant to bring comfort to those departing who could not face God. It was not originally the intent of the Shadowland to be a place of emotional darkness. It was meant originally to be a place of rest, comfort, and rejuvenation.

It was then discovered that the Shadowland had fallen prey to those who sought to dominate and perpetuate those thoughts and such as are found to be imbalancing forces in the Earth. Recently, they have departed, as they should have initially. Some have returned to the Earth. Others have moved on to find places where they might have done well to move to originally... levels within the Sea of Faces where they can righteously dwell as they wish, no limit of time or dimension.

They were invited to go and experience healing and love and forgiveness. Hundreds did this, then thousands, and then tens of thousands, and these have gone on to help others. And as the result, the Way is being made open and passable for many, many souls who have dwelled in fear and limitation and have not been able to find forgiveness because they have not been willing to believe and, from such belief, to ask.

> June 30
>
> *Sight* requires only that you free yourself from limited and reactive thinking... that you perceive from outside the " box."

[Journey 13 concludes:]
    From the inner knowing that all is well and all is aright, there is the capability of having the Sight, the Sight that is the capacity within you to perceive.
    To perceive the nature of the event, one must be willing. One must have the intent. One must have set themselves free from the nature of those things that might be offered to you as you encounter such an event. Of course, these are qualities that are of the Christ and, as such, they were demonstrated. They are a part of those things that are accomplished on the Path and that are associated with the major confluence of energies that have recently come together.
    So, in one sense, it is very simplistic because it requires very little from you in terms of an action. Rather, it requires that you free yourself from limited thinking and reactive thinking, and that you perceive from Conscious levels, which are outside of the " box." See?

> July 1
>
> Truth can be expressed, interpreted, applied, colored based upon thinking and intentions. Yet the core is the same: Truth.

Truth is Truth.

It is basic. It can be expressed in varying ways. It can be interpreted and applied according to the applier. And it can be given life and color based upon the thinking and the intentions of those who are called the practitioners, or adepts, of such.

Yet the core of it, the mainstay, the Spirit, the framework would be the same: Truth. See?

Some of all this that has been given may sound to some who do not have familiarity with this work as something that lies beyond the questionable border of what you call sanity. Yet who is the one who can stand on that border and say which side sanity is on and which side insanity is on?

(And, when one is in sanity, are they considered sane? Or when they are in sanity, are they considered insane? It is complex. We, as Children of God, find it humorous.)

> **July 2**
>
> For comprehension, Consciousness is perceived as moving at a certain pace, yet it has expanded before it can be thought.

    The Word of God goes forth as the continuum of Creation that moves (as you would perceive it from Earth) at such a rate it is inconceivable to contemplate. It could not be thought of in terms of light years or such because, before you could say it, it would be gone. It would be past.

    The Word is, in the fragment of a moment *before it can be thought*, gone.

    So the movement of Consciousness, which is the Word of God, reaches a point where it is joyfully expanding. This expansion is not as you would think, that the Word of God is moving at a certain speed or pace through Nothingness. It is only that the Children of God have chosen to perceive it and manifest it in this way for comprehension. See?

> **July 3**
>
> The Spirit is the pattern that formulates the image, and the mind chooses from the images. This does the creating.

God is the Creative Thought of existence. The Thought of God and the Word of God are that which God "spoke" (in the vernacular of those writings.)

But you speak words. You create, all of you. You are "God creating." Your consciousness, your free will, the gifts of God born in you, are choosing the creation, and your choices of creation are fashioned out of Color. (Again, not color as just pigment or light, or even beyond vibrations and all that sort. It is the Thought. See?)

The Spirit is the pattern that formulates the image, and the mind chooses from the images that are perceived or chosen in the expression of finiteness. Thus, this does the creating, interacting with other minds and mass-mind, mass-consciousness, mass-color... all participate in the creation.

The consciousness of Earth, or mass-mind thought or the mass-energy, always seeks to sustain itself in a consistent, recognizable, or modifiable format from a baseline. When the modification from that baseline goes beyond a certain point, that mass-consciousness, that mass-being, will seek to harmonize itself, bring itself back into modulation with the baseline. See?

So as you, as creators within the mass-mind, begin to create from your Spirit that which is not in the modulation of mass-mind thought, it will of course see this as something it needs to bring into harmony with itself.

> July 4
>
> See the blessings of God ever-present in all things. Pause to look for them in every day, every hour, every moment.

    Pause a moment and recognize that only a short distance ahead you shall find that doorway, that portal, that leads you to the passageway that will free you from your current journey. All that has been given to you will be blessings, and all that you cling to will cause you to return again and again, for in all that is in existence in and about the Earth, the blessings of God are ever present.
    It is the encouragement then of we here gathered that you would ever pause to look for these, to see them in all things, and to know that not one moment, not one hour or day shall pass without the thought of God's love for thee being present.

> **July 5**
>
> Release your reactions to conflict, lack of compassion, etc., that the potential that lies within them can be reborn in you.

How can there be conflict, in the presence of such immense beauty as has come to dwell for a time 'round and about the Earth? How can there be a lack of compassion in the presence of such sweet truth, such sweet and complete awareness?

If such is perceived do not dwell upon it nor consider it to be something in error. Rather, pause long enough to remember our Father's promise, our Father's love, and see these to be merely the choices of your brethren in and about the Earth, who are equally loved by your Father. So doing, release the reactions that would seek to find shelter within your mind and heart. Release them, that they can be reborn in and of themselves to become the full potential that lies within them, just as well as within that which you see as being of beauty.

> **July 6**
>
> Pause here and there to receive the prayers placed for you along your pathway by brethren who have loved you.

There is never a step that you take, wherein you are alone. There is a moment here and there that is special for you, special in the sense that these are pauses in your journey through life where prayers have been placed for you long ago.

In these special moments, feel them —a subtlety, a flush of energy, the twinkle of light in another's eye not known to you, a stranger passing by – pause and be the recipient of that blessing that has been placed here along your pathway by dear brethren, brothers and sisters, who have loved you from afar and who love you even now.

And as you look about and see the journeys of others, some whom you know and others not, pause and send forth a prayer to await them on *their* journey, that when they pause it can surround them and bless them, that they will know their path is not that pre-ordained but one that is flushed with choices as a spring tree flushes with blossoms of color.

Seek, then, that moment of peace and, as you do, recognize and affirm we are with you, we who have walked with you in past and who are here walking with you, unseen perhaps but in your presence.

> **July 7**
>
> See the potential within you. All paths are open and possible to you.

Consciousness is the reflection of the potential within self. As you open self to see, then that which is within you will be that which will be viewed first and foremost. And when you can see this and know it, and breathe it in and know it to be good, then the passage of your consciousness from that which was into this now which is will be filled with the grace of God. And your movement will be as swift and gentle as a spring breeze.

So then, know that you are the universe, that you are that force that brings into the awareness of Earth the Consciousness that is of your Spirit, which is universal. It is intended that, in the Truth of Consciousness, you will find that all paths are open and possible to you. As you traverse them, your presence and your passage will make the way open and pass-able for others. When two or more do this together with singular intent, then the power of the universe moves with them, and the harmony of their peace invokes the Righteousness that lies yet ahead and beckons to you: *Come. Be with me, and let me be with thee.*

> July 8
>
> The Pattern, the Way, Oneness, is in the meadow between the contrasts. Here, He awaits thee.

In the Earth, you know that which can invoke a taste of sour and another that is sweet. So you begin the process of categorizing certain things known to be sweet and certain things known to be sour.

You view and assess things as to be of beauty or not. You create a gradient of good because it has beauty and not so good because it does not.

In your walk through life you may hear sounds, some so calamitous as to cause a reaction to the entirety of self, while others begin their soft call and it is as though your body reaches out to be one with it. And you will group these, the less than joyful and the stunningly beauty.

And you may reach out and touch a thing and find it to be harsh, and another that is so velvety that it summons you to wrap yourself in it because it brings out a sense of wellness, and so, you categorize these as pleasantries or irritations.

As you walk upon the Earth in your journey called life, there are many more, we recognize. In which of these would you find God? And which of these would be that which you reject and that which you accept? When you can look upon them all and the reaction within you is one of recognizing these as the contrasting taste in the realm of definition and finiteness that gives meaning to it, as tools to guide and build understanding, then they will begin to flow in the river of life, giving unto it the majesty of creation that is builded upon these very contrasts and the beauty found within each.

So you would, of course, find God within all of these, for God is creation. And you would find our Brother, the Christ, Jesus, anywhere, everywhere, to lift one up who is in despair or fallen upon their journey. Then here is the Pattern and this is the Way, Oneness. You can meet Him in the meadow between the contrasts. Here He awaits thee.

> ## July 9
>
> It is you who *chooses* to dwell in limitation or to live in the beauty and limitlessness of a Child of God.

Whoever shall read these words, we offer this in utter humbleness as your brethren, your brothers and sisters:

There never is a time, in your world or anywhere, where you are separate from God. There never is a time when you offer a prayer, whether under duress or joyful, that God has not heard and answered.

Even though you have chosen pathways to journey in the embrace of finite definition, often pause to remember that you are still the Child of God you were and are before and after this current journey. You have simply, in terms of time and space (as you hold those for reference), paused for a moment to see and experience from another perspective, in order that you can Know the way no matter what, and that you can claim the power, which is the sweetness and Love of God all throughout.

There is not an ending in the sense of eternity, merely one step. Thus, as you see what you call news reports, think carefully before you consider the ramifications of these. Think, *I am the Master of my domain. I choose how I shall be after reading or hearing or seeing this news.*

It is true that the Earth is in a time of change. But change is a beautiful thing, in that it affords the opportunity for growth and progression. There are aspects that are a part of this that have been designated as bad and, indeed, the experiencing of some of these are less than joyful. But it is still a moment in time and space and, when it has passed, you choose whether to continue in a limited form or to return to the beauty and limitlessness of a Child of God.

> July 10
>
> The you that experiences and reacts has given Earth the right to impose, yet you have the right to react or to choose not to.

The nature of reality as you know it has conditional response associated with it because of the heritage that you have been given upon entry into the domain of the Earth. Therefore, these are those things you are dealing with in this current time and at your current position as you seek to progress in awakening yourself while yet experiencing in the physical body. This lies at the foundation of your thoughts as we perceive them, and as your questions are also seen.

It might be well to remember that your Brother Jesus did not suffer even though the body did. That portion of his choice to be expressed in physical body chose that in order to open the way to make it known and passable. This could not be done from a distance, for only "the chosen" (only those who believed) could hear Him, and their capacity to affect that guidance from Him to others in the Earth was minimal at best. Thus, His "entry" began as Amelius. We were with Him then and we are with Him now, but it is good to note that you were and are also.

The parts of you that experience and react have given the Earth the right to impose; yet your right to react or choose to not react remains intact. So this might be, as you would call it, the crux.

Finding the "groove" and living in the groove is a matter of knowing that you are a Child of God but not just when it is convenient or not just when you take time in your schedule to pray or meditate (though this is commendable and indeed worthy of your doing). To be in the groove, in truth, is to know who and what you are as you follow that groove. The question is, then, does the Earth permit you to move through its dimensions, its expressions, in a groove? Therefore, it must be an inner application.

> July 11
>
> When you have an experience that does not seem Godly, it is not separate from God; it is meant to be experienced as a *gift*.

Some clarity of understanding is still needed, though this we have given in past:

Satan, *Devil*, are terms applied to the misuse of the power of God.

Stepping back a moment to remember that in the beginning all was God, all was of God, what would you discern that it is now in your current day? Are some things *not* of God? Are some things not an expression of God?

Therein lies much to be discovered but utterly simplistic: When you have an attitude for a moment or an experience for a time that does not seem Godly, recognize that it is not separate from God; it is present to be experienced by you as a *gift*.

"How late is too late to accept the gift?" some would ask. We tell you this: If in that last moment of life in the physical body you call out with joy, "Oh, Father, I now understand. I now know that I am yours now and always," that is as wondrous as if one makes the same discovery thirty, forty, fifty years prior.

> July 12
>
> Without death, could you endure remaining forever in finiteness? Without birth, would you have the new opportunities?

Time is not a measurement here. It is a guideline that *you* use in the journey through finiteness, perhaps because without it you could become, indeed, "lost."

Without death, would you endure if you were to remain forever in finiteness? Without birth, would you have the opportunities such as forgiveness, and renewal? Even the trees, the plants, the animals, come into the Earth, into life, with a brilliance and hopefulness. One has only to look upon the young of any species to see their vibrant joy to be alive.

Then be alive in Spirit, always.

> **July 13**
>
> The purpose of interacting in the Earth is to find that point of intersection between you and the "forces of opposition."

Your intent, as you have stated it – to assume the position of unlimited-ness while yet expressed and experiencing in finiteness – for this to be made manifest for you, this must be the most important thing in your life. *All* else would be secondary.

Jesus journeyed through the incarnation in which He was called by that name, but he journeyed as a Child of God, a Son of God. There was not that issue from Him that was *not* of God.

When you began applying your truth and your belief, did you wish it to simply flow without challenge, without limitation, without contest? The question is, then, why are you in the Earth plane? What is your purpose (other than, of course, you wish to serve God and, thus, to serve and assist your brothers and sisters)?

It must be recognized that the purpose of interacting in the Earth is to find that point of intersection between you and the forces that believe they are in opposition such that they struggle to sustain their "dominion."

When you began your "journey to Consciousness" you asked God to guide you, God to strengthen and enlighten you. But when you were born into this lifetime you came from that enlightenment. Thus, the interaction of your Spirit asks, *Guide me that I might strengthen, bring unto me that which does not receive that I might know it and bring to it peace.*

The first test invariably seems to be to test your faith, your belief: If it does not manifest as you anticipate will you sustain? (Might reread Job.)

> **July 14**
>
> Earth is neither the kingdom of Darkness nor of Light. It is the meeting place of these two beautiful polarities.

Lord Michael and Lord Haliel are expressions of the Love of God, just as you are. They began their journeys just the same as you, as difficult as some would find that to accept. Their choice, immediately, was to remain in service with God and each did so with zeal. If you look at them you'll see powerful similarities – neither one will take much flack (as you call it).

Be thou just so the same. See? They are not in opposition. They bear powerfully the wonder of the contrasts that are the fountains from which eternal expression can flow. If you dwell utterly in the light, can you see anything? Similarly, can you see in absolute darkness? Think about that. There are many dimensions here. The misnomer is to think in terms of Darkness as evil, and those forces that have fallen prey to habit and to the familiar invoke the power of Darkness, believing that it is, in a singular sense, in opposition to the Light when, indeed, they are brethren, kindred souls.

The Earth is not the kingdom of Darkness. That is its own illusion. Neither is it the kingdom of the Light. It is the meeting place of these two beautiful expressions – polarities, if you will – have been focused by the children of God who sought, and still do, to express themselves.

There are those who would seek to misuse the Darkness, just as those who seek to misuse the power of the Light.

Michael is the Lord of the Way, and Haliel the same in the Darkness... not evil but polarity.

In the beginning was the Word, and the Word was one with God. And God spoke the Word, *Let there be Light*. So is the Darkness less than God? For the Light was born of God.

> ## July 15
>
> What can you do that you have not done? Look at self with sweetness, and see what portion of life is being repeated?

There is naught that can have dominion over you – naught means nothing – except that you permit it.

It can be argued for eons that those who are being slaughtered in various countries, those who are being stolen and sold into slavery, etcetera, have not chosen these things. This is the perspective that is in the now that does not consider what went before or what should follow. It does not consider that all are one.

In other words, who permits these events? Who looks the other way because they profit in the material? Who sees something, at a curious level, that it is exciting or exhilarating to be able to dominate and control or take away life? *They* are those who are being brutalized and *they* are the perpetuators of their own brutality upon themselves. For the Law is perfect, and this is their lot

The time is close at hand when it shall be heard – the Call – that those who choose will hear it and answer it. Those who do not will be given a renewal of opportunity to follow these pathways *because they choose them*. And the opportunities will continue: the aggressor becomes the dominated, and the dominated become aggressors, warrior against warrior, until they realize only the body physical dies, only the body physical suffers.

What can you do that you have not done? How can you become "unstuck"? Look at self from the sweetness of Spirit and see what portion of life is an illusion and is being repeated? Not that we would judge; this must be known by self.

> July 16
>
> Habit and fear are allies, calling to you every moment, in place to help you know that yours is the power to choose.

    The force of habit is seeking to perpetuate itself, not just in one moment in one day, in one year, but always.

    Imagine that always, every moment, every breath, Habit calls to you: *You love me and I love you. This is comfortable. I give you shelter.*

    Habit has an ally. It is as though habit calls again and again, stating, *And here is our friend, fear. If God does not answer in twenty days, surely there must be no God.*

    Yours is the power to choose, not habit. Habit brings you the beauty and the fruits of the past if it is in harmony with God; when it is not in harmony with God it must ultimately recognize its own discord.

    If you are oppressed and you come to accept that oppression, even find comfort in it, then you are building more of that which will serve you and oppress you again and again.

    If it does not begin with self, where does it begin? If it does not end with self, where shall the ending be found?

> July 17
>
> Habit seeks to perpetuate the attitude of domination and fear. Ever look with love to the broader perspective from Spirit.

Some depart the Earth and fall into what could be considered a deep, deep sleep. They do so because they are weary. In their weariness they are vulnerable. Sweet voices call to them, forces that appear lovely and embracing offer them nourishment and comfort, and then convert them into forces that will expand and perpetuate those wills of domination, those forces of habit that do not bear testimony to the accomplishments and fruits of the past, but seek to perpetuate the attitude of domination and fear.

We (through this, our dear brother) have spoken as asked and he has answered every call, not questioning, not judging, but merely offering to help. It follows, then, that those forces will never stop seeking to unsettle him, to distract him, to cause him all manner of effect because, though he is only the messenger, they see him as a destroyer. If the messenger is vanquished, then habit basks in the familiarity of its own perpetuation. We see all these things. We have been with him since the beginning of time. He is a brother to Haliel as he is a brother to the Christ and to Michael.

Jude journeyed in the Darkness, not because he was lost or being punished but because of his love for God and Jesus. The heart of Jesus is that which empowers Jude as it empowers this, our brother and, mark you well, as it empowers each of you.

If one of you stumbles, bring love, bring forgiveness, inspire hope. Yes, speak truth, but never let a modicum of love be diminished because of any event. See the influential forces and look to the broader perspective from your own Spirit.

> July 18
>
> Your intention in prayer goes before you. It bears the essence of God, borne on the love that is in your heart.

The hope that is found in a prayer gives it power. Your intention goes before you and bears the essence of God, and it is borne on the love that is in your heart.

If one turns in a moment of sorrow or pain or struggle and asks of you, then give it, but give it with the power as of a Child of God. Give it as you know in your heart is righteous for you. Never question another as they do the same, *nor* allow them to counter you in what you know and feel to be right.

There are as many pathways unto the Kingdom of God as there are Children of God. But when you agree to follow a pathway, then believe unto it. Do not let the forces of habit detour you or convince you that your path is incorrect.

The manifestation of who you are and what you are is yours to command, and the multitudes are at the ready to walk with you.

> July 19
>
> Christ Knows the glory of God manifest in all things, so He walks where you choose to the glory of God at journey's end.

Jesus did not wave his arm across the thousands that came to hear Him and say, "You are all now free, each of you. I command you now in this moment, know yourself to be an eternal Child of God and let the illusion fall away from you."

Do you believe that he could have? So great is His love that He endures their pain by their side as they stumble, His tears mingling with theirs, He gasps for breath as they gasp for breath, that they would know He is ever at their side.

But He feels not the pain, He feels not the sorrow; He feels the glory of God manifest in all things, so He would lie with them *where they choose*, and walk with them *where they choose*. And, when they call out and say, "Jesus, help me," it is His arm upon which they lean to continue the journey and to find the glory of God at journey's end.

> ### July 20
>
> To find the center of Be-ing, the Sacred Place within, is to find the Creator's Word that is defined in the Uniqueness of You.

The intent by our Channel and his mate has been to fully integrate their Spirit with their physical expression. The pathway to this, as it has been defined by them, is now complete.

It is not to imply here that there is but one pathway. In the beauty of the Earth and other energies that abound in and about it there is the construction of that which is often not seen, not known. To find the center of Be-ing – that which is holy, the Sacred Place within – is to find the Creator's Word that is defined in the Uniqueness of You.

There cometh the return of the Promise in many forms, not only as has been foretold but, that there can be borne on the reverberation of our Creator's Word, those great cycles that have come into confluence and that bear the Light now.

So it is a blessing offered to all who have the desire to seek it: that the gift of Consciousness cometh forth and is offered unto those who are seeking. And those who knoweth the Christ Spirit and Light shall feel It and shall seek within, and the remembrance of this will fill them with the golden Light of the Christ, this very pathway upon which we stand.

> **July 21**
>
> There is no ending, only a continuum of beginnings, affording the journeyer greater opportunity to claim the potential.

    If you seek to release that which holds a bond of familiarity and thus can veil the beauty and wonder of your true being, do so through the reclaiming of who and what you are.

    So is it, then, the beginning of that time wherein there is to come that which manifests as opportunity and, through the many translations, the many interpretations, the many prophecies, and all that and greater, there cometh that which is of wonder, purity, and Light. If there is not the eye to see this, nor the ear to hear it, then that is a choice, and it has naught to do with God's love or God's judgment. It is merely the expression of Free Will: the greatest gift of all given by God.

    There is no ending, only a continuum of beginnings. And each beginning affords the journeyer the greater opportunity to understand and, through the understanding, to claim the potential – yes, the power – as an eternal Child of God. But with this great gift of choice comes the right of each to manifest according to their choices and, where these come together in a certain familiarity, the choice and its power grows.

    Now, through the presence of the great keepers Michael and Haliel, the manifestation of this choice comes to its fruition in a time near at hand.

    We should look upon this with great joy and celebration were we in the Earth in form.

July 22

> You cannot look for a beginning that is eternal, for this is defining something that is infinite. There is no ending to God.

It is difficult, indeed, from the Earth to comprehend such a vastness as your goodly scientists and others seek.

In the beginning was the Word, and this was the beginning and yet ever shall be as such. But there is no ending to God and, thus, you cannot look for a beginning that is eternal, for this is as defining something that is infinite.

Just as there is the continuum of creation through every word, every thought, every deed by those of our brethren who dwell within the Earth, considered far greater than a singular place such as the Earth, then so is it expanding, for there is no boundary to Gods gifts. God continually gives to all of His Children.

> ## July 23
>
> Remember your brethren who cannot find their way. Many are calling. Listen, and you will hear them.

It is a very good time for you to decide what is the fire, the flame, that gives to you the joy of Being?

It is not one who comes from distant realms of great Light and that alone but all of you who have this flame within you. It is the spark of the Creator's Love for you that gives you the Uniqueness so precious unto us all.

So is it said here, "Tell them: Look for that Sacred Place within. It is there to be recovered and awakened."

Here is a great time, as you measure it in Earth, for you to follow the call that comes from within. This is that which gives you the opening of your personal Uniqueness, the personal power that is within your Sacred Place in order that this can give to you, as it is now and ever has been intended to do.

You could say that the Creator's Word dwells within you in the Sacred Place without limit. But you cannot grasp this, for its enormity escapes the boundaries of the thoughtform of the defined. And yet, here is the pathway, the portal.

And we add this:

Remember your brethren who cannot find their way, who know not of themselves. Many are calling. Listen, and you will hear them.

> ### July 24
>
> Prior to a work, place the awareness of your eternal nature and God's Peace before you, and then it is done with God.

It is good to always recognize that we are God's Children. As you journey with this affirmation, you bring into the fullness of your Consciousness – Spiritually and in terms of your expression in finiteness – this eternal Oneness.

Let us review just a bit, that you will have these thoughts to use:

• The word that you speak has power and, when you contemplate the words prior to speaking them, you bring into them the fullness of your potential. When you contemplate these from the Sacred Place within, thine own Spirit in oneness with God, then you add this power to your intent as the words are spoken. Remember this and use it. You call forth the power that is yours, your Uniqueness and your connection eternally with all that is as God's Child.

• If you summon the awareness of your eternal nature prior to a work and you place this before yourself, and come into God's Peace having so done, then what you do is done with God. Use this and build this into a strength that has substance.

• The "pathway is complete" that was referred to was brought unto Michael, for it is he who is Lord of the Way. As you brought the intent to open the path from the Earth, this intent is honored. And so is it. The continued focus and placing of energy upon the path will bring your goodness of intent into it, and where it passes through those forces of limitation they shall empower it all the more. And the workers of Light can now move along the pathway and will serve with you. Use them, for this is a gift to them, just as your own service to others is a gift to you.

> **July 25**
>
> No forces or power of limitation can limit you. Your belief in your heritage as a Child of God is the power.

- You are an expression of the Eternal Spirit, ever in oneness with it.
- No force, no power of limitation, can limit you.
- You have the power of your Spirit and the fullness of your expression as a child of God within you. You are this.
- Your belief this heritage as a Child of God brings it to its fullness. We are with you in this. Together we choose it. So is it.

These are the intentions of your consciousness, and thus they are awakened.

You who are our brothers and sisters in Earth have begun to reclaim your own oneness with God, your Father, and you will find the pathway opening unto you perhaps more than you can recall before.

Oft be in the stillness of your own Spirit, and ask of the Father. He will guide thee. Do this often and it will become natural and will become who you are.

We shall be a part of your intention. No separateness. Bring this into your being. We are gathered here in the midst of those who have pledged themselves in service in this time of hope and promise as lies as a gift before the Children of Earth.

Within the embers of hope and promise that lie within each is the flame of Knowing, awakening the beauty that is the gift of Uniqueness within each.

We celebrate you in a manner of this nature: For each joy and moment of wonder and love we offer many times that number to each who is open and seeking, in the recognition of no separateness between Spirit and flesh, in Our Father's Name.

[Note: In a series of readings put together into a book titled <u>When Comes the Call</u>, in which was given the history of the Children of God and of the creation of the ream called Earth, this was given:]

"There is a consciousness that is filled with the beauty of the original intent for the Earth and adjacent realms. This "place" is occupied by those souls, those Children, who moved to this realm in realization that some of the original intent, in their words, "went awry."
"While they do not judge, they chose to leave the Wheel of Life and live here in their true form. They know that they can (and some do) journey into Father's Word, into the purity. Some remain in the purity and some return.
"The Master can often be found here, for these are among those who will return with Him. And if the path is opened and made passable, when the consciousness of Earth reaches that point of receiving, then they will come to the Earth from this realm, without birth, with Him."

Susan began calling this the "Homeland" to represent a certain sense of belonging, being "Home" with Father even while within the Freedom of exploration and experience of the Colors of God. In the Homeland, nothing is mandated and all expression is free. The Lama Sing group often took the Channel to that consciousness, in order that he and the readings could build understanding and awareness for any involved in these works of what can be, was and is intended to be, for the expression called Earth. In the intent to build this understanding, many manifestations were shown to the Channel (and Susan and others who were able to follow along), expressions familiar from the experience in Earth. Expressed in the Homeland, such expressions – water, clouds, meadows, paths, even human form – are always free, as the expressions of God are meant to be.
The "Homeland" will now begin to be referred to.

> **July 26**
>
> Seek ye naught without. The true treasure is that which God placed within you the first moment He gave His Love to You.

We come to take you unto the place that is held now in the heart of our brother, this through whom we are speaking, through his many journeys here. And so, we come upon the beautiful rolling meadows. In the knolls and summits of the array of beauty that is here, we see others who are gathered in various places. We move with you and see them as they gesture to us, coming to us, and we join them.

The sisters are in song, celebrating that which is awaiting the claiming, and they call to all who are present herein to remember the Promise within and to offer it to the without. In this, come the Light of hopefulness and the joy of expectancy. Let us pause, then, and celebrate their song.
[Pause]

It is a time, dear brothers and sisters, to seek out those treasures that lie within, and not those without. For in the coming days, there are opportunities aplenty to find the hopeful promise awakening within you. This, then, is the true treasure and the hope for the morrow.

Unleash the joy that is your own Spirit and let it sing and dance, for in the beauty of its presence will come the harmony of others as they, too, look within and reclaim. And where thee are gathered together in this manner, find that we shall join in song with thee.

Be thou ever in the Peace that is thy heritage. Bear His Peace. For those who look yet in the Earth for the nooks and crevices that they believe will hold secrets give to them thy peace and love. But seek *ye* naught without, for the true treasure is that which God has placed within you in the very first moment of giving His Love to you.

> ## July 27
>
> Set free that which obscures the Truth within you and seek the power of your own will. Have the faith that will light your way.

Remember:

- Seek the power of your own will.

- Set free that which seeks to hold you and obscure the Truth that is rising to the forefront of your Uniqueness.

- Sing out with the joy of your own Spirit's beauty as it embraces you, as two parts of the whole coming together might sing a glad song.

- Reach into your being often and hold the Father's hand as it is outstretched to you.

- Hold not the moments of doubt or concern that are continually offered to you. Give to these, rather, the Light of your hopefulness and the truth of the Promise.

- Be in the peace that you have chosen and this shall guide you.

- Have not a doubt, but have the faith that has ever been yours. That is the Light with which you can illuminate the way.

> ## July 28
>
> There is the powerful intent set before your soul's journey. Call for this: *Guide me, Father, that I might fulfill my intent.*

We look upon the vastness of consciousness as it surrounds and embraces the Earth, the consciousness of the potential and the collage called mass-mind thought. Wherever there are those who are asking, seeking, one can see that the Light is growing much more intense, as though one would recognize that the Light is seeking to give to those who are asking.

Within the temples of the Children of God is that which can be awakened and brought to the fullness of its original potential. And while there are those occasional calls from within the lifetime that this or that might be the choice, there is this powerful intent as it was set before your soul's journey, and this has to be honored as well.

Thus, in your journeys, in your works, in your meditations and prayers, we should think it well to recognize:

That which I have sought by entering into the Earth in this journey, guide thou me, Father, that I might fulfill this. Let me be shown that pathway to fulfill this, that I might, in the present, know my self and my Spirit to be one. I pray of thee, Father, if it be righteous, that Thy grace complete the intention: that I would become complete.

So as you in the Earth would see this to be righteous for you, then call for this.

> July 29
>
> There is a Consciousness beyond the defined where creations and the glory of the potential of what *can be* are celebrated.

[Journey 14 begins:]
    We move. We move beyond the influences of the defined to the undefined, and to the beauty of a wondrous realm of consciousness, where the Children of Earth and the Children of God have come in their mutuality of Oneness to celebrate in the peace and glory of the potential of <u>what *can* be</u>.
    The Channel is in his Spirit and we have set aside the consciousness that is limited, that he can be free here. He is turning and speaking this way and that with others he is meeting, some he knows and others he is seeking to remember from the early times. It is not like one might suspect from the Earth; rather, it is without need of definition, confinement. Here, there is the intent that was and is held by those Children who journeyed here to manifest the gifts of God.
    Many here look upon the Channel with wonder that he has broken free from the realm of Earth into this expression.
    He asks about the Colors here. A spokesperson answers that, here, they are free, having taken form out of love for the Children here simply because the Children love them, so they are here freely, exquisitely beautiful. It is likened unto a heart that is open and in peace, that God's creations can move within and become one with such Children. It is not their intent to a take this to the Earth and attempt to over-manifest those who are there. They have sought to do this before and realized, in humble love, that it could not be so. So they rejoice here, knowing that those who will depart the Earth who yet hold this vision within their hearts can be guided here.
    The Channel has come here to join with that which his Spirit seeks, that the brighter pathway can be made for his mate and himself, and those who are willing to follow it.

> ## July 30
>
> Anything that obscures your Knowing that you are a *Child of God* and your authority as that Child, command it to be gone.

[Journey 14 concludes:]
    There is the Knowing that comes from be-ing, and the be-ing that comes from accepting that you are a Child of God. The acceptance is within.
    When the Earth realm obscures the Knowing, then take your authority and command these to be gone. And seek out that which brings you joy.

> July 31
>
> In the quest to understand, particularly when that objective is finite, one can become entangled in that very objective.

[Note: In this reading, the Elders came forward to comment to a discussion Al and Susan had earlier in the day. The following entries include a discussion between she and they.]

[The *Great Passageway* reading begins:]

    Elders: There is a Great Passageway.
    It is not *great* in comparison to existence or what you call infinity, so that term could be considered relative.
    Passageway implies that this is more singular, narrowed, confined, directed. So, in the usage of those two words, there is the recognition that this can connote something that is not generally seen by some as a good thing, yet those who can see this in our meaning of it will understand.
    This Great Passageway follows the intent of one's mind and heart.
    In our "journeys" we have followed this Great Passageway and we have used it to know it, to comprehend, its potentials, its meanings, its power, if you will. It was during such exploration of the Great Passageway that, in another "time" (as measured by Earth), we became entangled with those very forces we were seeking to know. It is in the quest to know and understand a thing, in particular when that thing or objective is finite, that one can find themselves being called to become it, perhaps only for sufficient duration as one could know and understand from that perspective.
    So, as we explored through the Great Passageway, we came unto that which was very diverse and intense in terms of the collage of focuses that were placed upon specifics: finiteness, and the interactive nature of those specifics and finite creations. All of this and much more we did through the Great Passageway.

> **August 1**
>
> You *generate* – with your thought, with your mind, and with your heart – according to that which you *choose*.

[*The Great Passageway* reading continues:]
   Susan: With respect to the meditation I had, that one does not have to "die" to regain our full potential and that this allows us to not be dominated by it [finiteness]... Is that correct?
   Elders: That is a correct statement and it is a truth.
   Susan: The film I was trying to describe, as an image, an example of what I could step through... Is this relative?
   Elders: You give permission to reference your thought?
   Susan: Yes, please.
   Elders: You are referring to the cinema with Miss Foster. [Contact] We are aware of this cinema, and it is relative, inordinately so we might add. That translucent, shimmering essence that she reached out to touch, you could define as the *field reference* of her thought. In that which we find as truth, what you saw in the cinema has its counterpoint in reality (and, of course, those who created it, on varying levels were and are aware of it).
   The essence of one's reality is similar to a sphere-like orb around them. The further one moves, generally, from the point of origin, similar to a broadcast, the more space that signal needs to occupy. (Unless, of course, there has been the evolution of intensely focusing it, directionally speaking.) But for the most part, you generate – with your thought, with your mind, and yes with your heart – according to that which you *choose*. Your Spirit's involvement is a variable that is dependent upon the individual. Trying here not to move from the singular to the plural. Nonetheless, having stated this, it is difficult not to move into the singular *and* the several-fold for this reason: These are not individual energy fields, not just one mind, heart, and Spirit sending out a broadcast, but many.

> August 2
>
> One can extend their Knowing beyond the beginning of their interaction with finiteness to the point of their very creation.

[*The Great Passageway* reading continues:]

    Elders: As soon as you reach a certain point in your own energy field, you will encounter other energy fields and, if you have a connection of heart, of mind, of Spirit (or through some remorse or regret, some other form of connective link that is looked upon as less than perfect), this creates *interference*, if you will, just as with your broadcast.

    So, referring to your discussion, you *can* bring your Spirit into the Earth. You *can* bring your intent to become that which is You. This will then, initially, create a field that is quite dynamic. By dynamic, we mean powerful. To a degree, it is likely to be predominant. In other words, other field energies would have difficulty penetrating it. The intent, the ideal is, at the onset, impenetrable in a manner of speaking.

    Your ideal, your intent, consists of a composite of who and what you are. It draws upon and builds upon the foundation of what has gone before. You have within you all that you are. Many in the Earth believe this, subscribe to it, but only within limits. Most, we observe, believe only to a certain point. That is not judgmental, merely an observation. They cannot extend their belief back to the *point of their creation*. See? So they extend their belief, their recognition, to a degree of variable nature only to *the beginning of their interaction with finiteness*. See?

    In your meditation and your expressed ideal and truth, to a degree you are knowingly (and to another degree you do not fully realize this yet) reaching back to the point *of creation*. See?

    To make this as clear as possible, this is precisely what the Master does. He draws upon the wellspring of His very creation.

> August 3
>
> It is impossible for you to not be a part of the All. It is a matter of the degree one's intention manifests that involvement.

[*The Great Passageway* reading continues:]
   Elders: Remember, the Great Passageway is your intent. What you intend would come from the wellspring of your *Being*-ness.
   While in Earth you have this field of resonance that will initially be seemingly impermeable. (In other words, that which is less than the intent cannot endure within it.)
   What is within an entity is seen in all that they say and do, in the product of their hand's labor or their words or minds or creative self. The key is, what is the intent in any or all of this, and do you believe that what you do is limited and finite and that it endures for only a time.
   You are not, as it has been given, of the Earth, but you are in its consciousness. Yet you *are* of the Earth, for there is naught that is apart from God, therefore, it is impossible for you to not be a part of the All. See? Thereafter, it is the degree to which one's intention manifests that focus or involvement.
   You have spoken of the polarities in finiteness. It is the very nature and existence of those contrasts, those poles, as you experienced them and mentioned, that gives definition. And definition gives meaning. And, through meaning and experience, one builds understanding. It's a chain. That understanding, then, can be woven with other understandings and it becomes, thereafter, if one is willing, wisdom. So you want the polarities.

August 4

> God is the Darkness and God's will is the Light. So the Will of God moves from the Darkness to become Light.

[*The Great Passageway* reading continues:]
    Elders: Within the Great Passageway is neutrality. It is at that form of expression where the creative flow of God can be found. This could be called primal in the sense that it has no boundary, nor definition, nor intention, as you know these words and their meanings. Of course, flowing from God there is a collage of intent, but it is the intent of God and, therefore, indefinable by its very nature.
    We know some of the facets of it, and we learn more of it with each experience. It is the essence of that which is still moving through what you call time and space, like a great wave of light coursing through the darkness, rushing through the void where, in the very moment before its presence, there was naught. The instant the wave of light of this creative potential of God intermingles with same, all exists. It exists because the Darkness is the counterpoint to the Light.
    The illusion is that God is not in the Darkness. We have come to know that God *is* the Darkness, and that it is God's *will* that is the Light. So the will of God moves from the Darkness to become Light.

   To our beloved brother, the Channel: This is why you see the Darkness first, for you have come to know the path to see God – and that is the Darkness – before you begin your journey to be a channel of blessings to the Earth. Then *we* come, in the sense that we make our presence known. (We have not always been permitted to do so, but of recent times this great gift was given us. So as you look back, you will note our presence mentioned here and there. But there is not one journey, not one, in which we are not at your side.)

> August 5
>
> The Great Passageway begins within you as your intent. What do you choose?

[*The Great Passageway* reading concludes:]
    Elders: In the movement of one's intent through the Great Passageway, it is the moment of conception that offers the opportunity to choose.
    What do you choose?

August 6

You bear a unique beauty by God's intent for you. Release the things that restrain the growth of your awareness of this.

In the journey called life in Earth many facets can be found of definition, form, and a somewhat universal understanding. Most all, for instance, would know that a tree is a tree and understand its definition. The great gift that is being offered to those of you who are seeking now is to understand beyond that which is the summarily agreed upon definition. This is often found only by a journey within.

The inward journey – or as has been called, the Great Passageway – is an eternal potential for all of you. Each of you bears the glorious beauty of Uniqueness by God's intent for you, and it is by way of this Uniqueness that you make discoveries, you have experiences, and you gain in every respect. And, as you ascend, you receive further and further, and then reflect these unto God and unto all.

The beauty you taste and experience is that which is found by the release of those things that lie in contrast to it. It is not the kind of contrast that gives opportunity for understanding but the contrast that limits, that tends to wish to restrain growth of awareness because of its own needs or fears.

Therefore:
- Keep a schedule, not harshly but keep to the openness.
- Know your intent, that Consciousness knows it with you.
- Honor the physical temple as an integral aspect of being a child of God. This has, by your nomenclature, tangibility.
- When you choose to have a functioning Consciousness expressed in Earth, Universal Law is then in harmony. This is the empowerment that makes the way open and passable for you.

> **August 7**
>
> Close the energy around one for whom you offer prayer. It is a statement to prevalent forces of the power of your faith.

Let us speak to prayer and to several issues that we are aware are often brought up in and about the Earth regarding that topic. We wish to state at the onset that what we give from here is offered as a gift, not a mandate. It is recognized that the greatest of all guidance cometh from that center within you, wherein you and God come to know one another in the intimacy of your Uniqueness. Ever would we step back to honor this, first and foremost.

The first action we would see occurring, as your prayer begins to manifest for an individual who has asked, is a surrounding of them with the light of your love and your blessing as a Child of God.

Then, to the center of their being, you might search for that which is willing to truly receive the gifts. If they are willing to receive, then the "energies" flow immediately to the center of their being. This is as a reflection to them of their own divine nature as an eternal Child of God. Should they be willing and have no outstanding "reasons" for that state of dis-ease to continue, wellness will be instantaneous. If there are moderate reasons, these move a bit slower. But the work is done that swiftly. In the event they cannot receive immediately, the intent of the prayer surrounds them until there is an opening through which the prayer might enter and do its good works, whether in this realm from which the prayer is requested, or a realm beyond, or in another journey.

We suggest that you conclude the prayer. Since you are responding to their request or a request on their behalf, you have the right to close the energies around them. As you do, you withdraw. This is an evidence to the forces that may be prevalent of the power of your faith and the recognition that, as it is asked, it is given.

> **August 8**
>
> Concluding a prayer ensures the prayer is intact and cannot be altered by, or be susceptible to, non-benevolent influences.

    Another reason for concluding the prayer is variable. It is dependent upon that one or those who are in prayer for the individual.

    If you are "accomplished practitioners," you would not keep an open pathway between you that can be susceptible to other influences in either direction. You would know that concluding the prayer does not mean that you cannot revisit the entity and offer your love, your peace, and any other gifts that have come to your consciousness to be given to that individual.

    If you are very devoted and conscious of works in the healing genre, then you can comfortably sustain a connection with the individual, continuing to nourish them (in a manner of speaking) with your love and your prayers for their healing. This must be determined by self.

    But succinctly, the reasons for concluding are to ensure that the prayer remains intact and cannot be altered by extraneous forces that may have less than benevolent intent for the entity and that doubt, concerns, and other such that are of the emotional power in the Earth realm cannot penetrate the purity of your prayer as its given. See?

> August 9
>
> When you know your Self and have set your Self Free, you bring forth the gift of You to all you meet and all you do.

    It is good to remember ever that the greatest of all celebrations comes when you know your Self and you have set your Self Free, for in so doing, you bring to the forefront that gift of your Uniqueness as an offering unto all you meet and unto all that you send your love, your prayers, to.
    It is good, ever, to celebrate often the affirmation, the confirmation, that you have come to know yourself to be God's Child.

Lama Sing offered the following for an easeful, productive journey and meditation to the Homeland Consciousness, where some Children of God create, and they and their creations experience one another, each and all utterly Free as intended by God:

———

    Be as relaxed and open as possible and put yourself into a state of as much ease as you can possibly do, such as a reclining chair. We would encourage a secure environment in which you can be undisturbed. Have the opportunity to simply *be* at the conclusion.

    It is good to have "breadcrumbs" on the path to find your way back (given with humor here), to build the pathway and that the pathway will be recognizable to you.

    It is good to make "real" the destination:

If you perceive grass, see yourself bending to touch it, or seating yourself on it or laying back upon it and feeling its embrace.

When you walk past some of the beautiful, flowering bushes, pause to take in their fragrance and see the glory of the color that they shower you with.

When you come to where the waters of Spirit dance down over the faces of the rocks and, with crystalline sound, land into the pool below, reach out and feel the droplets as they cascade off the edges of various rocks.

Touch the surface of the rock and feel its gentle response.

In greeting others, reach out to know them and open yourself to be known. Feel the rush of a certain, beautiful energy or the passage of something special between you such as sound, color, vibration, fragrances, and various beautiful transmissions of a sort that have no word in the finiteness of Earth.

Continued comments from Lama Sing for journeys and meditations in the Homeland Consciousness:

The beauty of the journey is not ended when you return to your physical expression in the Earth; you can feel the resilience of what has been gained. And, when you close your eyes to meditate, perhaps you shall feel the presence of it very close, very near.

The more you make these journeys, the greater will the awareness be that others journey with you (whom you may not know in the present), that others are following you along the pathway if you welcome them. And this is an opportunity for further service.

You have the right, through the Universal Law, to request assistance. You can request this in accordance with the Law and God's gift of your Free Will Choice. Because you are within the Earth making this request, it must be honored. And, as powerful as the forces are – the great sea of mass-mind thought and emotion – they cannot usurp the Law. They can give the impression, they can make one whose faith is not strong feel that it has dominion; but it is not possible. This is the intended illusion.

The perpetuation of your invitation makes it possible for millions of Light workers (who have been waiting for just this time) to join with you whenever you are about a benevolent work seeking to bring your love and healing grace to your beautiful planet, to bring the love of the Spirit of God (symbolic in the Earth as the waters of Earth), which is the purity of your being. Those who come in answer to your invitation will join with you through God's grace and Word, which is His Law. Whenever you might hear calls and you are in a state of rest or peacefulness, pause before you answer and call forth those who would joyfully serve with you, and you can do even greater works than might be presumed.

> August 10
>
> Freedom, in its complete sense, is your right. You will come to know what Freedom truly is as you experience its Expression.

[About the Homeland:]
 The quest for Consciousness is an eternal one.
 It is not to imply that in this very moment as we speak this word – *Freedom* – that you cannot fully accept that intention that lies behind that word as it is spoken. It calls out beyond Universal Law to the Truth of God's Word, for you are created in His purity and, as such, you have the right to claim your Freedom at any moment. It may seem, indeed, not so here and there, but if you are at peace and surround yourself with the love of God and your faith in Him, you will see.
 Once you have attained the Homeland, you will know what Freedom truly is, as you experience some of your brethren who await you there and who have even been in your presence. You will come to understand Freedom in the expression of all the forms that you experience, whether it be the trickling water, whether it be the fragrance of a beautiful flower or flowering bush, the wonder of the green that represents the grasses, and on and on. You will see, as you admire or give your appreciation, your gratitude, to them that they will respond to you. As you might lie upon the grass and caress it back and forth with your hand, you might find the grass responds and seems to be caressing you back.
 For as with all that is in the Homeland, the grass is comprised of the intentions of the brethren and the original intent to manifest some of the beauty that they felt from the Word of God in the form of His unlimited array of blessings. They have created of the Colors of God's Word, the energies, the vibrations, the sounds, and the plentitude of gifts that are beyond the nomenclature of Earth. And all of these expressions – here because the love between the brethren and the Colors and energies of God's Word are equal – are Free! So how can they be? What is the nature of them? Are they "real"?

> August 11
>
> The original intent for Earth was and is the free, unlimited expression of God's Word in harmony with His Children.

[About the Homeland:]
    All that is of the Homeland is so real, alive, and responsive that you might know yourself to be walking upon one of the beautiful pathways and know that you are walking in the embrace of God.

And those you meet will greet you without reservation, without hesitation, and completely give to you the fullness of their being... their love, peace, and grace that is theirs so uniquely that makes they, themselves the blessings.

You may hear the celestial sounds. You may hear the sounds made by the flowers as they sing out their colors. Yes, as they *sing out* their colors! And the fragrances will caress you with their intention to be a gift to you.

All that is present in the Homeland is Free. It sustains form only because there is joy and harmony in so doing. It is not confined. It is not limited. It is the unlimited expression of God's Word in harmony with His Children.

> August 12
>
> Holding the knowing that *you are,* and that you are one with Source can aid powerfully in the reclamation of Freedom.

[About the Homeland:]

Some of you will come to know that, beyond the Homeland, is the continually flowing expression of God's Word. Our brother, the Channel, has given this several names: the All, the Nothingness, the Pure Peace and Wonder with God.

It is possible for you (and, though it is not a mandate, we recommend that you have a good relationship with the Homeland as a first order) to journey into the All and feel the wonder of what might be called *not-being.* In other words, having no confined form, the utter Freedom of Knowing *that you are* and that you are one with God, and the sweet bliss and ecstasy of Knowing as God Knows, and Oneness with God as God is known to be yours.

Holding this knowing while in Earth can be a powerful asset in reclaiming your Freedom to move beyond the finite boundaries of your mind, your emotional constraints, and those constraints (whether loving or nay) that others have placed upon you in the sum of your journey to the present through your life. It is difficult, while in the confines of your physical expression in the Earth to know these as well as you can know them when you move "just a few steps away" and look back upon yourself: You can know the energies, the colors and light of your presence, and you will come to know that you can understand that which is the composite of your expression in the Earth in the present.

The power that you bring back to your physical form can set these energies – *any* limitations, *any* impositions – Free! We do not imply in any way that you destroy or eliminate them, but that you use grace, forgiveness, love, and compassion, and free your self from this by Freeing the individual who imposes the constraint. The greater you Free your self, the greater are the freedoms granted to others. See?

> August 13
>
> When you give love to another and it is felt with resonance, a line of light is made, allowing for the flow of God's blessings.

[About the Homeland:]
Now is the time to prepare for what lies ahead, and it is much closer to you now than ever before.

It is indeed a blessing of profound magnitude to be one with you, all of you, in this good work, this journey. It is not to preclude you from any other experiences in your intended journey in the Earth but, to the contrary, to heighten these; that the realization that what you are experiencing can be known on many different levels; and that the understanding of what is involved at a greater depth might be awakened, that you can be of such vibrancy that your presence with others will have an impact that will be endearing and enriching.

When you give love to the heart of another and it is felt with resonance as you give it, then a connection is made. We have referred to such connections as lines of light. You encounter a myriad of entities in your journey in the realm called Earth, and each of these has varying degrees of "lines of light." They are representative of interactions between two Children of God and they are often used to send blessings to one another, not necessarily because there is a call and a need, but simply because you are thought of and remembered with love. The giving of love, then, to another is to surround them with that which is an expression of your Uniqueness. And in many, many instances, since God's love flows through you, you are blessing them, often to a significant degree if they are willing.

August 14

> To truly be Free is to confine no thing. Pause a moment and think of this: You would seek to confine no thing... *nothing*.

[About the Homeland:]

As you seek it, it will be given.

The Homeland can be interpreted as that which is promised, or the "Promised Land": *utter* Freedom, utter Oneness with God. The pathway to here exists. It is *in expression*. We are keeping it in expression. It is offered as a gift to those of you who would build from your consciousness to that point of intersect between that which is finite and that which is infinite.

You can hold the thought that you are giving to this, building a gift for others — a gift of faith, a gift of hope — and it will be a part of the return of the Promise. The pathway will be for those of the faithful who choose it. (Those who wish not to, of course, can choose whatever else is in accordance with their consciousness.)

Consciousness includes the potential for the Children of God to choose and, in the choosing, to create and, in the creating, to bring forth those qualities that are ever within them. These qualities are of God, for they are God's Children.

You are God's Children. In the Knowing of this, you would realize that to truly be Free is to confine no thing. Pause a moment and think of this: You would seek to confine no thing, nothing.

In other words, all that is expressed in the Homeland is expressed because it brings joy to the source of the expression.

> **August 15**
>
> Regarding the question of animals, pets, they have no karma. They are free. Yes, they could choose to be in the Homeland.

[About the Homeland:]
    The animal kingdom, the plant kingdom, is a collective energy of sorts that is in the embrace of the Consciousness of the Children of God. This does not employ the same "mechanisms" such as the Wheel of Life, or karma, or those sorts, for these are simply the energies that can manifest into finiteness in accordance with the choices of the Children of God.
    Therefore, when they depart, they have no bonds, no mandates, no karma. They are free. If they would choose to be in the Homeland from a state of Freedom and the choice being an expression of joy, you will find them here. That simple.

> **August 16**
>
> Universal Law sustains the opportunity to journey into finite experience. The Homeland needs no Law, for it is Free.

[About the Homeland:]

Regarding the issue of Universal Law, consider for a moment that you are in the embrace of God completely and utterly, that there is no thing that separates you and that there is only your oneness. Would you think, in such an environment, that there would be need for governing law?

In the environment of finiteness, order manifests with the choices. In other words, God's Word invokes harmony. This is not to imply that the choices of His children must do this or that but that the environ in which the expressions are evolving or experiencing have a governing structure. It is defined as Universal Law. The expression of Universal Law is needed where there is the expression into finiteness or definition.

Universal Law requires no reference here in pure Consciousness, for the harmony is in the state of Oneness with God and, therefore, there is naught to govern here.

Do not misconstrue what has been given, for there is a potential of so doing... The Law is perfect. In its perfect expression you would not, were you to journey into its embrace, perceive it as such because it *is*. In the expression of finiteness you still do not perceive it in the literal sense, but you feel its effect. So journeying beyond definition takes you beyond the need for Universal Law to mandate.

Were there not the presence of the Law it is very probable that the expression that is called Earth would have long since passed and have returned into its originating forces. The Law is that which sustains the opportunity of the Children of God to journey into finiteness and to experience and express. It does not mandate to them in the literal sense, but it is that within which they dwell.

August 17

Your "pure form" is the You that ever bears the Light of God within, wherever you journey.

[About the Homeland:]
What is the form of water when it is heated to a boiling point and dissipates? Would you say that water has moved into Spirit?

Your *true form* is your immutable Uniqueness, the beauty that is the resonance of God's Word expressed as You. This is the true form in its purest sense. The form that is defined by many references, many sources and, indeed, many holy writings, refers to Spirit. The Spirit is when the Children of God move from their "pure form" to an intent. The intent, then, guides the purity of the Uniqueness of the Children of God to be expressed, in harmony, as they move into the embrace of Universal Law.

In other words, Spirit is ever in harmony with Universal Law and this tends to bring about the varying expressions. Your "pure form" is the You that ever bears the Light of God within. See?

One can be formless and be within the embrace of finiteness. Many who journey in finiteness with you are not in form. They are formless. Formlessness that is often spoken of by our brother, the Channel, is beyond definition in the energies of God's Word. As he and others journey into God's Word, or into Consciousness (capital C), they are closer to their true nature, which is the brilliance of their Uniqueness. Were you to view them, should you have that potential to see, you would see them as light or energy.

When one attempts to perceive that which is without form, without mandate or definition in the sense as it is known in the Earth, it is difficult to perceive it beyond that which is known.

To know Consciousness is to know utter Freedom and Oneness with God.

August 18

To know Consciousness is to know the utter Freedom and Oneness with God.

[About the Homeland:]

The Homeland is beyond "frequency" as you know it. It is in the pure state within God's Word. It is a gathering of the Children of God who hold a part of the Promise, which is their love for their brethren.

> August 19
>
> By journeying to the Homeland, you are building a benevolent gift. You will know the gifts you have given in the days ahead.

[About the Homeland:]
So in what ways does journeying to the Homeland benefit others? That which you choose and build becomes a part of mass-mind thought. The greater are the number of those who contribute to this intent, this thought, the more does its presence have "the right of manifestation" under Universal Law.

It is the gift of an intent that you are building, and that cannot be usurped by mass-mind thought. For again, Universal Law preserves the right of Free Will choice. You are building this intent as a benevolent gift. This, then, conforms perfectly to Universal Law. So the path continues to expand as you continue to choose it and intend it.

It is a beautiful work that you do. Perhaps difficult to comprehend in the moment, but we can assure you that you will know it and it's value and the gifts that you have given in those days which lie ahead.

> August 20
>
> If you can set aside all that limits you, you would find yourself capable of walking right into the Homeland.

[About the Homeland concludes:]

What is the "construct" of the Homeland? The stumbling stones here would be that, how can you look at this, pick it up and shake it, turn it 'round about? You run into difficulties because the resources for referencing and understanding are, when sought from the Earth plane, based upon the references that you have from within that. The Homeland has no beginning and no ending. Therefore, it may seem, categorically, it cannot "be."

It is not constructed. It is intended. In other words, think of yourself as rising up in a very beautiful warm-air balloon. The limitations are the ballast. As you jettison the ballast, the balloon rises higher. If you can set aside all that limits, you would find yourself capable of walking into the Homeland.

You could not bring form into the Homeland, you could not bring limitation into the Homeland, because these are "defined." They have expression.

The Homeland exists through intent. All within and about it are free. See? Freedom is the power here.

Freedom is that which gives you the opportunity to be. When you arise in the morn, dependent upon the circumstances that you have chosen prior to entry or that have evolved as a result of your choice or non-choice, you will have certain experiences. In the Homeland you are always free – *always* – to choose.

> **August 21**
>
> Your intent is like a substance bearing the qualities of you within it. In other words, what you intend has substance.

[About Be-ing:]

What is very valuable to know, we should think, regardless of where one has chosen to dwell in their consciousness, is the realization of the wonders that you possess within and about your being.

We have chosen the word *being* rather than your *self* or your *physical* or your *expression* because, wherever you choose to experience is where you will "be," for the focus of your intent brings about an action.

Your intent is like a substance bearing the qualities of you within it. It bears the sweetness, the uniqueness, the faith, the inquisitiveness, the hope, the love, and peace, and so forth.

Recognize that what you do, what you say, what you intend, has substance: Do not criticize yourself. Do not continue to carry the ballast that prevents your beautiful balloon from rising into the embrace of God. Set yourself free by choosing Freedom.

> ## August 22
>
> You are a Child of God! As you choose, you commit an action to occur. The intent goes forth and is heard.

[About Be-ing concludes:]
    Faith and the authority of *be*-ing a Child of God build a pathway of love that can connect you to others. While you may not know of a certain brother or sister who is in need, holding your authority and your faith and offering prayer, which is the giving of that which is yours to give, will be felt by them, by those who are in need.
    Seek ye that place of silence within and, as those thoughts that are a part of consciousness in the Earth come to ask of your energy, your attention, bless them and honor them, and claim the authority to have them take their proper place within the continuum of Earth. Yours is, ever, the right of choice.
    Remember, in all things, that you are a Child of God and, as You choose, you commit an action to occur. The intent goes forth and is heard. The greater you can make this a part of you, the more power does the intent possess. But ever be at peace in the doing of this, never with intensity, always with the peaceful knowing that all is aright, for you are the Children of God.

> ## August 23
>
> In this grand cycle of change and opportunity, you can contribute to the Light and the great harvest through prayer.

[About the Grand Cycle:]
    It is widely known, dear friends, that all of existence, as it is expressed through the Children of God and their choices, has great cycles, great waves of Light. And the results that come from having chosen – and *not* chosen – express themselves in varying ways. For the Earth, this is a grand cycle of change.

    We use the word grand to indicate that it comes as there is the readiness of those who go before, who prepare the way to make it open and passable, that this Light may engage with those who are His to bring the blessings of the great harvest to those who are willing.

    We should lovingly emphasize this to those of you who partake in the joyful works of prayer, for here before you are those times of great opportunity. For as there is challenge in the Earth, know ever that the *greater blessing* is also present. Those of you who hold the requests from others in your hearts and in your Spirits with joyful prayer on their behalf, give unto them of this great blessing equal and greater than their needs that they place before you.

    In these times, then, celebrate and be joyful with your prayer, knowing that He is with thee each step of the way. We, as we are granted the great joy to so do, shall be at your sides as well.

August 24

You have journeyed to the Earth to find opportunity to serve others and to gain the understanding of your soul's blessing.

[About the Grand Cycle:]
    There may be some challenge in perceiving the blessings that have been bestowed upon those who have endured hardship. Here we call upon you to remember that there are those influences that are rising up in their energies, their forces, for this time of great change. It is like the crescendo of a symphonic resonance before it begins its final aria or its instrumentation expresses the great conclusion of a work.

    Think of yourselves, then, often in the light of who and what you are and that you have journeyed to the Earth to find opportunity to joyfully serve others and to gain the understanding of your own soul's blessing.

August 25

> Within you is that Light of God, the same as when you *first awakened*. Cleave to that Light in these times of opportunity.

[About the Grand Cycle:]

In these times that are ahead there is the opportunity to gain much. Within you is that Light of God just the same as when you *first awakened* unto your Uniqueness. The moreso you cleave unto this Light, the greater shall its brilliance reach out to touch all aspects of your being, your consciousness, your actions, words, and deeds.

You have the power as you reclaim that you are His. By the claiming, all that is yours awakens in its beauty of Uniqueness and in its grand opportunity to serve others just so by way of that Uniqueness.

Let not the ripples of illusion inundate you as their precedence goes before the great change. It is most often in this manner (in the expression of finiteness) that there are those efforts on the parts of what could be called the status quo to resist change. It would be no different than attempting to tell a mighty oak tree to hold onto its leaves through the coming winter season. It is not created to do that. Neither are you, each of you, created to hold onto the past in a manner that limits the future.

Be brave. Step forward. And reach into the seeming unknown that is immediately before you, and you will be gladdened of heart and mind when you realize the great gifts of joy and wonder that await you. It is, again, as with the oak tree... Some of the past events, habits, memories, and so forth must be released to their source, where they can be reborn anew.

You stand before a time of calling that from within. Do this with a joyful heart and be at peace within. As you so do, you will find that all about you will reflect this peace back to you, and the way will be made open and passable for you.

August 26

> Bring forth that holy Uniqueness within you. This is one of the greatest works you can do.

[About the Grand Cycle:]
Believe unto that which is sacred within you. Look within yourselves to bring forth that which is your own truth and that holy Uniqueness, that it can be that which is seen and felt by others. This is one of the greatest works that you can do in these current times.

Hold the promise that you are His and that He is ever with thee.

August 27

> Give up habit and the familiarity that can limit, and Love and Peace will guide you into the dawning of the Promise.

[About the Grand Cycle:]

Some of you may find that the changes in consciousness are beyond anything that has true familiarity for you. As you encounter these changes notice that, as you affirm and bring peace to these changes, you will find understanding through that very peace.

Peace is that illumination that can be given to any situation of darkness, of doubt, of fear and, as you have the courage and strength to bring this to the forefront when confronted with the unknown, the greater shall be the illumination within you, and less and less will be the power of the unknown to create doubt and confusion for you.

In the beauty of the changes you will find yourselves choosing to release some things that are familiar to you. Not that they are no longer of value but that they belong in a certain place that comprises the foundation of who you are, not carried forth into the future of your potential.

Yet it is the giving up of habit and familiarity that tends to bring about uncertainty in so many. In this, then, ever be joyful in the silence of wonder that is found in the Peace and Love of God and, as you hold these in your heart and mind and let your Spirit be your guide, all things will fall into order and that which was curious, unknown and, yes, even something that makes you question, these things will come to be the new building-blocks of who you will become in the dawning of the Promise ahead.

August 28

Each day is a holy ceremony of life. In it, you are empowered to give the blessings of joy and peace to all.

[About the Grand Cycle concludes:]

We call to you to remember – *remember* – the beauty of your Uniqueness.

When you arise on the morn, look within and see the Light before you greet the day. And give thanks to the beauty God has placed there, and promise yourself that you will be true to this, that you will honor this beauty of your Uniqueness. Then when you open your eyes and look to the dawning, you will recognize the light without as that which is within. You will know it as God smiling back upon you.

There may be dark morns, of course. Perhaps you could take these as God's embrace, that you would dwell moreso on the Light within, that you would see this as the opportunity to bring it forth all the greater.

Then give your beauty to others in kind thoughts, in compassion and, yes, above all, in loving prayer. Pause here and there – as it is joyful for you, not as a mandate or as a rote or dogma that binds but as that which is the glorious opportunity – to give again and again.

And as the sun recedes below the horizon for that day, look to the Light within once more. As you see the sun's last rays settling upon the land about you, send your Light with the sun in its journeys around and about to bring its gift of light and warmth to others of your brethren, known and unknown, and celebrate the completion of this day's journey. Look to yourself for the goodness, and look at others as they have touched your day's journey and give thanks for them and bless them, as they are blessing you.

Each day is a holy ceremony of life and you are the one giving the prayers in that holy ceremony. You are the one empowered to give the blessings of joy and peace to all.

> **August 29**
>
> Paths of loving neutrality can be made for some to come to Earth for good works, sustained by those willing to receive.

Many of our brethren move along the pathway created by and with our Channel – and us, in harmony with all of the Laws in place between us – to be of service to those who are seeking, those who are calling out, and those who know not to ask. The loving neutrality of the pathway that the Channel journeys on is a great value to us.

When such – and other pathways of sincerity and truth in the prayer and meditation of others, for instance – it is possible for a group of good workers to remain after the work has been completed to continue their works. It depends upon the reception they are given. While this might seem curious to you, consider that they cannot dwell where they are not in compliance with the Law.

In the Earth, Universal Law is expressed in very defined and, in some cases, very finely defined, terms. Thus, there must be the reaction on the part of the recipients of their offerings that then forms a bond of harmony. That bond of harmony complies with Universal Law, creating an environment in which the gifts being borne can be shared with those receiving them. That sharing expands the consciousness of those who are being served. So, by their willingness, the bond is relatively straightforwardly made if they are sufficiently conscious and have sufficient belief and faith *in themselves*, see, to accept this. This points, again, to the to the importance of not dwelling in the quagmire of unworthiness too long.

Those who are in a state of dis-ease or who are in need and have known not to ask will feel the presence of that light which is brought to them and, then should they choose to accept this, in some cases those good workers will remain serving with those who are the guides of the entity in need.

> August 30
>
> One can help sustain a path for good workers by dwelling in Peace and intending only to serve as others ask or are willing.

One can make it their intent of service to help sustain a path of good works, as a sort of "doorperson." The intent must be set before one's self to become pivotal in that position and the intent must be in harmony. Some would call this: *Do no harm*. Others would call this *loving neutrality*. And some would call this being a pathway of pure Peace.

The intent needs be sustained, first and foremost. Like having an electrical light, you turn it on with your intent. If your intent goes off, the light goes off and the pathway will close. Straightforward.

You dwell in a sea of consciousness that does not welcome change and, wherever there is a line of light that is wavering, that sea of consciousness, the thoughtform of Earth, will occlude it. Reconnecting that pathway is not as straightforward as simply choosing once again, "Oh yes, I turn the light back on." What is required is a consistent attitude of faith and joyful ease, a Spirit that has love at the forefront. Most of all it would be that one *dwells* in an attitude of peace such that the Sacred Silence is held within self to such an extent that all that comes unto self would have to pass through this and become embraced by it. In other words, there is no intent to make decisions for others but only to serve as they ask or are willing to be served.

> **August 31**
>
> God's Grace is the pathway of immediately balancing with karma. Forgive and love yourself, as you would do for others.

The question has arisen again on the topic of Karma and how karma can be transcended.

It is good to understand, foremost, what is karma. The truth is karma is merely the opportunity. It is an opportunity for a soul, an entity, upon a journey through finiteness or elsewhere to make choices and then to experience the result of the collage of choices that entity has made.

There are denser energies in the realm of Earth than in many others. The density of energies, emotions and such, are (as the Channel often says) very sticky. The density of these energies that have been experienced in journeys and lifetimes in the Earth tend to have a greater "adhesive" nature to the experiences, the choices. The adhesion is largely based upon the emotional energies involved.

God's Grace is the pathway of immediately balancing with karma. But it must be believed that God's Grace is pure Love and that pure Love will make all things understandable. Thus, the opportunities that are present in the Law of Karma, in the karmic records, are met, for they are your choices, your experiences, even though they oft involved others and may involve others' "stickiness."

Forgive yourself and love yourself and you begin the steps towards applying God's Grace. See?

> ## September 1
>
> If an ancient teaching illuminates the Light within you, it will serve you; if it does not, return it with honor, judging it not.

As one considers the various and ancient teachings, it is paramount to recognize that there is but one God.

If you look about in your current time, in your current realm of consciousness, you can take the same records, give them to divergent groups and ask them to give an opinion, and you will find a collage of translations of the same writings. This has predicated varying sects and groups and diversities among the same basic teachings, whether Christianity or some variant upon same, or whatever religion.

There is but one God. Whatsoever you would seek to discover in the ancient works, bring it into the temple of Light that dwells within you and hold it in that Light. If it is illuminated in a spirit of goodness and joy for you, then keep it within, for it will serve you. But if you find that it does not serve you and your intent and your journey's purpose, then return it to its place of rest, honoring it, not judging it but only equating that which is of value and goodness to you.

> **September 2**
>
> Each one's journey was lovingly selected by self, with assistance from others, for the potential opportunities and value.

It is curious, isn't it, why so many variations on choices. But isn't it wonderful, too, that it is possible that each of you can do so and that groups and cultures, races, classes, and so forth, can choose to come together and work under a common cause or a common ideal.

The difficulty came to pass when this was looked upon with conflict. And this attitude still exists in varying forms in your current time.

You are in the Earth because you have chosen it. Because your Spirits have evaluated, along with wonderful assistance from brothers and sisters and Elders and so forth, you have selected carefully and lovingly the potential opportunities and circumstances that would make the pathway of this journey of value to your Spirit.

> September 3
>
> Throughout the day take time to reflect, to surrender and to receive, and to move between these, and to stay balanced.

It is important for you to take time to reflect upon your journey. Consider the varying aspects that you know, and hold these before you and feel them. Let them call to you and you to them.

• Look at your journey and your intent, and your willingness to surrender all. As you do this, there will be the offering that will come to you.

• In a manner similar to being willing to surrender all, be equally willing, and receive all that is offered to you of God and of the Christ.

• Take time to allow yourself to be between the two expressions periodically here and there – giving and receiving – not for prolonged periods but several times during an Earth day. This will endow you with the ability to recognize that which comes intending limitation versus that which comes intending you a blessing.

• Keep the energies well balanced but do this on a regular basis for body, emotion, mind, and Spirit. We have emphasized this repeatedly, thus, thou knoweth this to be of import. And not merely to sustain the wellness in the body but *as a part of your intent.*

> September 4
>
> Pause and feel yourself being embraced by God.

[Note: What follows began a change in these readings, and began a transformation for Al the man and Al the channel. Thus, the Journeys will be named, titled according to Al's intent for each.]

[*Journey to God* begins: His guides, Zachary and Sarah, lead the Channel:]

Zachary: The Channel was met by the Angelic Host of Father, Mother, God. He was embraced and carried into the golden Oneness of God. He was and is being given form for these interactions so that it will leave a clear effect upon the sum of his being, inclusively, his defined form in finite consciousness, which he lovingly calls his "Friend."

It is a glorious journey here. It was by the intent he stated in his prayer at the beginning of this journey, in which he stated, in profound love to God, "I want to talk with You and just be with You." So he has come to be one with God.

Many might ask an array of questions: "Is he really with God? Does he see Him? Can he feel God? What's it like?"

He *is* one with God. But you cannot equate this with an embrace of two physical forms unless those two physical forms were, in and of themselves, Complete. So what we have here is a son who seeks to return to his Father, bearing, as a part of his journeys in God's Name, certain gifts, as though to say unto Him, "I have gathered some of Your harvest. Look how beautiful it is! Oh, Father, thank you for this beautiful opportunity to experience and know these things from that definition of expression!"

God has embraced my brother. The embrace is like being one with vibrant, brilliant energy of light, color, and sound that I have only limited terms to share with you. But feel this, if you would, for a moment...

> September 5
>
> Release those things that strive to restrain you. Find the way to see that you are, ever, complete. And sing out.

[*Journey to God* concludes:]
    Zachary: There is nothing, no thing, nothing... just the incredible golden Silence and Peace.
    You know this to be the Spirit of God that passes through all that is, that offers to all greater than they can conceive. You feel the warmth and embrace of this golden Silence and you know it is coming from within and without.
    Then, at the moment of the embrace being complete, you *are* it. Hence, the term, "Glory! Glory!"
    The Golden Silence is the passive, loving, all-embracing Spirit of God. As you feel this and know it, let it become who and what you are. This is the balance point, that which is the love, the compassion, and the sweet, loving neutrality of God's profound Love and Oneness with you.
    From this attainment, from this reclaiming, much more can be revealed. Those things that may have been a question or a doubt, or that which lacked understanding within one or more of you, will be revealed.
[pause]

    The Angels caressed him, in a manner of speaking, to awaken, even more, the knowing of his Heritage.
    This is your Heritage, any and all of you. If you wish it, choose it... Choose the path that leads unto it:
- Release those things that strive to restrain you and keep you unto themselves.
- Find the way to see that you are, ever, complete.
- And sing out. Sing out with your very being, that, whatsoever you do and wheresoever you are, your song and the glory of your love of God is felt.

> ## September 6
>
> Let us be brothers and sisters seeing choices of experiences and intentions to serve but never seeing separateness.

Be thou ever strong of Spirit, and let the strength come *from the very "Beginning."* It is a line of Light, an eternal one.

But neither is it limited to this, for can it not be said that the line is also an ever-present Consciousness? The knowing of this awakens the potential to be it, to become it. Thus, where there was a line between a distant point and the present point, this is no more, for they are one.

We stand now at the threshold... all of us. Wheresoever you are as you are aware of these words, these energies, this communication, the Great Cycle is upon us. Let us rejoice and celebrate one another, and let us open to the completeness of our eternal Nature, cherishing the beauty of that Uniqueness that God gives as life to us eternally.

Let us do, as the Christ has promised: *all these things and greater.* Let us be brothers and sisters seeing no separateness, seeing nothing that limits, seeing that which is for what it is: choices of journeys, choices of experiences, choices of good intentions to serve but never seeing in separateness.

September 7

> The Christ Spirit is that infinite, eternal essence that is the continuity of God's intent borne in each of His Children.

- The Christ Spirit is that which is the promise of God within each of you.

- The Christ Spirit affords each soul a golden path of Light to return to the Uniqueness and purity in which they are created.

- The Christ Spirit is that infinite eternal essence that is the continuity of God's intent borne in each of His Children.

- The Christ Spirit is your torch, the Light that shall guide you throughout all of eternity.

- The Christ Spirit is ever present in all things.

    The omnipotence of God is also the omnipresence of the Christ Spirit.
    Thus, when one discerns the Light of God, they are simultaneously discerning the Light of the Christ Spirit.
    Wheresoever the Christ Spirit is expressed, there so is He.

> September 8
>
> Listen for it... Hear the blessings of the Christ. Let your faith be the vessel into which these are received.

[*Journey to Understanding* begins:]
   We move upon the blessing as it goes forth from our Brother, the Master, given at the beginning of this journey that reaches out, individually and severally, to touch those who are calling out. (All of you who can hear and know: Here are the blessings of the Christ. Let your faith be the vessel into which these are received.)

   We move now with the joy of our brother, the Channel, passing through a sea of our brothers and sisters who journey within the realm called Earth. We look upon them with him, as though we are looking upon a beautiful field of flowers twinkling in their sparkling brilliance, casting off the raiment of their color and fragrance, giving life to all that comes to them, nourishment and the hope for the morrow in their seed.
   Next, we come to an area where we see the entangled thoughts and intentions of those who know not to ask and, as we journey through these, we see them pass us by without a reflection of the love we offer to them. Yet the Master points here and there and smiles, and then we see the Light of our Father's Love within them, and we smile and continue our journey.

September 9

> It is possible to be defined in form yet be the unconfined expression of utter Freedom and the purity of Consciousness.

[*Journey to Understanding* continues:]

The Master guides us, with the Channel, to a place we know well and, as we come to touch the Earth once again and feel the love of its Spirit, given by God, we see the "Healing Spring" known to the Essenes but secreted to that community, alone. All of us are now expressed in form that we can see the definition and it can be in harmony with the Earth.

The Master, in His form, moves with grace to the edge of the Healing Spring and bends to gather handfuls of the water. We watch Him very carefully as He lifts these up unto the heavens. We hear Him – not in word but in Spirit – speaking to bless the heavens. He then raises His hands on high, and the waters from His hands are like many beautiful white fluffy creatures fluttering upwards. And we are in wonder as we look into the blue clear sky and see these white intentions fluttering up from the Master.

We smile, then, with understanding: The sky begins to gather in white fluffy clouds, growing and becoming brilliant in the reflection of the sun's rays and then gathering in their strength. And we know that the Master has answered a call for some healing rain.

He turns to look upon us with a smile and tilts His head with a bit of laughter, and we, with the Channel, join Him and become one again, leaving behind the finite expressions and soaring throughout the manyfold universes of expression until we come into the purity of Consciousness, and to God.

> September 10
>
> What are the boundaries of understanding? Who sets these?

[*Journey to Understanding* continues:]
Zachary: Sarah and I suggest to our brother that we might "chat" a bit. He glances to those with whom he has been sharing the joys of our Father, and then turns to us with a smile.

Sarah and I take our brother to that which he has called the Rim. It is that level of Consciousness wherein he has experienced the pure omni-Presence intersected with that which contains the pure Potentiality. As we look off into the All of Consciousness, God's Word, I ask my brother, "How have you experienced since our last journey together?"

He is looking off into the beauty of the Word of God expressing Itself. "I have been well. I am understanding but, yet, looking at those things that have no understanding."

I pause to be certain he is complete. "You know that all things have understanding within them."

"Those things that do not share their understanding with me... Would it be wise that I would persevere to find this, though they do not seek to offer it?"

It is difficult for me to withhold my laughter, as I find great joy in the clarity with which he has responded.

He continues. "I do not seek to know and understand that which does not wish me to know it, any more than I would wish them to know my understanding of my being if they do not seek it."

"Then what shall be the place of peace between these things that do not wish to be understood, or do not wish to share?" I counter.

"The place of peace is ever before them. It is not I who should cause them to choose it. As they choose it, I will offer them my understanding again and, if they offer theirs in return, the oneness and the understanding will be complete."

> **September 11**
>
> Being open to understand empowers us to be understood.

[*Journey to Understanding* continues. Throughout the readings, beginning in the 1990's, Zachary became very prominent, adept at reminding us of our true nature. He most frequently accomplished this not by explanation but through experiencing. He called these experiences "outings." – To the Channel:]

Zachary: "Let's go on an outing," and, once again, Sarah and I embrace our brother as we move with swiftness.

To his delight, we have taken him to the grassy hill of the Homeland. Some quickly acknowledge our presence with a gesture of love. Others are interacting with one another and some newly arrived brethren, so we do not intrude.

"Here is the holding of the Promise, brother. Do you find Understanding in it?"

With a quick assessment, he answers softly. "I find complete Understanding in it. Your point is what, brother?"

"Why would you differentiate between the Homeland and anything or anywhere else?"

"It is in the willingness they have to give and to receive," responds my brother.

> September 12
>
> Everything has Consciousness... everything.

[*Journey to Understanding* continues – To the Channel:]
 Zachary: "Let's go for another outing."
 Very swiftly, we are moving along some cluttered, war-torn streets. The Channel glances about and realizes that we have taken him to the midst of the challenges in the place called Syria. "See what *Understanding* you find here, brother."
 With but a pause, he turns and allows his Consciousness to reach out to a building that is barely able to stand erect as the result of hostilities against it.
 A soft smile appears on his countenance and I know he has gained the Understanding.

> September 13
>
> True Understanding is a pathway to Oneness.

[*Journey to Understanding* continues – To the Channel:]
   Zachary: "Now, look over there, across the street, through the walls and into that building."
   He does so, and we all perceive a small group of fighters huddled against the wall sharing a bit of nourishment. They looked worn and wearied of battle.
   "What understanding do you find here?"
   The Channel shifts a bit, beyond the call of the familiarity of finiteness, and reaches out again. His countenance seems serious, even a bit solemn. Then, but a few moments later, that soft smile appears again and he turns to look at me. I nod and Sarah laughs softly.
   "Now come," I say to him. We move very swiftly and come to rest by the side of a small stream. There are children splashing in the water as some women, cleansing garments, glance ever this way and that to be sure that they are yet safe. But the children have no such thoughts. They are playing and laughing with the water as it trickles past them, over toes and through fingertips. "Look upon them all. What understanding do you find here?"
   I see a flash of his knowing of familiar energies that are ever-present in the Earth, those that come from brothers and sisters who have lost essentially all, not only belongings but their love... their mates, parents and, some, a child. I watch carefully as my brother reaches out with his Consciousness and Knows these things and Understands them. And when I see that little smile, both Sarah and I squeeze his hand just a bit to affirm to him his accomplishment.
   Without another word, Sarah and I lift him and, immediately, we are back, seated upon the grassy knoll of the Homeland.

> September 14
>
> Understanding is ever-present and hampered by nothing for one who opens their Consciousness.

[*Journey to Understanding* continues – To the Channel:]
Zachary: "So share with us, dear brother. What understandings did you gather from this journey we have just been upon?"

We see him look down into his own Spirit and we feel the rush of who he is, the Uniqueness, come forth. It touches us, and both Sarah and I look at one another as we feel the love he gives to us.

"In the first building," he begins, "there were no windows. Most of the structure was damaged by the actions that had taken place. But as I used my Consciousness the building gave to me Understanding. I heard the laughter of children playing in the hallways of the building in times past. I saw the love shared between a husband and wife as they contemplated their children's growth. I felt the sweet nourishment of a warm tea brewed with loving kindness and given in honor to a stranger at their table. I saw the beauty of the hands of those who placed the décor just so to give color and warmth to those who might enter their home. I felt the sweetness of a mother's love for her child, and the father's pride in how quickly they are grasping the lessons being taught.

"But what endures in the Understanding that the building gave unto me were the times of prayer and the love of our God that these people shared here. The Understanding the building also gave to me was that all is not lost, that a time shall come when the intent of those who pursue it shall prevail once again. The building will rise and become strong, for it is not the mortar and stone but the hearts and intentions of those who dwelt therein. The building gave me Understanding that this is timeless. No weapons, no shells, nothing can take this from the building. It is here, ever, if one seeks to understand and opens their Consciousness."

> September 15
>
> Even within that which seems in opposition to our beliefs, through Understanding we can know that Love abides.

[*Journey to Understanding* continues – To the Channel:]
   Sarah: "Sweet brother, what Understanding had you as we observed the warriors huddled inside the other building?"
   Again, our brother looks down. We feel his Spirit rising up like a fountain of truth coming forth. "I saw the fatigue. I saw the fear. I saw the memory of those for whom they would give all. I saw the love that they hold within as they quest for freedom and a good life for those whom they love in heart, mind, and body. I saw the dreams of one to become creative once again, to build structures that are reflections of those who will occupy them; another who remembered his times of making music, and singing and dancing with the children as he taught them their lessons; and another who remembered brewing a pot of that special tea and serving it beside a meal he had prepared for those who were hungered. And I see their Spirits, even now, not as warriors but as my brothers, and as they gave to me Understanding I gave to them of my Spirit and the wellspring of Father within."
   The Channel turns to look at us and continues softly. "I felt it stir within them! And I saw those who remain ever with them, guiding them in this journey of their life, and they assured me that these will endure and that they will resume their dreams, one to build fine structures, the other to teach and sing and dance with the children, and the third to nourish again the bodies with food that is prepared through his Spirit and the love with which his hands prepare it."

> September 16
>
> When we open ourselves to truly Understand another, the line of Light can be a path of service at the purest level of Spirit.

[*Journey to Understanding* continues – To the Channel:]
 Zachary: Finally, I asked my brother, "What Understanding was given to you as we paused by the stream?"
 Without looking down, without hesitation, he glances from Sarah to me and smiles. "My Understanding was given to me by the Christ in His love for the children. I saw this shining around them, preserving them, giving them joy and peace, even if but for this hour or two of play and rest.
 "I was given Understanding from a woman who had lost her husband. I understood her contemplation of the path that lies ahead for her and her child. And from within our mutual Spirits – yours Sarah, yours Zachary, and my own since we are one – I gifted her with the knowing of the coming of another to care for her and her child, that she shall have joy again and a life that has peace, and that she can honor the one who gave all in his quest for freedom for them and yet journey on, that the love within her will have a place to be received.
 "Another of the women, who has yet not borne a child, was concerned over where her mate might be and of his well-being. As I touched her Understanding, and she gave it freely, I spoke to those who are with her unseen and they told me he is well, that he will return to her and they, together, will share the joy of the child that will come. The Christ Spirit was blessing the child that will come to her and I joined in this with you both, as I know you are aware.
 "The others I reached out to and felt through Understanding were equally strong and beautiful in their Uniqueness. One bore more sorrow than others and I saw, from the Understanding she gave me at the Spirit level, that she wished to pursue this sorrow a bit longer, so I placed the gifts of our love about her for when she is a ready to receive it."

> September 17
>
> See behind what the five senses tell us, and Understand where it is not easily found. This is a path to Consciousness.

[*Journey to Understanding* concludes – To the Channel:]
   Zachary: "Have you more, brother?"
   "Yes. I was given Understanding from the waters in which the women cleansed their clothing and the children played. I knew not, in that time, from where the waters came, but I knew them to be the same in essence as those waters there," gesturing to the spring here in the Homeland, the pool and the water cascading down over the rocks below.
   "The Understanding was given to me that the waters of Life are eternal, the waters of Spirit are eternal and, where we can give hope and the offering of peace and love, these waters will come to the surface eventually and will break forth to flow, even from those who aren't willing to share that which is within them."
   We arise and move down to the pathway and to the edge of the Homeland, a particularly familiar place where he has many times come and gone.
   "I want to thank you, my brother and sister, for the gifts you have just given me in this journey. You are helping me to See, this I know. And you are helping me to find Understanding where there is none easily found. I shall cherish this and I shall ask that my total being gathers the essence of this, that I can give it, where it is received, beyond this journey."

   We return to God, and we feel the immediate glow of God's Love and Light. It passes all throughout all that we are. And the Channel, my sweet brother, is now simply Be-ing.
   The Angels are touching him, as are we, and God's Love is embracing him.

> September 18
>
> As you reach out for Understanding know that you are not alone, and let your Consciousness receive what is given.

[*Journey to Understanding* concludes:]
    When you look about the Earth, as we so did with our brother, remember that we are with you.

    And, as you reach out with your Consciousness asking for Understanding of what it is that is before you, know that we are with you *and let your Consciousness receive it*, not with equation or judgment of any sort but in the sweet essence of your Spirit's Light.

    This gives the firmament to the Great Passageway, that you can proceed and build upon Understanding wheresoever you are and whatsoever you are about.

> September 19
>
> What is real to you... a dream? Yesterday? Tomorrow? *Reality* is that which resonates within you as the Truth of God within.

[*Journey to the Rim:*]
   Our brother has journeyed to what he calls the Rim of God. He discerned this as he sought Father and Father gave to him that which would build understanding and reference.
   Is it real? What is real to you? A dream? Is yesterday real? Is tomorrow or the coming year filled with reality?
   Reality is that which you know within. When you encounter reality, it resonates within you because you know Truth as God within you.
   The vastness of the Rim staggers the consciousness of the Channel.
   He turns to observe spheres of light come rolling upwards, spinning and dancing in radiant light up to the top of the Rim. They pause for just a moment and the Channel can almost perceive them laughing softly as they swoop down with such beautiful fluidness and, as though the Golden Sphere anticipates their entry, they become one.
   The Channel has soared among the heavens with the Spirit of his mate and, together, they have danced and sung songs and journeyed far, far beyond what "ordinary" consciousness can conceive of.
   Now, they linger on the Rim, looking upon God, filling themselves with the joy of God so that when they return to their experiences in the consciousness of Earth, they shall be infilled with this.

> ## September 20
>
> In seeking Consciousness, bring all within your "book of life" – memories, emotions, thoughts – to a state of peace.

[*Journey to Knowing* begins:]

There is ever that quest as a part of one who is seeking... that is to say, seeking their total Oneness with God. Should they be expressed in the finite realms such as the Earth, the collage of emotional reflections that are a part of same tend to bring about a coloring, a toning, a shaping of this quest, this intent for Oneness.

The coloring and shaping, the tones, with which thoughts are presented to you are, for the most part, connected with other thoughts, other emotions. Thereby, a single emotional experience or thought tends to invoke a collage of other perceptions, thoughts, emotions, memories. From all of these, one might think, "I cannot, in this time and this journey, reach the Sacred Silence, for I am too beset with thought, too inundated with emotional energies." There is validity to this. But those of you who have placed the intent before you as the ideal or as that which is the light guiding you upon your pathway, know ever that you are in command of all of these. For they are not without. They are within.

Therefore, as you find such an event where there are many crosscurrents of energies – colors of consciousness, emotional decor upon the thoughts – all of these are yours.

You could look upon your life and bring all of these into a state of peace, just so as one would close a book. For if the life is yours, then all within it is equally so. The interactions with others are not, in the general sense, yours, in terms of being within. You are connected, yes, in many instances, but for your journey, what you seek to do is quiet that which is the calling. Seek, then, to bring these into a state of peacefulness, into a state of being bound together as they are intended to be and as they will literally be upon your conclusion of the current finite journey.

September 21

The higher Consciousness is not separate from the aspects of the finite (form, emotion, mind) but part of that embracing it.

[*Journey to Knowing* continues:]

What is a thought? What is an emotion? To speak of these disarms them, for the speaking of a certain thought points to the fact (as you call it) that thoughts are not tangible. And if they are not tangible, where, then, is their power? How can they ever burden you?

To define what is and what is not is not meant here as a frivolous endeavor but only to point out to you that you are the master of all of these. The power that they seem to have within and/or over you is that which you have allowed them to possess. It is your choice, and you have the right to make them as you would: into that which is a building block, or that which is limiting you. You can seek the median point, which is the point of universal harmony, the point that is often referred to by our brother, the Channel, as Loving Neutrality. This point sees from the vantage as one who is not in finiteness but as one who sees from the greater perspective of a "higher" Consciousness.

The higher Consciousness is not separate from the finite or from the mind or emotion as aspects of same. The higher Consciousness is that which is in the sea of consciousness as a part of that which is collectively embracing the Earth.

September 22

Loving Neutrality is a pathway to God's Peace and Love and, therefore, a path beyond any thing that seeks to hold you.

[*Journey to Knowing* continues:]

Being in higher Consciousness in a state of Loving Neutrality is different than simply submitting one's will to that which is prevalent.

Being in Loving Neutrality – the balance point between polarities – is a pathway to God's Peace. Thereafter, it is a pathway to God's Love.

Therefore, when you seek to journey, for example, in a meditation or in a literal intended journey, the more swiftly you claim Loving Neutrality the more expedient shall be your movement beyond that which might seem to call to you and possess a part of you.

Remember ever, you have the right and, within you, the power to choose.

> **September 23**
>
> The comfortable and expected, the pathway of familiarity, needs to be set aside if one seeks the gift of Knowing.

[*Journey to Knowing continues* – Lama Sing to the Channel, ellipses indicating pauses in communication:]

... It is a good example to have been, dear brother, in the sea of experience as was so in your just previous journey [*journey to Understanding*], for in this journey you see the contrast. Think of these, then, as a sort of polarity: the busyness of consciousness in the Earth and the quietude that can come to it, and yours being the right to choose. ...

... It may seem curious for one such as you having made so many journeys, taking with you with a pocketful of requests by others in the Earth mandating some certain accomplishment, some good work that you are asked to bring back to the Earth. So, as has just been given, here too is a little contrast, isn't it? For as you consider a journey such as this one as being only for the joy of the journey, only to be one with God (and, of course us), it is somewhat out of the character, out of the mold of habit, is it not? ...

... As you look upon this from this vantage point you see that, no matter where you are/what you are about, some things can become comfortable because what is expected, that profound familiarity, provides a pathway that is, therefore, sought as one begins a journey. ...

... The power that you are now seeking is the power of Knowing.

Knowing is different from that of our last experience where you sought Understand. Knowing is like looking over a broad valley beneath you, seeing water trickling down a mountainside and beautiful trees, a green lushness down below, and the color of flowers reflecting themselves up to you by way of the sun's rays dancing upon their faces: Such a scene is, indeed, a gift to the one perceives it, but one who perceives that gift and *acknowledges* it, gifts it to all. ...

> September 24
>
> You can choose to move beyond so completely that there are no definitions experienced, only the bliss of *Potential*.

[*Journey to Knowing* – Zachary to the Channel:]
 ... Look you now here, my brother, in the *Nothingness*, (as you call it) and note what we have just described to you. ... [pause]

 In our oneness with my brother, we feel the scene as he feels, we see as he sees, we Know as he Knows. What he is Knowing is the *sum* of all the valleys, all the mountaintops, all the beautiful trees, and flowers. The streams, the rivers, the lakes... He *knows* them.
 Any of you can do the same: You can pause to be in the Sacred Silence. You can choose to allow those things that call to you to be at rest, and move beyond. And you can choose to move beyond so completely that there are no stimuli present, no definitions experienced, only the experience of *Potential* that is such that it invokes a state of bliss.

> September 25
>
> Knowing is perceiving of all the aspects of God in whatever is present.

[*Journey to Knowing* continues:]
Zachary: Sarah stirs a bit, by her intent, invoking a contrast for my brother. The contrast is that which is of her own nature: the spring-like fount of expectation and hope that comes from such a maiden, such a Child of God who has chosen to give life wherever she can. In the life that she gives are all of the essences, qualities, of God.

We know, in our oneness with our brother, that Sarah's intent to him has broadened his Knowing and he Knows now from within the Earth itself, the warmth and love of Father's Spirit. He Sees from the heavenly position, from the universe, the brightness of the Earth. And he Sees and Knows all of these in the moment she intends it, like a vast journey summated upon the dot on a page.

... So dear brother, look you now from your Uniqueness to ours, and see us in the Knowing that you now have. ...
[pause]

I speak now, not from within my oneness with my brother but here in a place of Consciousness that will not disturb what is taking place.

My brother is not seeing Sarah and me. He is not knowing the qualities of Sarah or the qualities of me. He is Seeing aspects of Father. As he Knows these aspects, a wondrous occurrence takes place: He is immediately within the golden embrace of Father and, again, being touched, caressed, if you will, by the Brethren of Father.

So a very beautiful Knowing has come to be his. And for you, who may have journeyed along with what we have given, the gift is yours, as well.

> September 26
>
> In the sense of eternity, experiences are a part of the journey's intent, and that intent is what governs what transpires.

[*Journey to Knowing* continues:]
　　Zachary: Listen carefully to what I now give to you:
　　Try as you may, you cannot dominate an aspect of God.
　　Try as you might, you cannot mandate another in the Earth. Only they can.
　　You cannot impose your will upon another. It can seem that it is so and seen by others that you are doing so, but it is an illusion.
　　What others experience is never by your hand but by their own choice. Whether they are as one of those we took my brother to visit in Syria, or have now crossed over and were welcomed here, or one of those who yet remains in physical body in hardship, no one can do this to them. They must choose it.
　　The illusionary aspect of the Earth is such that it would seem that others are doing to others, and others are taking from others; indeed, even to take a life from another.
　　The measure of the rod of Earth – which is jot and tittle, each thing according to a framework, each put into a certain mold of judgment or evaluation – that measure lasts how long? An Earth year? A decade? No more than a lifetime. And what is this in comparison to how time is measured there?
　　In the moment of an occurrence of an act of violence the days that follow are heavy with grief and loss, and we do not negate this nor deny it nor judge it. We speak only of it in the sense of what is in eternity. Such experiences are a part of the journey's intent, and that intent is what governs what transpires.

> September 27
>
> It is upon the challenges and the opportunities in life that one comes to know the power in their choices as a Child of God.

[*Journey to Knowing* continues:]

Zachary: If a child is born into the lands of Syria some 20-odd Earth years past, it has known at the level of his Consciousness prior to entry that such events as are occurring in the present would occur. So is it the ruler's doing that so many of these have perished? By the rod of Earth, it is measured as such, indeed, and that is accurate by the measure of the rod of Earth. But in the eternal measurement, as it might be conversely presented, the event is but a moment. If one chooses to Know it and it is looked upon from Knowing as one would look upon a single flower on a grand mountainside filled with flowers too many to number, that event is as one such flower. And its coloration and brilliance, its tone and fragrance, it's very energy, is unique.

So is it with the sum and substance of that which we have just given. It is upon the challenges and the opportunities for one to see and feel and know: that they can, the better, make choices; that they can, the better, call forth the power of their righteousness as a Child of God. And as that one we exemplified 20 years ago chose to enter in Syria has, in the day just passed, released his physical body (died, as you would call it in the Earth), he knows he has done a good work. His presence contributed to the awakening of consciousness, that all of God's Children are granted freedom: the right to choose.

The journey into Earth is a choice. The journey from Earth is a choice. Whether it happens to you or is called to you, or you by your actions predicate it, from the level of Knowing, it is a choice.

> September 28
>
> You are a facet of God. You are the sum of what has been and the sum of the potential that will be or can be.

[*Journey to Knowing* continues:]
    Zachary: Sarah and I are now bringing our brother into the past. At the beginning of this journey he saw and felt and experienced his life in the wilderness as "the Forerunner." As he lies back on the yet warm earth beneath him – one great beast lying beside him, head nudging him to have its ear scratched, and another just an arm's length away – he gazes at the sky and the grandeur of our Creator's heaven and universe. He feels the energy of the earth beneath him. He feels the life in the magnificent creature nuzzled up next to him.
    And he feels the joy of BE-ing. He feels the wonder of Freedom. The heavens above are his rooftop, the earth beneath him is the floor upon which he walks, and all about seeks to embrace him because he embraces all. As we show this to him with clarity, Sarah again reaches out with intent to him, and now he feels and knows the creatures, the earth, and the heavens, all as one, and that includes himself as he views himself lying there.
    Reflecting upon the sacred Peace of this time, looking upon himself, John, there is the immediate rush of some subtleties that want his attention. (*How can it be? How was it that this was I? How is it possible that I am viewing myself here?* And on and on.) But Sarah's intent purges this from him, just as one would sweep away a covering of dust on a beautiful gem, just as one would pick a child up who has fallen, dusting them off, and with an embrace, looking into their eyes with a smile, stating, "You are well and blessed."
    Ever is it possible for each of you to see yourself and the many aspects of your being that comprise the sum of the facet of God that is You. You are not singular in your expression as you know it in the current time. You are the sum of what has been and the sum of the potential that will be or can be.

> September 29
>
> You are the power that governs your life. The moment you claim this, you can be well beyond the limits of definition.

[*Journey to Knowing* continues:]

Right now in this moment, this very singular moment of measure in the Earth, you have the power and the right to choose: *How shall the potential of me, for me, manifest? Which of the things that I carry with me shall I continue to carry? What little fragments yet remain to be blessed with the love of God, which is mine to give?*

Knowing...

This is Knowing: to realize that You are the power that governs your life and that, in the moment that you claim this, you can be well beyond the limits of definition as they are known and being lived.

Here is the temple that is Holy. Here is the temple in which good worship is ever welcome: You.

Others may speak of you in this way or that. Others may love you, some may not as much so. But ever is there within you that which is always worthy of your love, for it is God's choice of your being.

> September 30
>
> True faith knows no barriers, no boundaries. Faith can enable one to Know all of Self's expressions and experiences.

[*Journey to Knowing* continues:]

Now we call upon our brother – in that "time long ago" –to sit up. He starts, as though he has heard someone speaking to him. A little smile comes upon his face. He thrusts an elbow back and rises up until he is seated, and he brings his hands out before him, holding them palms up, and greets us.

We then share humor with our brother as he realizes what has transpired: that, *in the expression past,* John knows that we are present. He does not, in the consciousness of his knowing, yet perceive who it is that has called him, but his faith is such that he heard the call and he arose to honor it. His head is now bowed in prayer.

Others of the Ancient Ones come to be with him in this prayer, as do we. And so, we shall pause to be one with him, and celebrate the glory of his prayer.

> **October 1**
>
> There are no limits to Consciousness... *no* limits.

[*Journey to Knowing* concludes:]
Zachary: We move our brother from this experience, this expression, and come to rest upon the greenery of the Homeland – I to my brother's right and Sarah to his left – and we study him, as he is yet reflecting upon the prayer of John.

"Greetings, brother," I say to him softly, not by word but in his Spirit.

He turns to look at me and we smile, and then he *Knows* Sarah's presence and turns to look upon her with a smile.

All this is transpiring, yet we are not in the forms that are seated upon the greenery of the Homeland. We tell you this because there are no limits to Consciousness. My brother knows he has a physical expression in the Earth. He knows he has a physical expression in the Holy Land seated on a gentle knoll in the wilderness, looking across the broad valley down to a dim glow that is called Jerusalem, hearing the animal calls and smelling the fragrance of the wilderness and the wildflowers now in bloom. And he looks further, and further, and can see himself embracing the Shining One and His brethren, dancing a dance of celebratory joy.

Now I touch his form that is here in the greenery of the Homeland, and he looks upon me again and smiles. We rise and walk down to the reflecting pool, where we reach into the water. We feel the goodness of it, as though it is caressing and purifying our very being. It invokes a pure Peace that moves all throughout.

> October 2
>
> You are Complete. You are the power. Call this forth and place it before you on the path. Choose it and move upon it.

    Let us all remember to often be in the joyful wonder of our own Uniqueness.

    Let us often look upon those who are with us in this journey, and see God in the reflection of the beauty that shines from within them.

    Let us command ourselves to be Complete, that naught without or within can diminish the beauty of God's love and intent that is us.

    And ever remember: You are the power. Call this forth and place it before you. And follow the path that is now open, the path of Light that is called *the Way;* you will be empowered by choosing it and by your movement upon it.

> ## October 3
>
> The experiences and influences of a life stimulate the parameters, invoking the contemplation to take a step or two beyond.

There is the pattern and the expectation that goes before one who places an intent before them in any journey. The pattern could be defined as the expected potential... in other words, the limits of one's ability to accept, to believe, to perceive. It is difficult for us here to give this to you in a manner that is clearly definitive for you, but perhaps this will suffice:

If you consider your lifetime to be a unit of measure and you see that measure as having boundaries, two of these would be the entry into that lifetime and the departure. Other parameters could be the things you gather during the journey in the incarnation of Earth comprising the sum of who you are/what you are.

The parameters of this unit of measure expand considerably dependent upon one's awakening to knowing themselves to be greater than a physical being or a living expression in the realm called Earth. Then, when one seeks beyond that which is defined in the sum of that lifetime, these form variable parameters that comprise the willingness of self as a Spirit, as a consciousness, to accept and believe. In the believing comes the expression of one's knowing, and in the knowing comes the profound expression of wisdom. All of these are within that unit-of-dwelling in a lifetime in the Earth.

The pattern, then, becomes those things an entity has explored, considered, contemplated, and so forth. Varying activities within the unit of that lifetime contribute to this: other individuals, brothers and sisters, writings, forms of Color, even the telly, movies, and such. All these provide a stimulation to the parameters, the boundaries, of your lifetime, for they invoke the contemplation that might take you just a step or two beyond the norm. We do not equate any of these. They simply are.

> October 4
>
> Does what is known form the limit of one's consciousness... a demarcation of what is known versus what is not known?

[*Journey Beyond Limits* begins:]

Zachary: We shall now bring our brother into varying experiences that will surpass the pattern, the definitions, of his current lifetime, much in the manner as we have of recent times in the last three journeys. The intent here is to add to the comprehension that will be gathered by so doing.

"Greetings and good cheer to you, brother. As you see, we have journeyed into the beauty of Consciousness. The swirling bands of Color that God's Messengers have placed here in this beautiful dance of the Colors are for you, that you might experience the Colors in a different way."

My brother looks upon me with curiosity but lightness, and as he does, Sarah herself swirls a band of color around him that passes all throughout him. "This is the nature of your *be*-ing in the present," I tell him.

All three of us pause, that he can grasp what I am giving to him. "You have had many journeys beyond the definitions of finiteness – in mind, in imagination, in contemplation, in meditation, and in your journeys. These have comprised the sum of your Spirit, and, with several of your past journeys, you made a connection of oneness, adding to the sum, the pattern, the boundaries."

"How is it that these form any sort of boundary for me?" he inquires.

"Could it be," I respond, "that what is known is the limit of one's consciousness, that what you have experienced forms a sort of demarcation of what is known versus that which is not known, and therefore, these are as a pattern?"

"I comprehend what you are saying, my brother, but were I to choose it, I would have no boundaries. Isn't that true?"

October 5

There is a difference between perceiving and reaching out in Consciousness to Know.

[*Journey Beyond Limits* continues:]
Zachary: "Let us explore your statement that, if you choose to have no boundaries you would have no boundaries."

In oneness, Sarah, our brother, and I move, without definition of movement for we do not need that. We "know" our brother and he knows us. We are inseparable.

"We should like you to recognize our current state."

He responds. "I do. I recognize it. I remember it."

"Very good. Do you believe that we have moved?"

Our brother laughs. "I have no reference of movement. If you say we have moved, then I believe you because you are my brother and your honor and mine are as one."

"Then we have moved. Let us now take our uniquenesses and make them separate."

The Channel expresses a wonder, for as he perceives all about us, everything is crystalline. Everything perceived is comprised of some form of crystalline structure. "Are we within something like a crystal? Where are we? What is this? It feels as though I am within something."

"Allow yourself to reach out with your Consciousness; not just perceive, but reach out with your Consciousness."

October 6

When seeking to Know the unknown, remember that Consciousness moves in all directions simultaneously.

[*Journey Beyond Limits* continues:]
Zachary: We move in Consciousness with the Channel, which is of no effort, for we *are* Consciousness.

"Would you say, dear brother," referring to what he is perceiving all about as being crystalline, "that this is outside of your knowing? Outside of your parameters, outside the pattern that is the sum of you?"

The Channel turns about to observe but in a manner that is familiar to him... in a more limited sense.

I gently remind him. "Use Consciousness."

He brings himself into oneness and Sarah and I, and others who have come to be a part of this, feel his Consciousness moving in all directions simultaneously. "This is beyond the pattern of my knowing, brother," he responds

"Very good. Let us move into oneness and journey again." We do so instantly, and in our movement, we reflect with our brother. "Could it be that we were within a single grain of sand, or within a single atom of some structure? Could it be that we were in a grand realm, too majestic to measure its size? What would be the defining point that would reveal this? Would it be size? Would it be the feel of it? What would it be?

"Now, dear brother, let us be in our uniqueness once again, and open our perception."

The Channel is startled, then a bit amused. Everything about him is varying shades of green. He reaches out with Consciousness to feel the definitions expressed in the green. Again, I ask him, "Is this within the pattern of your knowing?"

He smiles. "It is reminiscent of journeying into Father's Colors. But I cannot say this is particularly familiar. I feel like I'm inside a leaf or a blade of grass. I have a feeling of form, but all that my Consciousness reveals to me is *green*."

> October 7
>
> If we open ourselves to what is before us, Consciousness allows us to Know without limitation.

[*Journey Beyond Limits* continues:]
Zachary: My brother smiles, turns again to the green, and now expresses to it, "I love you. Here am I. I give to you that which is mine to give in the love that I have for you."

To the Channel's surprise it is as though he hears a response. "How do you know me?"

His focus is upon me, then Sarah. Then, "I know you because I am…" casting his Consciousness about, "within you."

"Then we are one."

"Yes, I would suppose so," stifling a bit of chuckle.

"Then how is it that you do not understand? And do not Know me?"

We wait, knowing that this is valuable to our brother. We see him move into his Spirit, into his own uniqueness, and as he does, he touches that place within that is Father and immediately *he is Conscious*… not of that which is green but the sum of all that is.

He sees the green as a potential. He reaches out from this (you might call it) God-level of Consciousness and speaks to the green. "Blessings upon you. Thank you for allowing me to be with you. I know you and I love you as a potential of the Color within Father's Word."

We are immediately embraced by God's loving warmth and compassion. We find others gathering here to welcome and touch us, and we pause to bathe in that which is our own Uniqueness, but this time the Uniqueness is one with God, its Source.

> **October 8**
>
> The wonder of Oneness with God is like invoking a sense of belonging, a sense of Completeness.

[*Journey Beyond Limits* continues:]
   Zachary: The wonder of Oneness with God is like invoking a sense of belonging, a sense of completeness. My brother is in the Consciousness of his Oneness with God, along the pathway of his own choice.
   We feel the Knowing of God and the wondrous depth of Love and Compassion. We *Know* it touching all that is, and we feel Consciousness responding to God's Love, and in the response, its uniqueness forms into wondrous colors, collages of sounds, vibratory energies, and so much more.
   We can feel the joy of one another experiencing this, and as we in our Uniqueness have chosen to experience just one aspect of creation responding to God, we slip back into the oneness with God and experience the Knowing of all of creation responding to God's Love. It is a grand harmony of expression. We cannot perceive it's ending. We are Conscious that it is ever moving, ever expanding upon its own knowing of Itself. We stay in this joy, this wonder, for a goodly measure of your time.
   Then Sarah, I, and several others surround our brother, sustaining God's Love as best we can, and move him from this expression of God to another, and as we come to rest in this other expression of God, we allow the individual Uniqueness of each of us to release our brother, that his Uniqueness can come into the fullness of its expression.
   Very quickly he casts his Consciousness about and perceives that we are, again, on the beautiful slope of the Homeland. Looking down, he sees a form expressed that is his, and then perceives Sarah, and then the Homeland in that expression as is familiar to him.

> October 9
>
> When there is an experience you don't understand, raise your consciousness, or be one with God and perceive the totality.

[*Journey Beyond Limits* continues:]

Zachary: Our brother sighs very deeply.

"Sweet brother and sister, I love you so. And I am so grateful to you. I now know the Homeland for what it is in the truth of Consciousness. Thank you for these journeys. Thank you, so very much."

We watch him bow his head and we know that he is making these experiences his own, so we pause and await his completion. Quite soon, his head comes up, and he looks at each of us and reaches to embrace each of us with a laugh.

"Would you care to share with us what you have discovered?" I ask him.

"You have shown me that I define and understand based upon the extent to which I *reach out* to know a thing, to understand it. And that I have levels of consciousness, and I use one level of consciousness based upon my familiarity with the consciousness as it is expressed in the Earth that I have perceived throughout this lifetime.

"But when I move beyond that level of consciousness, my perception expands and I come into Knowing of much more. When I was in the crystalline structures I perceived that as all there was. When I was in the green I perceived that as all there was. But when I chose to raise my consciousness I could see the green in an individual expression and knew it to be.

"Now, whenever I have an experience I do not understand, I can simply raise my consciousness and perceive from there. *But* I could also choose to be one with Father and perceive it all in its totality."

> October 10
>
> One can comprehend from finiteness, from the infinite, or from the finite and infinite simultaneously.

[*Journey Beyond Limits* continues:]

Zachary: "Well done, brother. So would you share what you experienced in the crystalline structure and in the green?"

"I experienced what could be. I didn't experience a grain of sand or a blade of grass. I experienced the potentials."

"You are correct, of course. But for your reference, what you experienced in the crystalline structure was actually a tiny particle within the building you came to love in Syria." This has a profound effect upon my brother.

"Why is this touching me so, Zachary. Why do I have such a feeling of oneness with a building?"

I place my hand on his shoulder. "Because," I say to him gently, "you knew the presence of Father in the building."

Both Sarah and I realize he is not fully comprehending this... understandable, for the comprehension of this is quite mighty. To grasp this from the infinite is easier, but he is perceiving this from all these levels – infinite and finite – simultaneously. This is a good thing, for as he does this, it will expand him.

The obvious here is that God is in all things, as the Creator of all. But when you perceive a building in such a sad shape as the one my brother loves, you do not immediately perceive this as an expression of God. Although he knows at a level of his consciousness that he communicated via the Spirit of God in the Earth, this is giving him an opportunity to step beyond the pattern, the parameters of his knowing as it was before this journey.

> October 11
>
> Shift your Consciousness such that you would know that you are in command of the wonders of your potential.

[*Journey Beyond Limits* concludes:]

Zachary: Sarah and I each take our brother by an arm (for we are still in expression) and we move with gentle ease, allowing him to experience the movement as we soar towards the Earth. Very swiftly we come upon a very beautiful high spring meadow.

As we come to rest in the midst of the greenery and the flowers and the creatures, we release our brother.

Sarah gently inquires, "How do you know yourself to be?"

"I know myself to be very well, thank you." Looking about, he draws in the beauty of creation, the springtime birth of life, appreciating and expressing gratitude for the beauty he sees all about him.

Sarah and I feel all of creation here responding to his gratitude, and he begins to laugh as he feels it, too... the spirit of this beautiful place touching and caressing him with its colors, its fragrances, and all its essences.

"You see? Shift your consciousness and this is what you will experience, and all the expressions about you will experience you. Just as you Understood the building, you are Knowing this, all about us, in its completeness... that which it has been and shall be."

We lie back against the greenery and look up into the beautiful sky and its great billowing clouds in the distance.

"Why is it that we are not in command of the wonders of our potential in our physical expression?" he asks.

It is Sarah who responds. "Perhaps you are and you just haven't raised your consciousness that notch or two that your would know that you are."

My brother is drifting off into Creation itself, feeling the wonder of this locale. So I begin to prepare a pathway of return for him to his physical form in the Earth.

> October 12
>
> We are the sunshine. We are the rain. We are the wind. We are all of Consciousness. In Oneness, we can Know that.

[Note: After this reading, Al shared the following with Susan:]
   Al: So Very Cool...
   We were the Sunshine, shining down on the plants and on the earth and on the creatures, and I could feel them as we shined upon them.
   We were the rain falling and giving nourishment, life, to everything.
   We were the wind. We blew the pollen from flower to flower. And we lifted the great birds under their wings up to be one with us. And we rustled the leaves in the trees and rippled the water.
   It's a level of Knowing... that I could feel the roots of the plants thankful to the earth, and the earth giving to the plants, knowing that they would return to the earth.
   Oh it's so beautiful, so perfect.
[pause]

   I never thought of structure in the way that Sarah and Zachary showed it to me. Amazing! I saw realms, other levels of consciousness, where other souls dwell. I can't imagine how many of them.
   They're not like the Sea of Faces. They are other expressions revolving around Earth, similar only lighter, different, more alive. I wanted to visit some of them, but I let it go.
[pause]

   The room is filled with shimmery sparkles.
   Maybe I'm feeling the room for the first time.
   Thank you. ...

> ## October 13
>
> You can move beyond the familiar... and beyond, and beyond, and beyond... all the way into the arms of your Father.

You can move beyond the familiar...

beyond the knowing you get through the intuitive...

beyond the edge of your dreams' journeys...

and beyond...

and beyond...

all the way into the arms of your Father.

October 14

The clarity of one's perception is heightened by the realization that one can be Complete and yet be in a singular expression.

There are, ever present in and about the realm called Earth, those questions and those inquiring minds who would seek to understand.

In the sense of that nomenclature it is good to realize that the reality of one's perspective is based upon the collage of those experiences that have gone before and the willingness of those who inquire, in the Spiritual sense, to open themselves to receive a greater potential and to have the insight beyond that current expression and into the infinite and to the Oneness with God.

The clarity of one's perception is heightened by the realization that one can be Complete – the sum and total being, no separateness – and yet be in a singular expression. Like the Master. See?

October 15

You've chosen a journey of detail, but you are the master of the *sum* of You. Move about that with deliberateness.

The same as though you were to cook a pot of stew, you deliberately go about the varying steps that are needed to prepare the stew and all of the actions that are a part of that, and when you have completed those actions, you have a pot of stew: Deliberateness. See? Be deliberate in what you do.

If you believe that you are a Child of God, then live with deliberateness that you are a Child of God. Be willing to raise the consciousness, not only of yourself, but to touch the Consciousness of all that is about you.

What is your physical expression comprised of? Aspects, elements, that are within the Earth as a realm of expression? That which is not of that Earthly expression in the specific sense is your Spirit, your Uniqueness, that which is eternal. This is the part of you that is having the journey. You have chosen the journey to be in the detail, in the specificity that would be likened unto the two examples we showed to our brother: the inside of a crystalline structure, the inside of the potential of green, as a color as an expression.

But you are the master of the *sum* of You. Move about that deliberately.

October 16

> The simple choice is to continue to pursue experiencing in the finite as opposed to experiencing moreso in Spirit.

You have now crossed the threshold into what we have referred to as the Grand Cycle. [given February 2, 2013]

This cycle is anticipated to be present upon those who are willing for at least until (your measure) 2018, at which point the diminishing intensity will begin to be noted.

The exception here would be if those who are His and those who awaken are sufficient to sustain it. Remember, this is always a potential.

There may be the separation of those who choose Consciousness versus those who choose to continue upon the Wheel of Finiteness, but none is ever lost, no one. See? Each is an *eternal* Child of God.

The simple choice is to continue to pursue experiencing in the finite as opposed to experiencing moreso in Spirit.

> October 17
>
> Individuals are guaranteed the right of Freedom even within mass mind, if they choose it.

Freedom of will – in other words, the right of choice – is given by God.

Journeying into definition is the acceptance on the part of those who choose to journey to accept the general agreement that is the expression of free will on the part of the group. This is how mass-mind thought begins.

So we have those who have gathered and who comprise the consciousness of Earth, the consciousness of Children of God dwelling in finite form on the sphere of Earth and those who dwell in non-finite form about the Earth itself... varying levels of participation in finiteness dependent upon one's choices, one's habits, one's own commitments to a certain decision. All of this comprises the group thought.

The assurance of the Word of God in the midst of mass-mind thought could be called Universal Law. In other words, that, as the individual chooses *from within the mass choice*, they are guaranteed the right of Freedom, *if* they choose it. The Law is the guarantee of right of choice. See?

There are many different pathways for those who find themselves within the mass-mind thought and this can be claimed from within that mass-mind thought.

> October 18
>
> Any journey one is about is to gain and to glorify the joy that is the wonder of their Uniqueness.

When one is upon a journey – whether that be a journey in some form as one might surmise from the consciousness of dwelling in the Earth in finiteness, or a journey that is begun from the state of what you call Spirit, or from the Freedom of oneness with God – these *journeys* (as we might title them summarily) are for the intent of one to gain and to glorify the joy that is their Uniqueness.

As one so does, this might become something of a lamp, so to say, that can be beheld by those willing to receive same. Even if there is not another to receive this Light, yet does it shine as the one claims it.

Unto all those who shine their Light forth in this manner, through the knowing and acceptance of this comes the joy of celebration in the Oneness of those who are choosing and who are willing.

> October 19
>
> What you are seeking is the freer levels of Consciousness: the attainment of cooperation between Spirit and form.

    The direction of one's Truth... Mind the words here now, please... The direction of one's Truth is in accordance with their intent, their will, their choosing. As one directs their intent based upon their Truth, then the manifestation of this follows in the expression in which it is given, according to the Law. The Law prevails and supports you in your right to choose and to hold an intent, and to fulfill this with choices.
    What this means is that the levels of consciousness that are involved with your intent will, in the spirit of Truth, respond to you. But the manifestation of that response will be experienced in accordance with that level of expression in which that result... (choosing the words very carefully here) in which that result harmonizes with its environ. In other words, where there is the harmony of your intent in the environ in which you dwell, it will manifest as you intend it, swiftly.
    When the intent is brought to a realm or an expression that has less in harmony with it, understandably there is some interaction involved before the expression manifests.
    When you are dwelling in a finite physical form, a "body," and you are claiming your Consciousness, some recognize these as individualized points of perception or function. In other teachings these are not so – there is one God, one consciousness, one truth, and so on. But within all of this, there is the right of those who are the Children of God to choose, and one of the Children's choices must honor the other choices in order for there to be harmony. Where these do not harmonize, the energies, the levels of consciousness begin (for understanding here) to lower themselves into greater density.

> October 20
>
> It is possible for you to *Be* Free while in finiteness...
> no prerequisites, no mandates, no boundaries.

God is the Law.

Only in those realms that believe they are separate from God does the Law manifest in, as called, Universal. This is not to imply that the Law is not present, for as we just gave above, God *is* the Law.

Reminding... Universal Law is God. Therefore, as one speaks the Word within the Law, they are in honor with Universal Law, for these are one. So there can be no violation of the Law against itself. This would be not possible. Self cannot be against Self at the highest level of expression, which is as a Child of God. There would no longer be that Consciousness of that expression.

You have the possibility to <u>be</u> Free. You are free now. The question is, then, is it possible for one to reclaim the true Freedom while dwelling in a finite or, as perceived, "lesser realm"? The answer is yes.

You were not *Spoken* by God – acknowledged, Known – without complete Freedom. That God would say, *"I love you, you are my sweet Child to whom I give all that I have to give,"* it would be illogical that Freedom would not be number one among those gifts. Therefore, Freedom *is*.

The topic of BE-ing Free from finiteness brings into the arena of contemplation all of the precepts, the conditional thinking, the habit, and so forth, that conditionalizes one's ability to accept Freedom. But *Freedom is yours*. It has no prerequisites, no mandates, no boundaries. Freedom is, for Freedom is, in truth, God.

As our brother, the Channel, is questing for Oneness with God, he is also questing for Freedom, as are each of you who seek Oneness with God.

October 21

> What are you willing to release in order to have Freedom? For you cannot claim limitation and Freedom at the same time.

You cannot bind God's Freedom, which is given to you. You can *believe* it is bound, and because it is believed, there are the <u>experiences</u> (see, underscore that) of *<u>feeling</u> bound*.

One can free their consciousness, their Spirit, their mind, and so forth and, yet they will return to those things that are a part of finiteness. Why is this? Because they have been chosen, because they are largely the intent of the journey for most.

For some, the intent of the journey is as you: to become Free and to express that Freedom from within definition, a finiteness that seeks, in some quarters, to deny it.

What are you willing to release in order to have Freedom, for you cannot claim limitation and Freedom at the same time, can you?

> October 22
>
> Those who know they can be Free have taken the first step into that Freedom. The Knowing of it is the beginning.

Those who believed in *death* (as is called in Earth) had what they believed by seeing the Master upon the cross and "dying." They had no room in their consciousness for the awareness of what occurred.

The Master demonstrated that you are eternal Children of God and that, so doing, the limitations of finiteness are not bindings upon you. Those who *believe* have Truth

Those who believe through the filters of finiteness or limitation or the familiar or habit are honored under the invocation of Universal Law: They have the right to be as they wish.

Those who know they can be Free have taken the first step into that Freedom. The Knowing of it is the beginning.

October 23

Truth is that which is within. As you set this Truth Free, you begin to become It.

Universal Law is God. God is Love.

You cannot violate God's Love by living that which He gives to you. Those who wish to claim a journey in the manner in which they are pursuing it have that right. But those who claim Freedom and follow in the footsteps of the Master have *their* right.

Insofar as one honors the Law and the right of their brethren, then the Law assures them that they are honored equally.

Truth is that which is within, and as you set this Truth Free, you begin to become It. And as you begin to become it, you are claiming your own Freedom. You may be seen or not seen as having attained it. That is the choice of the perceivers.

> October 24
>
> There is no limit to Consciousness, no limit to Freedom. It occurs by seeing what is and *Knowing* there is more beyond.

    Would it be believed that there is a little Freedom over here and another little Freedom over there, and on and on... that one can be Free in this way but not that?

    One who has claimed their Truth, their Freedom (these are actually all one, you see) has become what is called in some teachings a master, and has become Free. With this, comes knowledge, wisdom, and the perception is like wiping a clouded windowpane: That one can perceive, not the pane, but what is beyond it. As one Knows by claiming these things we are discussing here, the Knowing makes the way open and possible, passable. And there would be the willfulness of intent to serve and to serve in accordance with the choices of the masses who dwell in the consciousness in which that master is expressed.

    There are those who are demonstrating varying levels of this "Freedom" and you hear about them here and there. It's a question, then, of how do we measure the expression of this Freedom.

    There is no limit to Consciousness; there is no limit to Freedom. This is what you are seeking: the Truth that you are first, and ever, a child of God. You are upon a journey of your choice as a part of those who chose collectively in a similar fashion.

    You choose *everything* in your life. But the sea of consciousness that is in place in Earth tells you that's not true, so you are conforming to that which is.

    The beginnings of Freedom occur by seeing what is, and *Knowing* there is something beyond. See?

> October 25
>
> This should be a journey that is filled with the joy and the hope of one who *Knows* they are a Child of God.

The desecration of one's belief... How is this fashioned?

What is it that is within the consciousness of brothers and sisters who hold such intensity of exclusion for another's belief that they would "kill" one another over it? If you are feeling this as we are attempting to convey it, you begin to understand why the Promise was given.

What one meets out with their intent is what they experience; what one is willing to give is what they receive. We believe that has been given in most all teachings, yet why is the eye not opened to this truth? Where is the Truth that lives in those who hold such potential of violence against those who do not concur with their choice? These are outer. They are not inner.

Freedom is the precious gift from God. This is a Consciousness that is within you, each of you. Jesus is your Brother, and God and His Consciousness are one with You.

Look not to the right or left, but look to the center of your Being. Look to that which is calling You from within. This should be a journey that is filled with the joy and the hope of one who *Knows* they are a Child of God, not one who must be wrenched from the grasp of the consistency of finiteness but who gently and lovingly blesses all and Knows: I and God are one.

October 26

> Have a care not to judge the truth of your pathway and your good works based upon the outer.

Do not fall prey to making judgments upon yourself of what has or has not been done or accomplished, for these can easily, almost silently, be woven into a fabric of the limitation from which you are intending to release yourself. They can cloud the pane of Truth that is You.

Be gentle and loving with yourself. As you do this, you are honoring your Father, who is gentle and loving with you. Have a care not to judge the truth of your pathway and your good works based upon the outer.

The power that is within you can pass easily through the illusions.

> ## October 27
>
> If sufficient make the way open, the Promise will be fulfilled and the Master will be evidenced in the manner prophesied.

[More on the Homeland:]

The Homeland represents the choices of those who are Free and experience one another in the joy of their Freedom. As a part of this joy, God's Word expresses itself within the joy of those who gather about that center of that Conscious choice.

The interaction in the Homeland is the sum of life. It is the sum of the Children who participate in honoring and celebrating God and one another.

The Homeland is in place as an offering to those who choose from within mass-mind thought, those who are upon the Wheel of Incarnation or the Wheel of Finiteness

Great cycles, confluences of energy, are in place now that provide a pathway for the Homeland to express itself within the group-thought. The "requirement" is that there are sufficient of those within the group-thought who would choose it, so that there would be no violation of the right of the Law and the right of Freewill choice.

If sufficient make the way open and passable, the Promise will be fulfilled and the Master will be evidenced in and about the Earth in the manner as has been prophesied. This will occur as prophesied. Whether or not those who choose are sufficient to manifest within the group-thought, this will decide the outcome.

The potential is now awakened within the finiteness of the Earth. It is touching the Spirit of those who are seeking it. As more and more of those who are His – those who choose – call this forth, the greater shall be the manifestation. In other words, the path shall be made open and passable for the greater glory of the Homeland to be brought forth from within the Spirits of those who are presently within the mass-mind thought.

October 28

To realize that you are greater than a finite expression on the surface of the planet Earth is to begin to set yourself Free.

[More on the Homeland:]

The Homeland Consciousness is reflected within each of God's Children. It is the expression of the joy of knowing that you are a Child of God.

There are many different pathways for one to *realize* this, to bring it into reality. Dependent upon the environ in which one finds themselves expressed, these pathways will differ significantly and will be met with encouragement or resistance dependent upon those environs. Those who are choosing Freedom feel the vibration, the energy, the presence of the Great Cycle, the Promise. The presence of that which they believe in is the echo of their Oneness with God.

Each is a Child of God. The illusion presents itself in layers upon each other to form a density of illusion, but the potential for the Homeland Consciousness is ever within. As one struggles for Freedom, as one struggles to know themselves – to break free from habit, to realize that they are greater than a finite expression upon the surface of the beauty of the planet Earth – they are realizing that which is being offered in the Homeland.

Some will call the Homeland by differing names and will experience it in differing ways, but all who choose the pathway to Oneness with God will come unto the Oneness by way of the Homeland Consciousness, for the Homeland is that place of celebration and joy of those who *Know* themselves to be Children of God.

The choice to be Free is the pre-requisite (if one must have one for definition) to enter into the Homeland. You can't take a bunch of Earthly baggage with you. You simply would not be able to perceive the Homeland, for the baggage is like sheaths, layers of illusion that are like the clouding of the sky blocking the sun's rays.

> October 29
>
> How many ways will be attempted to give definition to that which is unlimited? The blessing is in the Oneness.

[More on the Homeland:]

It seems, from the consciousness of the Earth, that you would name a thing and that the name would represent the qualities, the essence of it. The title, *the Homeland* (given by Susan) was intended to represent the qualities of that *Consciousness*, for to say that there is *a Blank* awaiting you doesn't give you much to hang onto, but if you say there is a beautiful Heaven awaiting you, immediately the references for ages to the term Heaven or Nirvana or what have you stimulates something within the consciousness of those who hear those terms used.

So now, with the title *The Homeland*, there is the gift to the consciousness that lives within the mass-mind thought and it cannot be quelled. It will remain in accordance with your intent. *These things and greater shall ye do.* Believe unto yourselves. Know that you *are* that which You Are. Know that you have chosen to journey from God's embrace to God's embrace within the Earth as an expression of consciousness. And know that you are, ever, within His embrace.

To experience dimension, depth and breadth, one uses various criterion. What is the criterion to measure love? Truth? Compassion? Peace? How many ways will be attempted to give definition to that which is unlimited?

You can take a cup of water from a great sea and carry it far inland until a stranger might ask, "Good woman, what is it that you are carrying in that container?" Would you answer, "I am carrying the sea, good sir"? If you did, you would be speaking the truth. See? You are that cup, and the sea of God is within it. The water in the cup is still the sea, and the sea is one with the cup of water. Ultimately, these unite in their commonality, for the blessing is in the oneness. You are the cup.

> October 30
>
> You might need to meditate upon your separateness in order to find your Oneness

[More on the Homeland:]
When you step aside from physical sensory perception into the doorway of Consciousness, you are like the Promise. The consciousness of self is a part of the Consciousness of the All. The moment that you pause and set aside all else to contemplate that you are that part of the All, you are beginning to truly know God.

When the expression of finiteness has served its usefulness for the current journey, it will be gently, lovingly laid aside. As the Tree of Life in its season sheds its leaves, the water will leave the cup and return to the sea from whence it has come. If the water in that cup chooses to pause here and there along the way before its return, all this and greater are its right to choose. Where many, many cups of the *great sea*, which is God's Word, have come together to celebrate, you could think of this as the Homeland. And because they are not bound by the confines of a cup, the expressions are ever free and filled with the beauty and wonder of God's Word.

As each chooses, God chooses with them and celebrates with them, through them and, collectively, all celebrate the joy. It is defined in the holy writings in various ways. It is defined as the Great Peace, the 1000 years of Peace. We might we find that title to mean an unending peace.

You might need to meditate upon your separateness in order to find your Oneness. Once you identify your separateness, you have claimed your Uniqueness and you will soon find, in the Uniqueness, that which unites you all. See the power in the willingness to give up that which is ever urging in order to listen to that small voice within that speaks only Truth, with gentleness and the nourishment of life-giving waters. The truth and love that is in your hearts seeking is that which you receive in return.

> October 31
>
> How does one assess one's life... from within or without?

[*Journey of Non-Separateness* begins:]
    We have our brother in an old stone building. One of the sisters has been taken ill, and as we observe, we know it is not our brother in the current that we look upon but as expressed in past. To either side of the sister who lies cared for lovingly do we see Francis and Clare, each of them bent in prayer, each with a hand upon Maria Rosa. We look into the Spirits that are present to see the understanding that is offered to us, the intent to bring the Christ Grace to the sister.
    Many hours have transpired, and while food and liquid have been brought for both of them, it sits beside them untouched. In their silent companionship it is understood that they would take naught of the Earth until their prayer is answered.
[pause]

    We take our brother, now, up the mountainside to the cave where we find Francis, again. He is seeking confirmation for his Spirit that his path and all that he has sought to give in God's Name has been aright and that, as his body is weakened, might it be that God would lift him up.
    We ask our brother to look upon this representation of his former journey. What do you see here, brother? Is it that one believes that their work is complete, and so, they ask to be lifted up from the journey that they themselves have chosen? Or is it the seeking of one whose faith has no limit, that he would be guided to carry on further if it so be God's intent for him.
    Perhaps the greater question here is the pathway itself. Where there has been found a good work and good workers to bear the load with him, is this to be adjudged from within or without?

> ## November 1
>
> Who is it who determines an action "good" or "bad," a lifetime "worthy" or not? On what or whose basis is the judgment?

[*Journey of Non-Separateness* continues:]
The many churches that were restored by Francis, the many good works for the poor and diseased... Are these the measure of a work that is deemed good, or is the Spirit within those who have sought to serve that is the true accomplishment? Could it be said that each of these who were infirmed, diseased, did so offering the opportunity to this one and his brothers and the sisters, that they might have the opportunity to serve? And were the churches destroyed that the brothers and the sisters might come at another time to rebuild them and serve and their faith would be seen and known?

Rosa (as she was called by some in the familiar sense) arose the following morn to the gratitude and joy of all, and she became renowned for her grace and did many good works. And it was said by many that the vigil that was kept for her and the call to bring the Christ to be one with her endured throughout that lifetime. Would this, then, by the measure of the Earth, be seen as a good work? How would it be described? As something that was given to one who was worthy? As the good service of two – and yes, the many others who were in prayer – who held the faith and believed and called out in our Brother's name?

As Francis knelt beside Rosa he knew that only his asking of God in his beloved Christ's name and all would be well. Similarly, Clare was without doubt. In the purity of her compassion, she poured the life of her own being into her sister, in Mary's name. And, together, the faith was answered.

November 2

How does one measure love? Is there a gradient? Or is love just love with many ways of expressing itself or being known?

[*Journey of Non-Separateness* continues:]
As Francis sequestered himself, believing that his days to remain in the Earth were few in number, his realization awakened and the *Truth of Being* came to the fore. So when a brother came to bring him simple nourishment, Francis rose up and walked with him, arm in arm, to choose service, not in the nature as one who is obligated but in the nature of one whose very joy and life are dedicated unto same.

It is the journey of Spirit and the call to hear: Truth is ever present. It remains only for one to open self, that it can be made possible.

[To the Channel:
... When within the great crystalline structure as you first perceived it, there was only wonder and awe at the beauty of the magnificence of what was surrounding you. Is there still that wonder and awe if you see it as a grain of sand upon a simple beach? Would you journey to find that single grain of sand and move within it to behold its beauty, or do you realize that the beauty and wonder that you experienced is yours and lives on, and is an offering to all who wish to know it? ...

... There is another grain of sand. We take you now that you can see it clearly. ...

... See the Light upon it and the brilliance of it. ...

... Look upon its wonder, and let us give it a name for you.

... Some call it Earth. ...

... Would you journey to be within it now, to know its beauty, knowing you have journeyed within it oft times in past? What is the measure by which you would adjudge its beauty? How does one measure the nature of love? Is there a gradient of love? Or is love just plain love with many ways of expressing itself or being known? ...

> November 3
>
> Look at the essences of the past and let them shine, just as one who ascends a mountain gives thanks to each foothold.

[*Journey of Non-Separateness* continues:]
It is very difficult, if at all possible, for one to deny their past. It can be of obscured. It can be covered over by layers of illusion. But within self are the beautiful embers that glow from the fire of a previous journey or lifetime. These are eternal and they give warmth and nourishment forever to the one who has the journey. The denial of these is to deny the warmth and nourishment of them, that these are the beautiful opportunities that grant one the growth of consciousness and the greater knowing of self to be as God intends you to be.

When one remembers that they are a Child of God, it is possible to realize, step by step, that you just might be greater than the experience you are now within.

God sends us to tell you: What value is there to a Light that is hidden under a bushel? Look at the essences of the past, and let them shine forth, just as one who willfully ascends a mountain gives thanks to each foothold that enables the climb to be accomplished.

> November 4
>
> Reference can be gained by way of definition but also through expanded Consciousness. Honor both.

[*Journey of Non-Separateness* continues:]

There was a young boy who knew not much of the outside world but knew much of the outside world from the great teachers. Is the knowing gained from the teachers equal to the knowing that might have been experienced had he not been given unto the temple?

One could say that, had he journeyed in a lifetime as a part of the peoples, the masses, he certainly would have experienced every jot and tittle of being "human" in those times. He would have labored and perhaps done good deeds here and there, offered the prayers and so forth, and it would have been deemed a good life. But he was given unto the temple, and was taught and initiated. Both are good pathways, but the one in the temple became enlightened. Would the experience in the midst of the people have surpassed the enlightenment gained in the Temple?

The one in the temple learned to see obstacles as only what they are... a passing expression of finiteness. In the normal sense, some obstacles may be thought of as impenetrable. When they are thought of in the Spirit of one who chooses to be Free, Love opens the way and the freedom to be one with that which is otherwise impenetrable makes the one who chooses to be free one with it. The obstacle is *not,* because you *are.* If you are Free, it is Free.

The simplicity of Consciousness is such that it cannot, in finiteness, be grasped without definition. Therefore, definition is given because it is known by those who are Free to be of value for those who are seeking Freedom. Thus, if you choose to give reference to others using definition, honor that; if you choose to give reference to others using the expansion of Consciousness itself, then honor that as well.

November 5

The point is for you to *Be*.

[*Journey of Non-Separateness* continues:]
In the immensity of God's Word is the glory of the potential that is ever flowing as gifts from God. You have but to call upon the Knowing and they are yours. Is that a shift in Consciousness? Is it a *journey* into what is Known? Is it calling forth Understanding? Is it *Be*-ing (with a capital B)? We here should vote almost unanimously for the latter (with a note of loving humor).

The point is for you to Be.

The Veils of Separateness cannot withstand your continued quest. They are failing in their attempts to separate you from the fullness of your Being.

Neither you nor we wish to vanquish them, so let us pronounce this to them now: You are the visions and dreams, the thoughts, emotions, and experiences of those who are and have been experiencing in finiteness. We are your brothers, your sisters, and we love you. We wish to set you free. We journey into your midst deliberately with this intent, alone, going before us – that we love you and we seek to free you. If you greet us upon our journeys toward you, then we will give you these gifts. If you do not wish them, then you may part before us, and when you are ready, these gifts will await you.

Note: After Al's return from a reading on Feb 2, 2103, the reading prior to *Journey to Non-Separateness*, he described how that journey had begun. He said, having made his usual transition for the reading, it was like waking up in a lucid dream. This is background for the November 6 excerpt:

Al: I began looking around, as anyone would probably do if they were to awaken in strange surroundings. In my periphery vision, I could see the corner of the neckline of what I was wearing and knew in the back of my awareness that I was wearing a robe. I was seated at the head of a very long table and I knew, as I looked around at the surroundings and the people gathered, that I was in the courtyard of Nicodemus. But I was seeing it all *through the eyes of Jesus!*

Then I blinked and I realized that I was seated several people down to the right of Jesus, and I knew just as surely as I'm sitting here in this time that I was John! I looked down at my hands that weren't my hands as I'm familiar with. My fingers had been absent-mindedly feeling the smoothness of the table until I consciously began to admire it. When I started wondering how they could have crafted such magnificence in this time, I realized I was wondering this as 'Al'!

At that point, I looked up and over to Jesus. He had evidently been watching me. I felt such a bond of love for this man and knew that He was, of course, totally aware of all the intricacies, and much more, that I was experiencing and thinking in this event. With a gentle smile, He began to impart to me the details of the steps taken to achieve the smoothness for the table surface. Of course He would. He's the Carpenter.

When this exchange between us was completed, I realized I had received one of the greatest teachings of my life – I had literally experienced non-separateness. I had experienced a time long ago, the time in the present, and simultaneously, *no-time* through observing myself as the observer.

November 6

The more you see God's Love in each person, the more you know God from the Consciousness that is outside of time.

[*Journey of Non-Separateness* continues:]
At His request, we have returned to the table to sit with our Brother, Jeshua, Jesus, once again.

[To the Channel:]
... Look at your hands, as you did in that experience, and make the bond with the table. ...
... Feel your Brother's eyes and love embracing you. ...
... As you see Him, you feel the two of you becoming One. This Oneness, dear brother, is that which is given when it is sought. Is it there for any who seek? Why would it not be? ...
... Let us embrace, that we can become One in that way. ...
... Now, as we return (after some Earth-time has passed) to seat ourselves at the table again, we turn to look at the brothers and sisters seated around the table. Look at them with your peace and just that. ...
... See them. See them as you did when you saw through the eyes of Jesus. Do not waver! Do not fall back! If you wish to *Be* that which you say, look now and See, through the Peace of God, those who are seated around the table. ...
... When you, just now, turned to look at Jesus, and He nodded and smiled, do you not know what is here? What you see before you and the realization coming to you is the beauty of God's Love, the facets of His Love, *expressed*. ...
... Look about at your sisters and brothers. See their inner beauty. Feel it and know it. Remember it. Make it yours. As their eyes meet yours, accept what they give to you. What are you doing in this? You are doing what you have sought – You are Knowing God through that part of the gift these before you bear of His Love. The more you see this in each of them, the more do you Know God from this level of Consciousness, which has no relevance in what you think of as time.

> November 7
>
> There can be the simultaneous Knowing of where one is expressed presently and of being expressed elsewhere.

[*Journey of Non-Separateness* concludes:]
 Zachary: Come with us now. ...
 Here is the beauty of the Homeland that is so loved.
 I would tell you, off to the side a bit, after that experience, my brother looks dazzled. He is lying back on the greenery, for he has chosen to be expressed in form here. Sarah and I are bringing him the sweet peace and balance that is ever present here in the Homeland. It isn't that he didn't have an abundance of this, but the sum of his Being is coming into balance with itself. It's something anyone might find value in doing.
 There is such sweet purity here. It is filled with the potential that seeks only to give, filled with the joy and beauty of brothers and sisters who have chosen to be a part of this simply out of the joy of being. Some come and go here and each leaves a gift of themselves and receives gifts in return, and there is such joy in the discovery of how these gifts interact with one another and the resonance of all manner of sensory perception, inclusively those from finiteness, of course.
 My brother stirs and rises up on an elbow. Looking himself over and glancing at Sarah and me, he marvels that he is truly here because *he knows he is also elsewhere.* The knowing of this is a part of his quest and, perhaps, the quest of many of you. We quickly follow as he rises and moves down the slope to the little pool into which the waters of Spirit are cascading. He bends to look into the pool and many facets of his being pass before him as he remembers sisters and brothers. He reaches down, cupping his hands to bring the waters up and he takes of them, stands, and pauses in silent gratitude. And now, we shall guide him to return to his expression in the Earth.
 This recounting is meant as a gift to all of Consciousness in the name of the Promise. Let those who would, partake.

> **November 8**
>
> Can you love who and what you are at present enough to set it Free?

It has been asked of our brother, "Where do we go from here?" measuring Consciousness relevant to time.

One can contemplate that the *going to* point is whatsoever you desire. So the question is, is it not, how would you measure or know your own desire? Is it a thing you can take from someplace within self and place it upon a measuring device of any nature? Is it that which you can taste or smell or feel? Does it have some substance to it?

What is desire? Is it not the calling from your own Spirit? Then the answer to this question is that where you should go is to your own Spirit.

You will counter with, how might this be accomplished? The manner of accomplishment is the measure of whether or not the *who and what you are* in the present wishes to be sustained, or whether you can love it enough to set it Free.

The fabric of one's being is that which can accelerate or limit depending upon the recognition of it and the choices one sees within that very fabric. Where does it begin? Where does it end? Or does it?

Can you remember?

[Note: The next journey began with the following:]
   If you can perceive the light, then know it to be the Light of thy Father. If you choose, come unto it, and all that has been is forgiven of thee. We call to you as your brothers and sisters, offering only love and Father's gifts of forgiveness and His holy grace. Fear not the Light but know it to be that same as is found within you. We await you.
   Greater is the joy and glory that lies ahead, if you will but lay aside that which you cleave unto of the Earth. Labor not in question or doubt. Set yourselves free and come. We will carry you and lift you unto the love eternal that you so long for.
   We leave others now this beautiful work.

[As background:]
   (Those souls who have been aware of the works with this Channel and who have in past sought to limit same have seen the transformation, not only referring to that which is of our brother and sister and those who are gathered about these works but a transformation in the opportunity. They know that this path of Light, rather than being anything that is demanding or requiring submission, is that Light that is the same that gives life to them.
   They are being gathered by our brethren as we move now to welcome our brother the Channel and those of you who journey with him. Thank you for this opportunity.)

> November 9
>
> The good works done in prayer, meditation, and intent do awaken those dwelling in illusion adjacent to the Earth.

[*Journey of Gratitude* begins – To the Channel:]
 ... Where there is Light, Darkness is; where there is Darkness, Light is. As you brought forth your own Light, the Darkness has surrounded this. ...

 At the onset of this journey, there were remnants of a past encounter on the part of this our Channel and those with him in works you call "The Borderland." Some of these remnants were set free by the works done at the onset of that experience, and then, by the Brotherhood who engaged them by way of this pathway of Light that yet exists. So a goodly number are in rest, freed from the illusion of their own remorse.
 As one continues to sustain the Light, it not only brings the greater joy of knowing the Truth as a Child of God, but it will, by way of the power of the manifestation of the Promise, reveal the Light, that others who are lost in the darkness of illusion and see it can choose it, some who have not known it for greater periods of time than you could surmise.
 When you seek to do a thing from the embrace of finiteness, there is the measure and questioning of the doing: What is its nature, where is its direction, and all the sorts of things that are natural to the consciousness present in Earth. The breaking free of this consciousness is merely a choice. It is, we understand clearly, not always a straightforward one. In some cases, it may seem that there must be a work of *un*-doing before this can be *done*. But we come to share with you the glory of the accomplishment of setting brethren free, that there would be gladness within you in the knowing that, upon any journey here, you may greet them and they will know you for the good service you have offered in God's Name to them. This is given that you can know that your good work does awaken those dwelling in the illusion adjacent to you.

> ### November 10
>
> If you seek Consciousness, there must be the willingness to give it, and as you give, you give to yourself.

[*Journey of Gratitude* continues:]

What would you do if you were suddenly here and we were embracing one another? What would you do as we look upon one another? You would ponder, "What do I see?"

Do this with one another where you are. Move to that place from where you are to a notch or two above the norm, and look upon one another. And as you reflect in the Sacred Silence, allow the Consciousness to awaken and allow your own Spirit to be that through which you perceive. The greater you do this the more will be the clarity of what you seek.

Share with one another in the meaningful way of contemplating each other's Spirit and each other's presence, and see this, feel it, know it. Not in the ways you have in past – to think and use the mind – but use the Spirit. See?

And remember us... again, not with the mind but through the Spirit. As you do, we can reach out to you. How do you do this? To do this you must set aside that which seeks to fuel the separateness and rise above that which is the norm. Some of you will find this facilitated first by prayer, then, by the quietude of peace within. Then hold us and we will hold you. Hold the consciousness of us, and as you hold our presence in your consciousness, we will hold your presence with ours. This will help to open the way for you, and it will give us a pathway to you that is only partially present in the current for, if you seek Consciousness, then there must be the willingness to give it, and as you give it, you give to yourself.

Where is the presence of your consciousness in this very moment? Where is it? Is it in some sacred place within you? Is it surrounding your physical expression there in the Earth? Is it right here, perceiving back at us as we perceive you? Perceive one another and ask and answer from those levels, and in the doing, become the Be-ing. See?

November 11

If you accomplish the journey that is You – that being oneness with God – you have accomplished all else.

[*Journey of Gratitude* continues:]

The *nation of consciousness* (as it might be called) that surrounds the Earth believes it is what it is.

Though you are dwelling in that nation of consciousness, you are not a rebel to the nation of consciousness by choosing your own individuality within it. That is a part of your reason for journeying and it is your right.

Your reason for being is you. Your journey begins and ends with you. If you accomplish the journey that is You – that being oneness with God – you have accomplished all else.

> November 12
>
> Stay true to your intent and stay focused. And then give of it as you are asked.

[*Journey of Gratitude* continues:]

When a good worker comes unto a work which is intended to be the very best that worker can accomplish, they do not choose to do many, many, peripheral works along with it, do they?

So here is a gentle caution... Consciousness will call to you, and say to you, "Might I have a moment of your time, your thoughts? Could I have a bit of help over here?"

You can answer, "Yes, look you upon this work that I am doing. Take from it as you would. It is without limit." Then, you see, you are saying to all else, "Here is the answer to that which you seek. I do not come to you to give it to you, because it cannot be given without it being asked for."

Their asking is the coming to the well to get the water that you know is within. It is not asking the well, "Dear well, I'm over here on this hilltop and I thirst. Come and bring me some water from within you."

See? Be true to yourselves and to the good intent that you have built. Then, as it is chosen, they will have it.

There are so many who are in need. We say to them, "Here, let us fill your need." And they stand immediately before us, not even perceiving us (can you imagine that) and say, "Help me. I have a need." And we say again, and again, "Here, take as you would."

Do you see? We walk among them, as we are permitted.

November 13

Now is the time. This is the hour. The knock is upon the door. It is yours to open.

[*Journey of Gratitude* concludes:]
>Now is the time.
>This is the hour.
>The knock is upon the door, yours to open.

> November 14
>
> The power of your journey is based upon that which you are willing to allow yourself to believe.

    It is good to ever remember that the power of your journey is based upon that which you are willing to allow yourself to believe.

    In the believing, Truth becomes a revelation to you and will, in the time that follows, reveal itself in a way that will make it known that you have, indeed, "journeyed."

> November 15
>
> In Consciousness, choices do not have the imposition of finite limitation, the mass-mind consciousness that sustains itself.

[*Journey to Being* begins:]

Zachary: The intent in this journey is several-fold for each of you and for the continuity of our brother's intent, which is the freeing of that which separates, *anything* that separates, him from God. The reality is there is naught that separates. Therefore, we are looking moreso at how we can assist our brother in the owning of that which is. So, as each of you find yourselves here exploring and experiencing joyfully with others, know that you have no limit... that you can do just that.

My brother, the Channel, is in a state of Consciousness intended by him to provide the freedom for the communication with those of you he loves so dearly, remembering that any choice you make is filled with the power of your Spirit as you are journeying here.

To make that as clear as possible for you: Your choices here do not have the imposition of finite limitation... or the *beauty* of mass-mind to sustain its status quo, if you will.

We now take our brother to a favorite place for him, the gentle green slope of the Homeland. Sarah is focusing her Consciousness upon my brother, and this creates a stirring in him. He will probably ask, where is he stirring *from*? The levels of Consciousness are not necessarily in need of definition. It is simply that you could think of this as a choice to be in a Consciousness that is moreso a neutral observer. It is much akin to the loving neutrality that has been spoken of.

> November 16
>
> If one activates freedom in order to journey forth and gather understanding, freedom could be considered separateness.

[*Journey to Being* continues:]

Zachary: Sarah's Consciousness now touches our brother's Consciousness. I reach over to do the same with mine, and there is the growing awareness, and Consciousness and we become one. In this present state of oneness there is nothing to perceive in the sense of the familiar. There is no expression of definition. There is only the beauty and warm embrace of pure Potential. It is a Oneness that recognizes that we have never been apart, and yet, we have chosen various individual experiences that create the paths to Understanding.

We had given our brother an opportunity... not a lesson, for he needs no lessons, only to call forth of his own volition that which he knows within. So it is merely that we reflected to him, in the form of understanding, that which is Known.

In the present Consciousness we are aware of the All. In the awareness of the All is the Understanding that we are also one with God. Why is this different than in the journey where it was unto God, guided by the brethren, the Angelic Host, into the warmth of His embrace in the more literal sense? The difference, here, is that we are experiencing Freedom.

Freedom *could* be looked upon, in one sense, as separateness, if one activates freedom to make a choice that is to journey forth and gather understanding.

November 17

True Love for a thing radiates as true Love for all... no exclusion, no exception.

[*Journey to Being* continues:]

Zachary: "So would it be possible, dear brother, for you to think that you were separate from Father when you asked the building in Syria for its Understanding, and proclaimed unto it that you loved it?"

The Channel stirs a bit, having been enjoying the bliss. He ponders for a moment, within Consciousness, the individuality of himself, sufficient that I can direct a question to him. In that moment of his recognition of this, Sarah and I (in a manner of speaking) re-energize our oneness with him. This gives him the polarity of balance that enables him to claim from within that he is an eternal son of God.

Now he is in that state of Knowing that he *Is*.

With the intent of a warm embrace to me in answer to my question, he responds. "No, never separate from Father. It was by my choice of Oneness with Father that I was *able* to awaken my oneness with the building."

"And your love for the building is evident, expressed even here. Now, isn't that interesting! The conversation you had in your group discussion about loving a single grain of sand, do you truly suppose that there is something inappropriate about this? I heard you state that perhaps the other grains of sand might feel left out, or something of this sort. In your current state of Knowing, do you still believe this?"

He smiles. "No, of course not because, as I saw the single grain of sand, I saw them all. My love for the single grain of sand, therefore, is a love of all of the grains of sand and all of the buildings that contain those grains. And indeed, what I feel, in answer to your question, dear Zachary, is Father's Love: There is no exclusion. There is no exception."

I like his answer a lot.

> November 18
>
> If you ask something for its Understanding, first accepting that you are one and you love it, the Understanding is instant.

[*Journey to Being* continues:]

Zachary: "So then, dear brother, why do you suppose that, earlier in that Earth Day measure, you would make a statement like that? Did you not mean it?"

I have elicited a bit of humor from him on that, of course. But he merely looks at me with his beautiful Consciousness and embraces me. In other words, of course, he knew the answer. Isn't that interesting... He *Knew* the answer!

My, my! Doesn't it make you wonder how many of you who might be reading this also Know the answer to your questions? Is it that you are seeking some confirmation of that Knowing? If that's true, of course, there's not a thing to be adjudged as "wrong" with that. But if you realize that's all you're seeking, then you could save some time and energy by just Knowing that your answer, as you Know it within when you asked the question, is already true. This is not a little game. It's not meant to be lighthearted, really, even though it may seem so, for if one is a Child of God, then whatsoever they seek, if they ask, it is given.

"So back to you, my brother. Could you tell me why you spoke those questions if you now realize that you know the answers?"

My brother does not speak but, rather, shows me.

Translating what he shows: If you "name" a thing in the Earth, you have brought forth the Knowing of it. And if you have Knowing of a thing, then you can reach out and ask for its Understanding. And if you ask for its Understanding by first professing that you are one and that you love it, the Understanding is instantly yours. It requires no thrusting or parrying. It requires only the Claiming and the Knowing.

> November 19
>
> Beyond the illusions of mass-mind there is no competition for prominence.

[*Journey to Being* continues:]

Sarah: "Do you remember the green, my brother?"

The Channel affirms this, and immediately we are surrounded in a myriad of expressions of green. The beauty of the expressions have no limit, and as we find joy in the experiencing of the green as potentials we see other colors moving to the forefront as a sort of dance of expression. We are in delight, the three of us in one expression moving through the colors as they come to celebrate Sarah's call of the Green.

It is not as a gathering might be seen in the Earth, where one color would compete for prominence. Here, all the colors come to celebrate the color green... to lift it up, to love it, to adore its potential. We feel the potentials as a collage of expressions.

Sarah and I smile very broadly in Spirit, in oneness, for we know that all of these expressions, dizzying numbers of them, are coming from our brother, this, the Channel. He is Knowing the green as God Knows green. He Knows the green of a leaf on a plant in a place called Borneo; another green, a bit darker, with some fuzziness on its surface, on a flower in a pot in New York City sitting on a windowsill; and on and on. Wherever there can be joy for green to express itself we perceive it, we *Know* it.

"And what does this mean to you, my brother, all of this *potential* that you and Father are bringing forth in this dance of expression? What does it mean? Why are you doing it?"

Oh, you will love the Channel's response to this... He is *Be*-ing. He is Be-ing one with God.

> November 20
>
> Blink. Just that quickly, because we choose it, it is so.

[*Journey to Being* continues:]
   Zachary: The limitations you perceive are relevant to understanding based on that which you know or have experienced or consider as potential. Again, these are the lessons of the journey into patterns and shapes and forms as we recently examined. But here, in the beautiful collage of expressions that flowed through my brother, the Channel, all of these were free. The green essences weren't told by intent from a child of God, "You must be this blade of grass."
   Beyond finiteness, it is through mutual concurrence that the grass is, and it is God who makes it possible. You could say the grass is an expression of your oneness with God; and you could say even further that, because you and God are one, you and the blade of grass are also one.
   We could do similar wonderful works with the myriad of Colors that are constantly flowing from God's Word, but we are called now. Do you hear the call?
   So we return (blink, just that quickly, because we have chosen it) to be standing beside our Brother, the Christ, the Master, in the beauty of the Homeland and with the Maidens and many of our fellow brethren as we listen to them sharing. We see Jesus turn to look at us and gesture that we join Him. And so, we shall.

> November 21
>
> Be open, choose and claim, and all that you have read and experienced here and greater is yours for the asking.

[*Journey to Being* continues:]

When we come together in a manner such as this, in an expression of Father such as the beauty of the Homeland, such "songs" and "dances" of celebration of joy are living gifts given to all of Consciousness.

Invariably, when we do as we are doing here now, many, many of our brethren come from distant experiences in Consciousness to join with us in the joy. Much of this, in terms of the intent of the celebration, is also manifesting itself within the consciousness of Earth.

Some of it is known by the faithful who have dedicated themselves to seek it. Others (who may be even reading these works) will be at the point where they might be tilting their head this way or that to figure out, "My, these are curious occurrences. I see the forces of nature in a different way. And I am noticing something once in awhile just off in the periphery of my consciousness." (You know it's there until you turn and the force of mass-mind dominance precludes it, so to say.) But the more you open yourself and the more you choose and reclaim, the greater is your potential to perceive, to know, and to realize that all that you have read here and experienced here – and greater – is yours for the asking.

> November 22
>
> The common intent emerging is the desire for Freedom and to reclaim the heritage as Children of God.

[*Journey to Being* concludes:]
    Zachary: I release my brother to the care of Sarah and several others, for I would like to speak for the recording (as you call it) to you, brother, upon your awakening and to those of your group and others... all of you who are listening or reading

    Some of you have journeyed here and we can see you. We know you. We see a common intent, a singular ideal, emerging: The quest for Oneness with God, the desire for Freedom, the wish to Know yourselves and to reclaim your heritage as Children of God.
    Make no mistake, you are eternal. The reclaiming of this eternal nature and oneness with God as His Child brings to use the harmony with Universal Law. As some of you seek to do works within the expression of the Law, this is the pathway: the belief and the reclaiming, the Knowing.
    This journey has been intended to make the way open and passable for those of you who are seeking in that way. Believe unto yourselves.
    To say that if you believe unto yourselves you are believing unto God is a truth. For you are one.

> November 23
>
> Consider all things from the truth of your own journey, for therein lies the gift of God's Uniqueness within you.

Thoughts and words could be likened unto bricks. One can take these bricks and make a fine pathway or build a sturdy wall. If one is upon a journey, then perhaps a pathway is better than a wall.

It is well to understand the beauty of each one's contribution unto the good work, and wherever there is a resonance within you from these contributions, then this is good.

It is also simultaneously well to remember the truths upon which you have built your current position in Consciousness and not to abandon these for something that is borne on the winds of change. It is good to consider all things from the truth of your own journey, for therein lies the great gift of God's Uniqueness within you.

One can say various words that can build a pathway along which you can travel with ease and rapidity, or these words can be as blocks within a wall that you must surmount in order to continue your journey.

November 24

In the journeys to discover greater aspects of self beyond the known, pauses help affirm the truth of what you discover.

    In one of your meetings, we heard one of you mention places of rest or pause, reflection, contemplation, along the journeys beyond finiteness in your meditations.

    We would see these to be of considerable value to all of you and should think the logic here to be self-evident.

    Do find places to pause and to acquaint yourself with your own being. For, as you journey beyond the known or the defined of self in the current, you are discovering with each breath of movement the greater aspects of self. Giving one's self places of pause helps to affirm these and put them into the foundation of the truth of who and what you are.

> November 25
>
> Honor the body equally to the quest for Spiritual Consciousness
> It is your vessel, the instrument of your Spirit.

It is good to have a schedule for one's self built out of a love for self. That love should include the wonder and blessing of one's temple... body, if you will.

To place the honor of the body equally beside the quest for Spiritual Consciousness should not be minimized in regard to its importance. For if you honor the body, you set it free. By this we mean you *care* for it, you give it the love and respect that is appropriate for it as the vessel within which you journey in this incarnation.

You also make it possible for the body to become the instrument of your Spirit.

Honor thy temple as you honor your Spirit. But as you set schedules for these, set them with the compassion of a loving parent for their child, as God thinks of you: with love that, if the schedule is met here and bent a little over there, it is a source of love and understanding.

> November 26
>
> You and God have never been separate. Summon the Completeness of your Being, the power of your Love.

The Consciousness of Self can awaken to the realization that you and God have never been separate. This awakening flies into the turmoil of consciousness expressed in the Earth.

We call it turmoil because it has so many eddies, crosscurrents, swirling movements that can all have impact upon the intent.

If you summon forth the Completeness of your Being, you can build a Consciousness that not only is impervious to these crosscurrents, but contributes the blessing that is your divine Uniqueness unto them.

You do this first by recognizing what the influences are that can be activated within you by these crosscurrents. You could call them triggers or buttons or some such, but they are those points in you that need to be given complete Freedom through the power of your forgiveness, through the power of your love, and through the power of your compassion.

> November 27
>
> You can linger in what you consider to be affects that the energies have had upon you, or you can give thanks for them.

    Where you are now (many of you, if not all of you to varying degree) is seeing yourselves among the influences of Earthly consciousness. We would be aware of this and see this only as a transient experience. You do this by focusing on what is to be rather than what has been, what is to be built by way of your intent, and hold this open-handedly before you in all that you are and do.

    Some of you have met the crosscurrents of energies and have found some residence within the physical, emotional, the mind and even, to a degree, to the Spirit. Some of you will set yourself Free *because* of this. Which shall it be for you?

    You can linger in the crosscurrent and the affect it has had upon the collective assembly of who and what you are in the present. Or you can give thanks for it and see it as an opportunity to rise up and reclaim, all the greater, the Truth of who you are and the power of what you Know.

> ## November 28
>
> Any challenge you face you have *asked* for. Step up upon each one with faith and bless it with the Light of God within.

If you fall into the space that so often comes when one meets a challenge of finiteness, that space is a place of action; it is not a place for you to linger in remorse or confusion or doubt or hesitation, or such as these.

This is that which you have *asked* for. When it comes, give thanks for it and rise up above it. No matter what the crosscurrents or the influences and trigger points may seem to counter with, the greater is the power of your faith in these times or challenges as you stand upon this new threshold, the greater shall be the accomplishment of your intent.

Now then, what are these various things that many of you who read these words will know about? Are they punishments? Are they indicators of wrongdoing? Are they Karma, good or bad? What are they?

They are step-stones of your current journey. If you pick up the step-stone and hold onto it with remorse or confusion, you won't be able to journey much further because of the burden of that step-stone you are carrying. Rather, place it back down and step up upon it. Meet each challenge with a joyful heart and a faith that cannot be limited by any contrasting energies. Rather, bless these energies with the Light of God within you.

November 29

It is good to know what things are good for your body, mind, and Spirit. It is even better to do those things.

    It is good to know what things are good for your body, mind, and Spirit.
    It is even better to do those things. See?

November 30

> In the waves of change are the opportunities for all to ask, "What is it in this beautiful container of Self that I can give?"

You will see great waves of change in all quarters, in all respects. This has been given for many millennia. It has been prophesied that there shall come those times of change that shall shake the foundation of the familiar and become the great opportunity for peoples, groups, classes, masses, races, nations, cultures, to look upon themselves with a humbling eye and ask, "What have I to give to my God? What is it that I am carrying in this beautiful container of Self that I can give in this time of change to all that is?"

Look at the traditions, the habits, the conditioning factors that have fashioned you into who and what you are in the present, and be willing to see these as no longer needed, for that is truth. By what measures shall you evaluate these? By the Truth that is within you.

All manner of words and teachings and ceremonies and rituals and beliefs can be given unto you, and if you are not cleaving unto the Truth within, these can be as the ever-changing winds of consciousness. They can sweep you up and support and encourage you to be as they wish it to be and to nourish that as a belief within you. But in these times, you shall see the fruits of each teaching, each labor, and you shall find Truths speaking to you.

There may be cause to lament. There may be cause to criticize self and self's actions in past. Dwell but a moment in that activity should it occur! For the moment before you is greater in its potential, if you will only claim it.

December 1

Dwell in the Consciousness that God and you are One. Stop. Welcome Him. And take that Presence with you in all things.

It is good now to recognize that you are, indeed, Children of the One God, and therefore, within you does He dwell. The more you can dwell in this Consciousness – that God and you are One – the more you will realize the power of your thoughts, your words, your actions.

You will hear more and more truth and of more and more of your brethren who are manifesting these truths. Has God favored them? Does God love them greater than any one of you? Were they be given this special gift that was withheld from you? Of course you cannot even contemplate such a thing, for this would not be your Lord God we are describing.

God's love – His gifts, His grace, all that He is – is offered to you in this very moment as you read these words. Look to yourselves to see what separates you from Knowing this. Is it habit? Then make manifest a plan to change each little habit that rises that you see is like a cloud between you and Him.

Or do this: Simply stop, open yourself, and welcome Him and the Presence, and take that Presence with you in all that you are and do.

December 2

There is not one of you who doesn't carry the power of the Promise. Listen for the call. Bring forth the Presence.

What is healing if not the calling forth of the Perfect Presence within each and every Child of God.

Listen for the call if you are presently out of harmony with God within you. If a crosscurrent of Earthly consciousness has set you awry, listen for the call as others gather together in prayer in your name. For, as they bring forth God within themselves, they bring forth God within you. You can turn away from that call. You can disbelieve it. You can move into the space that is ever-present with dis-ease. Or you can listen for the call and answer it.

No choice, no decision, no action, thought, word, or deed that might come forth from any of you is ever met with anything but love and compassion by God.

You are in a journey of experiencing. The experiencing you have chosen to be within builds an understanding and, at the forefront, an opportunity of service.

There is not a one of you who has not the power of the Promise.

December 3

> Consciousness contains all that is. If you send forth a blessing, all of Consciousness feels it and reverberates that blessing.

You may find this a bit too vast contemplate, but it is, nonetheless, true: If you say a word and believe that the word you say comes from the center of your Being, from God, from Father, then that word is felt by *all of Consciousness*.

If you pause and become one with God's Light within and you say... ... *Love*... ... it reverberates throughout all of Consciousness, and there is not one Child of God who doesn't feel a shimmer of joy at your speaking it.

Consciousness is as a great Sea of Oneness. It contains all that is. One could say, accurately, it is God. Or if you prefer, for understanding, it is God's Word having been spoken.

As you call forth and (in your terminology) re-*member*, in this Consciousness, you will strengthen it each time you do. By that we mean you will strengthen its presence within you, your awareness of it. It has always been and ever shall be, but now you have Knowing of it.

We would encourage you to use this, the word *use* being meant very lightly. First, to expand your own ability to Know and See. As brother Zachary gave the Channel with the color green and the grain of sand, let yourself *be* the great Sea and feel its nuances, it's subtleties, its colors, it's variations in energy and vibration, the undulation of its waves, the pulsing of the varying elements that are ever within it.

As you use this in meditation or in prayer works you will find returning back to you what you have given. If you send forth a blessing, all of Consciousness will reverberate that blessing.

December 4

> What is beginning to be felt and Known is the grandness of your own BE-ing.

Remember the military officer who came to Jesus and said, "Good master, if I give a command to my men, they will go forth and carry it out. I know that, if you say the word, my servant in my home, distant from you, will be healed." Jesus admired this man's faith, given in the simplest understanding he was capable of expressing. It wasn't from years of ritualistic study or psalms or prayers. It was simply that which he had grown to know as a truth for him. So, Jesus spoke the word, and said, "Your faith has healed your servant." And the officer thanked Jesus and turned and went to his home, knowing that that he would find his servant healed.

When you send forth a prayer, such as for a child you have seen in the news, your faith at that point is likened unto the Roman soldier... It is heard by that Spirit called Christ and honored by Consciousness, within which the Spirit of Christ lives. See?

Where goodness is given, goodness is received. When it is given in a manner of faith, simple and from the truth of one's being, then, the path is open for the receipt to be manyfold greater. It is the Law of Just Return. The Sea of Consciousness that you experience in such Return is You.

You are everywhere in this Sea. You cannot know this in the complete sense from a finite consciousness, but remember the colors and vibrations and such we've spoken of? These are awakening your Oneness. What you will feel (and perhaps have already felt) returning to you in so many ways could be explained to you as the grandness of your own Being.

This is given to you to build understanding and to affirm and strengthen your Knowing of it: The truth of your intent is that you are "seeking" to *Be* Free, to *Be* one with the Sea of Oneness, to *Be* One with Consciousness.

December 5

> To Know Consciousness while yet finite requires that it is the number one focus in your thought, word, and action.

To obtain your intent – Consciousness:

- It would be your number one focus.

- It is to Know that you are what you say you are.

- It is to place the Knowing of it at the forefront of all that you are about.

Whether you go to the market or put fuel in your vehicle or cook a meal, it is to know that you are one with God in the doing of all these things. It is like you are a finger of God touching all of these things.

If you Know this, then you are a blessing in all of these things, see. Just so as you have said a blessing to a child on the news, if you walk about a market in the same Oneness, you are blessing all the hands that have ever been a part of bringing that which is in the market before you.

> December 6
>
> Know the Spaces and honor definition but cling to none of it. Set the definitions free within yourself, then *be* the Spaces

The Knowing of the Spaces will enable you to create.

Know the Spaces that you are experiencing. Know the opening of Consciousness as the opening of what Is.

Give definition complete honor but cling to none of it. You are meant to cling to no definition to the extent that you must carry it into the Spaces.

Be very clear in this: Set the definitions free within yourself. Then *be* the Spaces.

Very swiftly you will be awakening your Knowing of the Spaces and how to utilize these for the fulfillment of your intentions. We have said this intentionally plurally, for we see that these will expand as you truly Know the Spaces.

Yes (to answer an unspoken question), the Sacred Silence is one and the same as the Spaces.

> December 7
>
> In the Sacred Silence, we can be with you as you choose it. Then we can accomplish with you through our shared love.

    Review the Colors and make them your own; be one with them. To do this is to Know the creative power of the Word of God. See this?

    Each of the Colors carries varying potentialities. Each one is unique, just as each Child of God is unique. Each of the Colors consists of all that you know in the knowledge of the Earth and much more. If you consider the Colors as varying forms of expression that can be directed to manifest, then you will have the beginning stages of interacting with them. Let them be One with you and you with them. This is to be one with Consciousness but adding the potentialities of God and the Christ.

    The Christ is the master of the creative aspects of God's Word. In the mastery of this, then, where there is the Sacred Silence, the Colors of creation can be directed. In the just previous passages, there were the references to the use of these in a different way, by sending love and blessings to a child in need. (The Sea, and the Spaces, and the Silence, could be simply different names for the same thing, but know it as you know it through your Uniqueness.)

    We would like to be with you within the Sacred Silence as oft as possible as you find joy in so doing, that we can accomplish with you through our shared love. Know that we are with you before you take the very first step.

    Remember the building, the warriors, the women and children in the stream, remember the color green, and the crystal realm. Build on these. These are no different than as when Jesus said, "Lazarus, come forth."

December 8

> The more you can release things considered to be flaws, faults, the more open you are to receive your greatest expansion.

It has been spoken often here in past of the great cycles of consciousness and energy, some that are known and some that are on the fringe of the known in consciousness in the Earth. Each of these has its importance to contribute to all the others. When such a confluence of Spiritual and eternal cycles of the flow of God's Word come into a certain convergence, there is an opportunity of profound blessing for those who are seeking and willing to receive same.

The message given to our brother, the Channel, earlier in this Earth day's measure – in which he was awakened and told that "As of sunrise, a new Consciousness is with you; sow seeds of hope" – and he sent this message out, this was to announce to all that this new gift is directly from God and is His blessing to those who are seeking in this time of heightened potential.

As you relieve yourself of those things considered to be flaws or faults, doubts, guilts, sins, or any such categorically as you might bear within, this leaves you open and receptive to the gifts being offered. The greater can you release these, the more you are open and free to receive that which is the greater expansion of your consciousness... indeed, to the uttermost should this be your willingness to so do.

> December 9
>
> The time of the Prophecy is upon the Earth. The Promise is manifesting. The Spirit is awakening.

The time of the Prophecy is upon the Earth.
The Promise is manifesting.
The Spirit that is one with all of God's Children is awakening.

Seek ye, then, that kingdom within that is eternal and, therein, shall ye find His Light growing in Its brilliance and beauty with each moment that passes.

Do not fall prey to that which would call you off to the side or whisper to you this or that but believe unto that truth that is yours and ever dwells within as the very life that you are experiencing in the present. Any guidance or words spoken to you that would call you to believe that which is external from you, have a care and look upon this with caution. For the Word of God is that which You are. You are His being, His expression, His love, His compassion.

So, measure by that which you hold to be the highest within and this, alone, knowing this to be that which is that temple of Oneness with God within you.

And feel these words:
A new Consciousness is given you.

As you feel and know this within, let it be those seeds you sow in the intent of hopefulness in your journey through life.

December 10

Set free the habits that no longer contribute to your journey and let Consciousness reflect to you what remains of meaning.

Now, as you open yourself to see, "What is the nature of my being, in truth, and how might I manifest this in the journey that remains before me?" seek only this: to find those things that you are carrying that are the habits that have been accumulated throughout the journey to this point that no longer contribute to your intent. This does not mean that you must adjudge things in the sense of good or bad but only: is it of contribution? If it is not, then set it free.

As each of you seek within your own being, your own consciousness, those things that remain that have great meaning for you, consider how these might be reflected back to you by all of Consciousness. For, as you seek these and find them within yourself, all of Consciousness seeks with you and strives to reflect that which is an accomplishment, a discovery of truth.

In the nature of the reflection, the meditation, and the times of quietude, the celebration of your Uniqueness is ever present. In this celebration, you will find that those who are of close proximity to your Spiritual journey may come forth to guide you to be of contribution to that which you are seeking,

In this, then – stating, before you do, "I accept that which is given in God's Name and in the Spirit and Love of the Christ" – ever be open and receptive, knowing that, as you do, you will find the greater is given as it is openly received.

> ### December 11
>
> We are in that time of the return of the Promise: the manifestations of Consciousness and the awakening the Christ Spirit.

Many of the prophecies have been recorded, written, and distributed. Some are known by tradition or by certain teachings, and others are known widely.

As there has been the question of the meaning of these two terms, collectively, then:

The Prophecy - is that which foretells the return of Consciousness in cycles that are noteworthy.

The Promise - is that which is of the Christ. It is the return of the Master and the Christ Consciousness as an offering to those who are seeking, those who are asking, that this Consciousness can be given and received so as it is chosen.

We are in that period of the return of the Promise, and the Christ Spirit is awakening all throughout among the faithful and among those who are opening themselves to know same. There will be the outer manifestations that will be, not so much so reactions to, but moreso the product... as one sows a seed, then, expecting a harvest from same.

This is that time that has been told many times over of the return of the opportunity to raise your consciousness into oneness with your Brother, called Christ. See?

> December 12
>
> In Knowing the Colors, you Know your Oneness with God as the unfolding Word of Creation awakening within you.

[*Journey to a New Consciousness* begins:]
　　Zachary: Sister Sarah and I are journeying with... A moment, please...

[Note: This might be interesting to some of you. There was a long pause here. After the reading was over, Al spoke about being greatly "jostled" about, and also of being moved from place to place by those watching over him.]

　　Very Well, we continue...
[To the Channel:]
　　... You may detect shifts in the "energies." Be patient with self in the movement of these energies, for there is that predictable shift from the finite resonance to the infinite. ...
　　... In the messages given to you, the intent is to call forth the realization that the possibilities before you are limited only by your belief in them. As in the previous journeys to green and to the sand, you were given the opportunities to see much greater levels of understanding. These have had an impact upon your consciousness, jostling it a bit to make it more flexible. Continue in the Peace and in the Space, and we are with you every step of the way. ...
　　... Do a bit more with the Colors. In Knowing these, you Know your Oneness with God. It is difficult to give commentary to others in the sense that it has been given to you, unless they are willing to set aside their familiar reference points of finiteness in order to understand these. ...
　　The Colors of Creation are much more than anything we have described to the present. God is the Colors. The Colors are God's Spirit. When it is said that God's Word goes forth and that the Colors are opening and awakening creation, unfolding, this is an offering that can take place *within you.*

> **December 13**
>
> The awakening Consciousness is impacting many souls who had lost their way. Call to them often. Serve them.

[*Journey to a New Consciousness* concludes – Zachary to Al:]
  ... Seek the Silence. Seek the Space, the Peace, and then Oneness with God. ...
  ... Let us move now, that these energies can be placed in better alignment, better meaning, more harmonious for the consciousness that yet remains in finiteness. ...
[pause]

  ... Very good. This day's measure is the beginning. It is not the beginning in the sense of the first and only, but the beginning of the journey that is an inner one and that can be made manifest in the outer as soon as you find you are complete with the aspects of this as was previously given. ...
  ... The power of the Consciousness is wondrous, and the beauty is having an impact upon many souls who had lost their way. Let us call to them often, that we can be a part of serving them should they choose to wish Freedom. ...
  ... Keep your faith.
[pause]

  We have nothing further for this meeting.
  As you continue to open yourselves and seek (speaking to any of you who choose to so do), there are many beginnings awaiting you, little journeys, little discoveries, and wondrous awakenings.

December 14

One can call essences of the infinite and allow them to be a pathway.

The movement from Spirit into deeper and deeper focus upon finite realms brings forth the Uniqueness of the individual who is on such a journey. One can shift to move, and as one moves, they make choices using God's gift of Free Will. These bring about an accumulation of uniqueness for each soul upon a journey into definition. The further the journey takes them, the deeper into definition they journey, the more there is a unique essence that is the reflection of all of the choices that are made upon the journey.

It is not to imply that this uniqueness is not, at the moment of awakening, God-given, but rather that this is *worn*, so to say. The collage of choices that have gone before the present incarnation brings about the diversity of consciousness among your brethren in the Earth.

As one "elevates their consciousness" to a position where they are above the collage of that which colors the Uniqueness of the entity in the Earth, from this greater level of perception one can call for those essences that are of the infinite. And as self is willing to receive these and allow a pathway that these might manifest in the lifetime, then it is so.

> ## December 15
>
> Free Will is fashioned by the Children of God as they choose to reclaim the Heritage or to contribute to the status quo.

As one progresses along a pathway of the reclaiming of their Spiritual Heritage, it is possible that they will encounter an array of resistance or challenges. Some of this is the result of the reaction from the collective thoughtform of the Earth resisting such change because of their own fear of the reaction to the works which they have perpetuated. But these come from within as well as without.

The relationship between the energies, the consciousness of the collective thoughtform embracing the Earth and that which is within you, have the same Source. They are as fruits from the same tree. So that, as you have journeyed through life and gathered emotional memories and fragments here and there of judgments upon self and others, all of this is from the experience of the collective energy of mass-mind thought in the Earth and the Earth itself.

While the Earth is ever offering in the purity of the Spirit of God, it has the dizzying array of choices made historically and presently by the children of God who dwell in and about the Earth that contribute to the sustaining of the status quo. And that would include each of you who might be embraced by the mass-mind thought.

What comes forth — whether it is the upon a memory that you would just as soon not claim as yours or the reaction and/or judgment of self against self — is nourished by the surrounding life force of mass-mind thought.

All of this, you see, comes from the source of God, but it is fashioned, in accordance with Universal Law, by the choices of the Children.

> **December 16**
>
> You are the masters of your life. Illusion would have you think contrarily. Seek the Peace and you will discover who you are.

Even a subtlety from the past that you might find bitter to review is energized by those forces that seek to sustain your bitterness. Know this. And realize that you have the power to pass through these and even to transform them, for the Law gives you the right of choice. They can sustain and nourish these thoughtforms and cause them to be seen this way or that to their benefit only so far, for if you exercise your right of Free Will choice and God's Grace, you become the master over all of these. The beauty of this is that you can set all these energies *free*! Whatsoever you held with remorse or guilt or any such is an energy that becomes free to take on a more beautiful form of expression, or to be used to quell an attitude of dis-ease, and on and on.

The beauty of the current time in the Earth is such that the call has gone forth to you, all of you.

Hear these words, these thoughts, as we offer them: You are the masters of your life. The illusion would have you think contrarily. That simple.

Remember, seek the Peace of God. So doing, you will discover the truth of who you are.

Note: These are comments Al made after the last reading that might interest to you. In this section of the audio, it is very difficult to recognize who is speaking, Al or Lama Sing, the voices and accents normally distinctly quite different from the other. Here, the voice and syntax sound like a combination of Al and Lama Sing, yet the message apparently comes from Al.

[very long pause after the reading]

Al: I return to the Earth surrounded with the Grace of the Christ and the Love of God.
These are the gifts I offer to all who are present. All of the spirits... Come and take of this, these gifts of the Christ.

[long pause]

Channel/Al: I ... am ... that Spirit ... that comes before.

[Another long pause and then it seemed that Al was returning, making slight movements and adjustments to his body. Suddenly, Al — or someone — whispered, very rapidly and nearly inaudible, the Lord's Prayer, followed by another pause.]

Al: This is really unique for me. It's like coming back to nothing, no expressions of finiteness. I know I have a physical form sitting in this chair and that, if I open my eyes, I will see the physical room of this physical house. But these are only thoughtforms. They are not real. The impact of that is, perhaps, as profound as I've ever experienced it.
In this moment, it would be easier to just slip back... a very strong pull to the other side.

[end of reading]

Note: This was Al's request as stated in his prayer at the onset of this next journey: *Father, show us how You Love us, that we might know to Love ourselves in the same way. Show us, in this journey, Father, what true Love is and what It means. We want to be Conscious of our Oneness with you in all that we are and do while we yet journey in this beautiful realm called Earth. These things we ask of You in the name of our Brother Jesus the Christ.*

Al and Susan prepared for several days in advance of this journey to Love. Compared to other readings the recording is mostly silent as they experience this Love. (A line of dashes denotes this silence.) The intent was not to obtain more information, but to experience. What follows are comments offered during that journey for the recording, while Al and Susan were off experiencing the Love of Father.

> ## December 17
>
> You are the master of your destiny. Only you control that which you experience. The power lies within you.

[*Journey to Love* begins:]
    It could be said that the request presently before us has changed very little from the intention held in the meeting one Earth year measure previous: *Journey to Father.* Yet so much has been accomplished that were we to attempt to narrate each and every item it would require many of your hours to do. The most significant we should like to humbly point to is the realization that you are the masters of your destiny. That it is you, and only you, who control that which you experience.

    It is true that having a physical expression (body) in the finite expression of Earth places it within the collective thought of that environ, and therefore, some subjectivity to that thoughtform is a part of the journey therein. This is known well in advance and, quite frankly, is prepared for. Yet the power, in its *complete* expression, lies within each of you.

> December 18
>
> There is the joy of Consciousness in knowing Itself to be of God, as Love expressing Itself to Love.

[*Journey to Love* continues:]
Now comes before us the delightful opportunity to attempt to express the unexpressable in finite word...

It could be said that a sincere quest to know Love is a quest to know God. That is the intent that goes before this journey.

[silence as the Channel and Susan journey]

So very much could transpire here that would be in response to questions that come from the mind. Yet mind in and of itself can know not of Spirit unless mind unburdens itself and comes to the realization that it is the expression of Spirit into the realm of intent in which it exists.

You might perceive that which embraces our brother and his colleagues as a warmth of golden light. You might define it as a resonance that echoes all of Consciousness as an expression of Love unto Itself. You might define it as the embrace that surpasses all description. Or you might simply call it the warmth of remembering your Father, and your Home.

Our brother and colleagues are without form and yet are perfectly expressed. Their expression is embraced by all that is and they embrace in a similar manner. There is the essence of joyful laughter, not as you would hear from a collection of children at play, but from the joy of Consciousness in knowing Itself to be of God and, so Knowing, Knowing God. -----

> December 19
>
> Learn to open self and receive. *Then* shall you know God's Love. And when you do, in this manner, you shall Love Self.

[*Journey to Love* continues:]

Our brother and sister are presently Free, as can any of you be should you so choose and place that intent before yourselves with the authority of that which You are and with the resolve that naught shall take this from You.

Now there is the wonder of Consciousness, and the sweet harmony of all that Is.

The Brethren come to gather together in joyful remembrance of many journeys and many joys that have been shared.

It may seem to some that might hear of this interesting, if not curious, that our brother and sister hear a call, and with a deep fondness and love they soar off to be one with the Colors, the very Color of God's Word. This is the pure Potential, the unending expression of God's Love in response to our brother's request. Can there be anything greater than this?

Freedom — beyond comprehension — to be or do as you would or to simply flow with the undulation of the expression of God's Word ever reaching out to create and embrace and to give love and compassionate opportunity to all that is.

Imagine for a moment a large flower bud that begins to open its petals before you... one, then another, then two, then 20, then an hundred, and soon it seems as though petals are opening everywhere and within them more flowers appear, and the colors and the fragrances and the sounds of harmony caress all that you are. Every particle of your beingness feels the delicate kiss of fragrance and color, life and joy. And the sweetness of that which is seeks only to give to you.

Learn. Learn to receive. Learn to open self and receive.

Then shall you know Father's Love.

And, when you do, in this manner, you shall Love Self.

> ### December 20
>
> As you choose, you are chosen; as you love, so are you loved.

[*Journey to Love* continues:]

It might seem to some that our brother would choose to remain here — in this sacred dance of Love, with the Colors of God's Word – forever. Yet he and the many others do not. They receive the gifts of God's Love expressed in the wonder here of all potential, all opportunity, and then they seek to carry this to those of their brethren who have journeyed into the shadows of *not-knowing*.

There are many contrasting philosophies and perspectives on such works that we know exist in the realm of Earth, and we honor these and each of you who hold them. Perhaps you might honor ours as we offer it to you...

The joy of Oneness comes about for many of our brethren through interaction with one another. Some choose the simple state of Be-ing. This is not a state of being that is as a hermit of some sort, but the Be-ing of Consciousness of God's Knowing. Others journey within this Consciousness to be of service, to give that overflowing abundance of that which they have to those who have (in your terms) lost their way. The giving is in a manner that is in harmony with our Father, else they would fall into a lesser state of consciousness themselves, not to imply this is some great loss that is irretrievable or some punishment, merely the result of choices.

So we find, we are where we started an Earth year ago with our brother and sister. In that time period past (as you measure it), they chose: Now, we claim you as our brother and sister.

So doing, we invoke God's Law, the Law of pure Love.

As you choose, you are chosen.

As you love, so are you loved.

> December 21
>
> Who is it that holds the reins to your destiny? What *is* your destiny'

[*Journey to Love* continues:]
Not all will understand this, and it is not our concern here if that is so. It is, again, merely a choice to open one's self to Know or (in your terminology of Earth) to see with eyes that can see and hear with ears to hear:

The Path is now in place.

That which was originally called by Susahn the Heart Realm (to symbolize the brothers and sisters who intended to bring the very Heart of God's Love as an offering to those willing to receive it, and now perhaps aptly retitled by she as the Homeland) is a part of this Path. It is yours to choose.

We shall pause now, that the completeness of our brother's journey may be made even more possible by discontinuing, for a time, the use of this Channel.

What is the true value of an accomplishment if it cannot be shared?

What is the value of wisdom if it cannot be employed in service?

What truth can be found in a teaching that seeks to confine or dominate?

Who is it that holds the reins to your destiny?

Why are you separate from God in this believed journey?

> December 22
>
> A rudderless ship is adrift, subject to the winds and tides of the sea of finiteness. Let your intent be that which guides.

[Journey to Love concludes:]

    Believe only unto that which seeks to set you free. When you encounter truth, honor it, give it your love; when you encounter something untrue, let it be.

    A rudderless ship is adrift, subject to the winds and tides of the great sea of finiteness.
    Let your intent be that which guides, not which mandates but that which chooses the destination.

    Those who seek to dominate, shall be, by their own actions, so affected; those who are dominated are the ones who can set them free. It is the Rod of Forgiveness and the staff of Truth that are borne by those who seek only God's Love.

    Do not think of forgiveness as erasing one's history, one's background, but that which builds upon it, transforming it into a solid firmament.

    Believe in that which sets you free. Let your intent be your guide. Allow past "errors" to be your firmament.

    We are through with this work for the present. The Peace of God goes before all of you. It is yours to choose.

> **December 23**
>
> No matter what you are about, the River of Light is always within you. You are never separate from It.

[*Journey in the River of Light* begins:]

[Note: Again, Al's and Susan's intent was simply to be in the space of the experience. Hence, once again, there is much silence between messages from Lama Sing.]

Some might ask, "What is there for us to focus upon, to celebrate, in our journey through a life in the Earth? It would seem that the beginning and ending are very narrowly divided and that the journey itself is one that has very little support or encouragement from that which is believed, that which is eternal."

It is unto such thoughts, such considerations, that we proceed in this journey, knowing what shall be given and that the intent would be to offer the light of understanding not only to our brother and sister here, but to all who would read these words. This shall be our prayer.

Our brother journeyed unto this meeting in the River of Light. The River of Light is an eternal River of Life itself, and thus it is used interchangeably by him and we, alike.

In the journey, he (he would say) gazed off to the side and perceived the Homeland and reflected upon leaving the River to be one with his brethren in the Homeland. At that point, he found that a part of him nearly chose to continue on in the River of Light.

We would offer to our brother and to all: No matter what your choice is, that River of Life is always within you. You are never separate from It.

December 24

I am neither here nor there; in my Oneness, I am in all that is.

[*Journey in the River of Light* continues — To the Channel:]

Having made the breakthroughs you have is a credit to your willingness to release and to move forward in an attitude of faith. By so doing and by your continued focus on what you consider to be a good work, you are setting yourself Free. It may at times be difficult to discern movement, and yet you know that movement is taking place.

This, then, is ever good to recall:

I am neither here nor there; but, in my Oneness, I am in all that is.

And, as I would choose, which is my right, then this is all that is required for my movement according to my choice and the destination in same.

> December 25
>
> The original intent for the Earth was for the utter Freedom and joy of all involved. This intent yet remains.

[*Journey in the River of Light* continues:]

The Homeland Consciousness is the potential of the Children of God to demonstrate their Love, each in their own divine Uniqueness in Oneness with God's Word.

The Homeland Consciousness is a state of harmony that constantly assures Freedom in the complete sense of all of aspects involved in the demonstrations of Love. So that when there is the intent to bring something of joy, of beauty, to a brother or sister, *all* that is involved in that manifestation participates *because they choose to be a part of that*.

This may be looked upon by some as one of *the* significant differentiations between the Homeland and that which is present in the structure of the Earth consciousness:

The original intent (from which the Earth and surrounding realms moderated to their current state) was for the utter Freedom and joy of all involved. This intent yet remains.

> ## December 26
>
> The willingness to release *all* is the destination being sought — that by releasing all, you become one with All.

[*Journey in the River of Light* continues:]

[Note: The following occurred for the Channel, having then a profound impact on him in his life on Earth. He was taken to a portal and told, if he wanted to move through it, he would need to leave everything there, which he did immediately, no hesitation. The following comments are to him, but they can apply to anyone who would wish to choose utter Freedom:]

[To the Channel:]
   ... That which you were invited to do — to leave <u>everything</u> at the portal — involved, as you know on some levels, the release of experience and the resulting effects and responses from the memories to those experiences. While the process involved in doing this obviously required no concerted effort on your part, it is to the joy — and, indeed, much more — for us to participate in such an accomplishment, for it requires the willingness to surrender. ...

   In regard to how others might accomplish this: Begin, first, by considering: What are you willing to surrender and what do you wish to retain.
   The willingness to release *all* is the destination to be sought after and the realization that, by releasing all, you become one with All, and the knowing of this to the extent that your Spirit can awaken to the Consciousness that is present at that point of choice. In other words at that point to choose this surrender... Yes, very well, a moment please...

> December 27
>
> That which one willfully gives is returned to them far greater than as they have given.

[*Journey in the River of Light* continues:]

[very long pause in silence]

    For your reference, a discussion is taking place in regard to what can be given on this topic [of what the Channel did in his surrender] that will be understandable for those who might become aware of this and attempt to apply it. ...

    The Elders have stated it requires that the primary turn of that choice – which is *a pivot in direction*, see – is that one is willing to return to God and to release that which are the joys and the sorrows, the happiness and the anger, the guilt and all that sort that give the flavor to life in Earth itself. This is not, as they point out, to indicate any form of judgment but only to indicate these things as a part of the activity needed to leave all here at that portal, as our brother did.

    Now in order for him to do a "reading" he, indeed, places all aside. So in this journey he had already placed all aside, and then it was asked of him again, at the doorway, to place all aside.

    The differentiating point is that leaving for one of these good works together has, as a part of its intent, to return to life in the Earth; at the point where he was told that he must leave all here, there was no condition. And he was willing to leave all, including his life in Earth, here at this portal! That is a quality that the Elders have as a hallmark.

    Be mindful of the Law: That which one willfully gives is returned to them far greater than as they have given. What our brother knew and knows is that the true Life lies beyond that portal.

> December 28
>
> To reach Consciousness the requirement is to set self Free. To know Self to be that which thou art is to be One with God

[*Journey in the River of Light* continues:]

Exploring the nature of Consciousness is best done through the experiencing of it. If it is sought after through the intellect, it may be of diminishing result because the nature of consciousness involved in the intellect requires definition.

[To the Channel:]
　... That which you perceived as the intersect between Father's cloak and Father's Word is a perspective. Understand this very clearly, dear brother. That which you gained through your journeys, through your experiencing, is the making real of Understanding (capital U) through your perspective of it. And as you have perspective in Consciousness, comes the Knowing (also capital K). ...

　Perspective, here, is differentiated from terminology that is probably associated with same in the Earth as a free *observer*, so to say. To set one's self Free is required, of course, to reach Consciousness. And to know Self to be that which thou art is to move to the state of Oneness with God, that thou art in the Knowing.
　And because you are a Child of God and not God, the Knowing becomes the Observer.

> December 29
>
> The Observer can Know that which is constantly in motion; in attempting to define it, the Intellect may stumble.

[*Journey in the River of Light* continues:]

Consider references to the continuing expansion of Consciousness...

The Observer Knows these expansions and can experience them because they are One with Consciousness.

But to move from the Observer's position of experiencing (which is in the form of Knowing) raises the potential for definition. This requires some shift from the utterness of Freedom into the more defined.

That process can bring about a shift, the results of which cannot be predicted, of course, without knowing the factors that are involved. But generally speaking, it would move one from the pure state of Consciousness into that which is being "examined." The Knowing of that from the Observer's position brings the value of Knowing without the boundaries or limitations, which are required by the intellectual definition.

Attempting to define that which is constantly in motion from any perspective other than in Pure Consciousness would require some very rapid movement on your part... basically, in all directions at once. The humor here is: the Observer can do this; the intellect may stumble.

> December 30
>
> Know Self and the Uniqueness of God's Love that is You, that it can be clearly known by all of Consciousness.

[*Journey in the River of Light* continues:]

Whenever one embarks upon an intention, take a look about to see what, if anything, you are bringing with you. For the moreso you free yourself totally to the intention, the more likely are you to accomplish it.

Know Self, and in that Knowing there will follow the Knowing of God and, more precisely, the Knowing of the Uniqueness of God's Love that is You.

Then, reaching out to Be in the beauty of Consciousness becomes not only an intent or quest, but also a gift and a blessing that God gives through You to all of Consciousness. This is an active aspect to Be-ing in the expression of Consciousness. In the opening of Self to the uniqueness of God's intent, a pathway follows by which your own Uniqueness, given by God, can be more clearly known by all of Consciousness.

For there is the continual preservation of the right of Free Will, and reaching this state of Be-ing has been preceded by the release of aspects of self. Knowing Self in this manner, then, fulfills the Law of Free Will and opens that gift of your Uniqueness: Your being that one that is a gift to all that is.

This is the way in which the Elders can be one with their brethren and be anywhere, elsewhere, simultaneously: The sharing and experiencing of the song and dance of the Colors and the wonder of the unfolding of Creation and the embrace of God... all of this in the one *moment*, as you measure it.

> December 31
>
> Claim your Freedom. Set the Peace of God before you in all things, and Know the Presence of God every step of the way.

[*Journey in the River of Light* concludes:]

Zachary: Our brother has shifted to celebrate the knowing of our presence with him. We find great humor in this, for if he were to pause a moment, he would remember that we are always with him. But we comprehend, and embrace him mightily as we return with him to the Homeland.

As we rest upon the greenery of this gentle slope, our brother pauses to literally collect himself.

Then we stand, feeling the laughter of the green on our being, and my brother moves to greet those who are here to celebrate with him, including of course the Lama. As we walk together towards the edge of the Homeland and pause to reflect about his journey before we move to return him, we offer this in closing:

In your journeys to Free your Selves, whatever comes, first *claim* your Freedom, and the Knowing of what follows will be accomplished in the greater sense.

Whatsoever you are about, do it with utter Peace, in the knowing that Peace clears the way and opens the path. *Be* a pathway of Peace, Pure Peace.

And Know the Presence of God every step of the way in your journey in Earth or beyond, for truly, there is naught but God.

It has to do with BE-ing.

On behalf of all here, we thank you for this opportunity to share with you.

The Peace of God goes before you.

Fare thee well, for the present.

And remember...

A moment of laughter
is a moment of embracing God.

Books by Al Miner & Lama Sing

The Chosen: *Back Story to the Essene Legacy*
The Promise: *Book I of The Essene Legacy*
The Awakening: *Book II of The Essene Legacy*
The Path: *Book III of The Essene Legacy*

In Realms Beyond: *Book I of The Peter Chronicles*
In Realms Beyond: *Study Guide*
Awakening Hope: *Book II of The Peter Chronicles*

How to Prepare for The Journey:
    Vol I Death, Dying, and Beyond
    Vol II *The Sea of Faces*

Jesus: *Book I*
Jesus: *Book II*

The Course in Mastery

When Comes the Call

Seed Thoughts

For a comprehensive list of reading transcripts available, visit the Lama Sing library at www.lamasing.net

About Al Miner

In 1973, a little more than twenty years after a near-death experience, a chance hypnosis session triggered Al's reconnection to the other side and began his tenure as the channel for the Lama Sing readings.

Since then, over 10,000 readings have been given in a trance state for groups and individuals from around the world, answering questions on a virtually unlimited array of topics. Individuals, professionals, and institutions have substantiated the precision of the information, and those who have received personal readings continue to refer others to Al's work based on the accuracy and integrity of the information given.

Al has quietly served individuals and groups for over forty years, dedicating his life totally to this work. His focus now is research on Consciousness and its application in daily life. He currently has 15 books in print.

www.ingramcontent.com/pod-product-compliance
Lightning Source LLC
LaVergne TN
LVHW020925090426
835512LV00020B/3200